Europe and International Migration

1855672979

Europe and International Migration

Sarah Collinson

Pinter Publishers, London and New York
for
Royal Institute of International Affairs, London

First published in Great Britain in 1993 by
Pinter Publishers Limited
25 Floral Street, London WC2E 9DS

Revised paperback edition published in 1994

British Library Cataloguing in Publication Data
A CIP catalogue record for this book is available from the British Library.

ISBN 1 85567 297 9 (PB)
ISBN 1 85567 296 0 (HB)

Text designed and set by Hannah Doe
Printed and bound in Great Britain by Biddles Ltd, Guildford and Kings Lynn

Contents

Table

Foreword

The original edition of this book, which appeared in April 1993, was the first substantial piece of research to be published by the Royal Institute of International Affairs since the classic studies of 1939 by Sir John Hope Simpson – *Refugees: A Review of the Situation Since 1938* and *The Refugee Problem: Report of a Survey*. In September 1993 the Institute published a second book, *Beyond Borders: West European Migration Policy Towards the 21st Century*, which deals with contemporary refugee and asylum policies. A third research project, on migration issues in the western Mediterranean, has also been initiated, thanks to generous funding from the ESRC. Chatham House has clearly demonstrated its commitment to the study of international migration, and for this lively programme of work we have our Senior Research Fellow, Sarah Collinson, to thank.

For this second, updated edition of *Europe and International Migration*, I would like once again to congratulate Sarah on her contribution to the field. This volume, I am convinced, will remain a valuable addition to the literature on migration studies for years to come, and now at a price that a general audience can afford.

I would like to thank the Le Poer Power Trust for its continuing support of research on international migration at the Institute, assistance that now spans four years.

August 1994   Dr Philip Robins

Preface to the First Edition

Since the end of the cold war, international migration has risen rapidly up the political agenda in Western Europe. A number of developments have coalesced to create a high degree of anxiety over the issue, an anxiety which is not confined to political circles, but now stretches across virtually every sector of society. The lifting of emigration restrictions in the former Eastern bloc, coupled with growing economic instability in the region, appeared to set the scene for millions of economic migrants moving from East to West in search of a better life. More recent events in the former Yugoslavia have raised the spectre of further future mass dislocations of population in Europe stemming from a resurgence in ethnic tensions and generalized political instability following in the wake of the collapse of the Soviet Empire. In addition, an increase in asylum applications and illegal immigration from outside Europe, together with a rise in extreme anti-immigrant attitudes in Western Europe, have intensified longer-standing worries about migration from the 'South', particularly from the less-developed countries of the Mediterranean rim and sub-Saharan Africa. Suddenly it appears that Western Europe is under siege from its poorer and less stable neighbours, and that a new threat of mass population movements has come to replace the old and more distant peril of a Communist Eastern bloc.

To an extent, fears of a 'mass influx' have served to obfuscate level-headed analysis of the migration issue in Western Europe, and have therefore worked against balanced appraisals of just what kind of migration challenges Europe might come to face in the decades to come. All attention is focused on the innumerable pressures building up in existing and potential 'sending' regions that are deemed likely to drive movement into Western Europe in the future, such as rapid population growth, growing unemployment and falling incomes. As a result, other factors which are important for shaping migration have not received the kind of attention that they might seem to deserve. Migration policy is one of these. While it has been the subject of some considerable debate in a wide range of intergovernmental, media and other public sectors, the direction, focus and impetus of discussions have been determined more by immediate immigration fears and concerns than by efforts to assess just how state action has influenced, and will continue to influence, the outcome of intensifying migration pressures in the past and in the future. This deficit is also reflected in the academic literature, which, although vast, is curiously disjointed. Surprisingly little attention has been paid to the international and national politics of migration, and to the role of state intervention in the migration process. As Myron Weiner observes, a number of important questions remain inadequately explored: 'How do state actions shape population movements, when do such movements lead to conflicts and when to cooperation, and what do governments do in their domestic policies to adjust to or influence population flows'?[1]

The intention of this study is to take a step back from many of the preoccupations dominating current discussions of the issue in Western Europe. By tackling the question from a historical, and to a lesser extent global, perspective, the study aims to contribute contructively to a debate which has in many ways tended to treat international migration as a new phenomenon and as a problem unique to Western Europe. More specifically, by focusing on state action and inaction – on migration policies and the role that such policies (or the lack of them) have played in shaping migration flows in the past – it aims to draw attention to the part that states now have to play to influence migration flows.

The purpose of the book is not to downgrade the importance of migration pressures acting around Western Europe and throughout the world. Indeed, it is emphasized in the conclusion that those very pressures which hold the *potential* for creating large-scale migration – whether resulting in migration or not – need to be addressed urgently, if for no other reason than to avoid the prospect of much wider economic and political destabilization in Europe and in other regions of the world in the years to come. It is argued, however, that when action is taken in the future, it is likely to prove most effective when based on an understanding and recognition of states' capacity and responsibility to deal with migration pressures and to cope with migration flows.

The subject of international migration crosses numerous disciplinary boundaries and presents a bewildering array of different levels, directions and methods of possible approach. All this study, like any in the field, can hope to do is throw light on one corner of what is a much larger and more complex picture. Certain omissions have proved inescapable and a number of issue areas have not benefited from the close attention that they might seem to merit. The main focus of the book is on state action in respect of voluntary, as opposed to involuntary, migration. It therefore follows that emphasis has been placed on migration which may be broadly categorized as 'economic' (and voluntary) in motivation, and migration which is connected directly with such flows (family migration), rather than on refugee flows and other forms of forced movement. While it is sometimes difficult to make a clear distinction between refugees and migrants or between voluntary and involuntary flows, the distinction is an important one, and, when separated conceptually, the two phenomena raise very different questions. The scope of this book is not sufficient to do justice to both issues. Therefore, with the exception of Chapter 3, discussion touches on refugee issues only in so far as they have recently become entangled with policy questions relating to international migration more generally (Chapters 2 and 7).

The study begins by setting out the major types of international migration in the world today, outlining current broad trends in international 'economic' migration, and providing some pointers as to how these trends have affected migration into Western Europe in recent decades. The second chapter looks at three specific categories of international migration in an attempt to determine to what extent current trends reflect the singular position of Western Europe as compared with other regions of the world. This comparative perspective is developed further in Chapter 3, which examines major historical trends in European migration since the emergence of sovereign states (and thus the first strictly 'interstate' population movements) in Europe after the thirteenth century. This chapter looks, in particular, at the role of the state in influencing migration, and, in so doing, highlights elements of continuity and change in states' involvement in the migration process. The theme of state action is expanded in Chapters 4 and 5, which concentrate on how the policies of certain major migrant-receiving and migrant-sending states of the postwar period have influenced trends in voluntary international migration in Western Europe over the past four decades. This theme is also developed in Chapter 6, which focuses on policy influencing the settlement of immigrant communities in receiving countries (as opposed to the migration process itself). All three chapters throw light on aspects of similarity and difference in the policies of different states in Western Europe, and thereby provide a backdrop for Chapter 7, which critically examines current moves towards the harmonization of migration policy within the European Community and wider groupings in Western Europe. While this chapter considers in some detail a number of specific obstacles lying in the way of harmonization, the concluding chapter suggests that the single greatest obstacle to the future development of an effective European migration policy might prove to be states' reluctance to look beyond traditional concepts of migration control – concepts which have guided state policy for decades, and to some extent centuries, but which in the late twentieth century and beyond are likely to prove increasingly ill-equipped to deal with a phenomenon that has the potential for taking on a scale and complexity wholly unprecedented in the history of international migration.

I would like to thank a number of people for their help in the preparation of this study. First and foremost, my departmental head, Dr Philip Robins, who read and commented upon every draft, and who, with our programme administrator, Jill Kalawoun, demonstrated untiring support and commitment throughout the project. I must also thank my colleagues Professor Helen Wallace and Professor Jack Spence for their many valuable suggestions, and Pauline Wickham and Hannah Doe for all their patient work on the publications side of the project. I am also grateful to the numerous academics, officials and practitioners who were consulted during the course of the study, and whose comments proved invaluable. Needless to say, I take ultimate responsibility for all the ideas and views expressed in the book. The study, of course, would not have been feasible without the continuing support of the sponsor, the Le Poer Power Trust, which I would like to thank not only for financing the project, but also for its help in developing the shape and focus of the study. Finally, I would like to add a special personal thanks to Chris Sylge, Jenny Wilson and my family for all their encouragement.

January 1993   Sarah Collinson

Preface to the Second Edition

Although this second edition follows close on the heels of the first, much has happened in the intervening period, and thus more work had to go into revising and updating the original text than had initially been envisaged. Of course, the historical perspective developed throughout the book, and thus the overall balance – reflecting an interest in the historical and global background to current preoccupations with the migration issue – has been maintained. Moreover, the overall direction of migration policy in Western Europe has not undergone any drastic changes over the past two years, so that many of the conclusions reached in the first edition remain valid. Nevertheless, numerous policy developments at the European level, including the entry into force of the Maastricht Treaty, have meant that considerable work has had to go into updating and amending Chapter 7, which examines current cooperation and policy harmonization among West European governments. I hope that in the process I have succeeded in further clarifying the discussion of institutional developments affecting migration policy and its harmonization within the European Union – developments which have proved confusing not only for students of migration policy, but also, at times, for policy-makers themselves.

As for the other chapters, all except Chapter 3, which is entirely historical, have been amended to a greater or lesser extent to take account of recent events or changes in policy and migration trends. Moreover Chapter 6, which examines policy questions relating to the integration of immigrant minorities in Western Europe, has been expanded to include a more detailed discussion of integration policy in the Netherlands and to include some discussion of the increase in racial violence and harassment in Europe over recent years. The statistics in Chapter 6 have also been updated where possible.

The material in the book has not merely been updated, however. Much of what I felt needed amending related to the tone of certain parts of the first edition, and in particular, areas of the book where I may have fallen into the (common) trap of exaggerating actual and potential problems or crises associated with migration into Western Europe, despite the overall aim of taking 'a step back from many of the preoccupations dominating current discussions of the issue' (Preface to the first edition). To a large extent, this reflected the general climate of uncertainty and insecurity which prevailed in Western Europe during the first few years after the fall of the Berlin Wall – particularly after the break-up of the Soviet Union and the outbreak of war in the former Yugoslavia – and which characterized much of the academic debate on the issue at the time. Of course, many of the challenges connected directly or indirectly with current and future migration are enormous, whether they relate to migration into Western Europe or, just as important, within neighbouring regions or in other areas of the world. One need look no further than the ongoing conflict in Bosnia-Herzegovina and the current Rwandan refugee crisis to be reminded of that. Yet the development of effective and humane responses to these challenges will not be aided by discussion or debate which reinforces or contributes to a siege mentality in Western Europe, or which – wittingly or unwittingly – encourages short-term defensive responses to problems whose resolution requires the long-term and active engagement of governments.

One thing that has not changed since the publication of the first edition is the importance of international migration on the West European political agenda. I hope that this book will prove a useful starting-point for readers interested in the development of migration as a policy issue in Western Europe. It is an issue which has always been complex, but is now perhaps more so than ever.

I would like to extend my thanks again to all the people who helped me with the first edition of this book and who, through their continued involvement, have helped in various direct and indirect ways with the production of this second edition. First, I must express my enormous gratitude to the Le Poer Power Trust, without whose continuing interest in and support of my work neither edition would have been possible. My colleagues at Chatham House deserve warmest thanks as always, and particularly Philip Robins, Jill Kalawoun and Jack Spence for their unfailing encouragement and assistance; and Margaret May and Hannah Doe who – against a very tight deadline – have succeeded with their usual aplomb to do a wonderful job on the publication side. I would also like to thank all the academics and practitioners with whom I have discussed my work over the years, and in particular Annette Bosscher, Gil Loescher, Nuala Mole, Anne Owers and Ann Singleton for their invaluable comments on the first edition. Of course, responsibility for the views expressed and for any factual errors rests entirely with me.

August 1994   Sarah Collinson

Chapter 1

Introduction

'The migratory movement is at once perpetual, partial and universal. It never ceases, it affects every people ... [and although] at a given moment it sets in motion only a small number of each population ... in fact there is never a moment of immobility for any people, because no migration remains isolated.'[1] Eugene Kulischer wrote these words in 1943 when Europe was still suffering the ravages of war and a massive dislocation of millions of people across the whole continent. By that time, Europe had experienced virtually every kind of international migration discernible in the world today – forced and voluntary, economic and political, seasonal and permanent, regional and transcontinental, bonded and free. Moreover, Europe was not the only continent of the world to have experienced massive population movements, nor, indeed, were population movements in Europe isolated from developments elsewhere in the world.

Yet today, the international migrations of people are greater in magnitude, more complex, more diverse and more interconnected than ever before. The worldwide picture reveals millions of people displaced by war and conflict and persecution – some within countries, others across borders, some with assistance, others with none, some crossing land borders, others fleeing by air. Millions more are displaced by desertification and other kinds of ecological degradation and disaster – some natural, some man-made. Incalculable numbers of people move periodically across borders, as seasonal or frontier workers or as transient traders. More and more businessmen and professionals move from one country to another. And as international communications develop further and the mobility of and contacts between individuals of different countries and continents increase and multiply, so more and more people migrate as foreign spouses and foreign-born children of 'indigenous' residents. As always, there is the international migration of workers – some permanent, some temporary, some legal, some illegal, some skilled, some unskilled, some headed for agriculture, some headed for industry; and, as often with the movement of workers, there is an accompanying movement of families, some outward, some returning.

Towards a classification of types

International migration is so complex a phenomenon that any attempt to categorize the many different types inevitably proves a reductionist exercise. Nevertheless, for the purposes of discussion and analysis, a degree of classification is called for. An approach which is central to the process of policy formulation is that which distinguishes migrants according to the basic cause and intention of movement. Thus it is common to distinguish between migration caused by factors that can be described as being broadly 'political', and migration caused or motivated by economic factors. It is this distinction, for example, which guides the definitional division between refugees and other kinds of migrants. The distinction between migration which is essentially voluntary in motivation and that which is involuntary is also useful.

Taking the two dimensions together, one can visualize a matrix within which to place the many different migration types. The extremes would be (1) migration which is strongly economic and voluntary in cause and motivation (e.g. worker migration); (2) that which is strongly political and voluntary (e.g. migration of Jews to Israel); (3) that which is strongly political and involuntary (e.g. 'classic' refugee flows); and (4) that which is strongly economic and involuntary (e.g. refugees from famine and ecological disaster). It should be stressed that such categories are always blurred and that most migration flows fall somewhere between the four extremes. Thus, for example, the expulsion of workers from the Arab Gulf, or the movement of 'distress' migrants in the Horn of Africa would, though for different reasons, fall somewhere between categories (3) and (4). Similarly, the 'economic' and 'voluntary' movement of migrant workers never takes place in a political vacuum, and thus worker migration incorporates elements of category (2). Furthermore, the fact that many worker migrants move to escape or avoid extreme economic hardship means that category (1) frequently overlaps with category (4).[2]

Although excluded from this matrix, certain factors which may be broadly defined as 'social' and/or 'cultural' usually impact on migration to a very significant degree. Thus the migration of families and dependants may be described as 'socially' determined, although the original migration which gives rise to this movement (and sometimes the family migration itself) may be largely economic in motivation. Even worker migration itself is very heavily influenced by the operation of social and cultural factors such as networks of communication between migrant-sending and migrant-receiving countries, or by more general cultural and linguistic links between sending and receiving countries. It is also worth mentioning that the increase in 'South/North' migration witnessed over recent decades has almost certainly been influenced by the spread of Western culture throughout the world.

One can take the categorization a stage further by distinguishing, for example, between the movements of professional and of unskilled workers, between documented or undocumented (illegal) movements, and between transient, seasonal, temporary and permanent migrants.[3] All fall within the same broad category by virtue of being 'economic' and 'voluntary' in character, but all are very different in terms of specific causes, motivations and impacts. Each general category includes a myriad of specific types. This diversity is important, and has led some analysts to argue that the causes and consequences of international migration should be evaluated only within the context of specific countries and specific migratory situations.[4] Indeed, even in a specific migratory context, factors determining and arising from migration may be very difficult to identify. It is perhaps this more than anything else that explains why international migration has eluded research-ers and policy-makers for so long, and why clear policies are so difficult to formulate and clear conclusions so hard to reach.

Global trends

Like international capital and product flows, the international flow of people has undergone a marked expansion over the past four decades. One estimate puts the number of people currently resident outside their country of citizenship at some 80 million.[5] If account is taken of (1) high numbers of people who are or have become citizens of the receiving country, (2) those who are now outside their country of origin after the collapse of the Soviet Union, and (3) huge numbers of seasonal, frontier and transient migrants worldwide, the figure can be assumed to be much higher (upwards of 100 million).[6] The international significance of the phenomenon is most easily demonstrated in economic terms. Although the total revenue created by international labour flows is impossible to evaluate, crude estimates of the scale of international remittance flows (capital sent by migrants from their country of residence to their country of origin) provide a rough indication: in the late 1980s, the total value of international remittances, put at some US$60.9 billion in 1989, came second only to trade in crude oil. Its value exceeded both global flows of official development aid (US$51 billion in 1988) and the global value of trade in coffee (US$9 billion).[7] Given this scale, it is somewhat surprising that it is only in the past few years that the issue has received the level of international attention that it would seem to deserve.

Although migration has affected all regions of the world throughout history, it is only in recent decades that international flows can be said to have become truly global. With the spread and advancement of modern communications, the expansion of the global economy, and the intensification of regional and international economic and demographic disparities, every continent of the world is now touched by the phenomenon. Furthermore, the past few decades have seen a remarkable expansion and diversification in transcontinental flows, such as from Africa and the Caribbean to Europe, and from Asia to North America and the Middle East. Much of this migration is driven by economic and political forces – such as world trading patterns and capital flows – which have become increasingly global in their genesis and development. The global causes and impacts of international migration have become increasingly intertwined. Thus, for example, migration flows from Asia to the Middle East have caused both economic and social changes in the sending regions, which in turn have given rise to further migration flows, e.g. migration into areas benefiting from development on the basis of remittances, or out of areas where a migration 'psyche' has developed or where traditional social and economic structures have been eroded by prolonged emigration.

However, while it has become progressively global in scope, the process has also undergone a degree of regionalization. To begin with, certain established patterns of movement between contiguous and proximal states have become entrenched, such as that between Mexico and the United States, or that between states in West Africa. At the same time, a number of new regional patterns have emerged or are expected to develop in conjunction with the strengthening of particular regional economic groupings. For example, the past decade has witnessed a marked diversification and increase in levels of migration between East and Southeast Asian states, and the next few years may witness higher levels of migration within the so-called 'European Economic Area'. As described by one analyst, 'we are observing ... the same phenomenon as in the global product market, namely a combination of globalization and regionalization, of outward-orientation and inward-orientation, of free movement and barriers, analogous to the combination of free trade and protectionism'.[8]

In connection with the process of regionalization, it is perhaps most important to note that over the past few decades international migration has become progressively concentrated in just a few areas of the world. Out of the estimated 100 million international migrants worldwide, over a third are in sub-Saharan Africa (at least 35 million), and of the remaining 65 million, most are concentrated in the Middle East and South and Southeast Asia (15 million) and in North America and Western Europe (15 and 13 million respectively).[9] Concentrations are often particularly marked in the case of particular countries. Saudi Arabia, for example, accounted for around 4.5 million of the estimated 6–7 million international migrants in the Arab Gulf prior to the Iraqi invasion of Kuwait; of the total 7 million or so refugees in South Asia, over 6.5 million are concentrated in Pakistan and Iran; of the 17 million or so people in Central and North America who are citizens of a country other than that in which they are resident, over 14 million are in the United States; and of the some 13 million 'foreigners' resident in Western Europe, roughly 8 million[10] are in Germany, France and Britain.[11] Furthermore, many transcontinental migration flows, although indicative of a globalization in migration, are, on closer examination, highly regionalized in terms of sources as well as destinations. Thus particular sending countries tend to dominate flows to particular receiving countries (e.g. Egypt to Saudi Arabia, Algeria and Morocco to France), and flows out of any one sending country may be dominated by emigration from particular regions of that country (e.g. Kerala in India).

Trends affecting Western Europe
All three of the principal global migration trends outlined above – escalation, globalization, and regionalization[12] – have characterized migration to Western Europe over recent decades. However, these trends are not entirely new or clear-cut. For instance, inflows of workers from other regions of the world rose at an unprecedented rate during the two to three decades following the Second World War, reflecting both an escalation and a globalization in international movements of migrant labour. But this was not Europe's first experience of large-scale transcontinental labour migration. Indeed, Western Europe had already been directly involved in two of the largest transcontinental migrations to have taken place in history – the Atlantic slave trade and the subsequent population of the New World. Nor did the postwar arrival of

foreign workers signify an entirely new phenomenon, since migration patterns in Europe before the two World Wars were characterized by high levels of international labour movement, including that out of areas of Eastern and Central Europe.

International migration, however, is a phenonemenon which is simultaneously constant and ever-changing. Although sharing many attributes of earlier flows, recent migration to Western Europe has departed from previous trends in a number of important ways. It was not until the postwar years, for example, that any West European states experienced large-scale inflows of foreign workers from geographically, ethnically and/or culturally 'distant' countries outside Europe. Hence this was the first time that a globalization in migration flows (coupled with regionalization) had come substantially to affect migration patterns *into*, rather than out of, Western Europe. While not signifying the emergence of a new region of immigration, this influx brought about new migration patterns. Poorer Mediterranean countries which had hitherto been isolated from the labour markets of Western Europe became linked into the West European migration 'network'. These links subsequently gave rise to new migration patterns, such as flows to Southern Europe from North Africa. And while the overall magnitude of, and the generally negative reaction to, the immigrant populations of the postwar years may not have been substantially different from those of earlier years, the implications of migration changed considerably owing to shifting economic, political and social conditions in both sending and receiving areas.

Migration trends have undergone further changes in Western Europe since the period of labour immigration following the Second World War. Although many of the same countries are involved, new players have entered the fray. Eastern Europe, separated from the labour markets of Western Europe for some thirty years, is once again a source of economic migration to Western Europe. At the same time, improved global communications and intensifying migration pressures outside Europe are giving rise to a diversification in flows from more distant regions, such as sub-Saharan Africa. Much of this migration is now directed to Southern Europe – Italy, Spain, Portugal, Greece – which has traditionally sent migrants abroad, rather than receiving them from elsewhere. Moreover, while postwar labour immigration took place at a time of economic boom in the most advanced industrialized countries of Western Europe, the environment today is one of economic recession and rising unemployment. Whereas migration during the postwar years was encouraged, or at least sanctioned, by the receiving states, much migration taking place today is 'unwanted' and, to some extent, unregulated by the receivers.

Nevertheless, current migration trends should not be divorced from the patterns of previous periods. First, as already discussed, the fundamental forces shaping migration have remained remarkably similar over decades and centuries. This applies not only to voluntary economic migration, but also to involuntary refugee movements, as discussed in Chapter 3. Second, migration flows and the policies that shape them are frequently linked very directly to previous patterns. One can point, for example, to the importance of Mediterranean migration in current flows to Western Europe – flows which may be attributable as much to past policies of labour recruitment as to current migration pressures operating in the sending regions. Third, a consideration of past trends and policies can prove informative for the formulation of new responses. Reference to the past may not only demonstrate areas in which state policy has had, or could have, a decisive role in shaping migration; it may also reveal areas of convergence and divergence in the positions of different states – an important consideration at a time when moves are being made to harmonize a wide range of laws and procedures relating to international migration in Western Europe.

Chapter 2

Western Europe in a World of International Migration

As noted in the Introduction, migration is now a global phenomenon which affects virtually every country of the world, whether it be the movement of workers, refugees, highly skilled professionals or traders, or other forms of migration. This chapter aims to look a little beyond the confines of Western Europe to consider, on a broad level, the extent to which trends today reflect the singular position of the West European region. It focuses on three main migration categories: documented labour migration, undocumented or 'irregular' migration, and asylum flows.

The first category is one that dominates the postwar history of migration into Western Europe (as detailed in following chapters), but which has come to affect the region less and less in recent years. Despite this decline, Western Europe continues to be seen by many among its own population as one of the most important destinations for economic migrants in the contemporary world. By focusing on the emergence of new areas of international labour migration elsewhere in the world, the first section challenges this perception, demonstrating that Western Europe and other advanced industrialized countries can no longer claim to be the primary 'honeypots' of international economic migration. Nevertheless, worker migration into Western Europe continues today. Apart from the (increasing) international movement of highly skilled and professional workers, 'economic' migration to Western Europe now takes place principally through undocumented channels. At the same time, the number of refugees arriving in Western Europe has increased. These two categories have become increasingly important in the European setting over the past decade, and now dominate current concerns over migration into the region. Undocumented migration and asylum/refugee flows are now worldwide phenomena, and thus the challenges they pose for a number of West European states are in many ways not unique. However, the situation in one region can never be compared directly with that in another. The second and third sections of this chapter compare some of the particular problems facing Western Europe in connection with these two categories of migration.

Documented labour migration

According to World Bank data, the world's main destination countries for international migrants in the late 1980s, or, more precisely, those countries which experienced the highest rates of net (documented) immigration during this period, were (in descending order) the United States, Australia, Saudi Arabia, Canada and Côte d'Ivoire.[1] This list supports the perception that countries of the industrialized 'North' are a major pole of attraction for international migrants in the contemporary world, but challenges the common impression that these are necessarily today's most important immigration countries.

The level of net migration to the United States during the second half of the 1980s was higher than total net immigration in all other countries of the world combined, reaching 2.9 million during the period 1985 to 1990.[2] Indeed, the United States took in almost the same number of permanent settlers and temporary workers in the 1980s as it did during the first decades of this century (around 7 million, compared with 8.8 million in the period 1900–10).[3] But despite standing out in terms of overall numbers, recent migration trends to the US reflect general patterns that are common to a greater or lesser extent to all the Western industrialized immigration states. All these countries have introduced policies which leave little room for the legal and independent immigration of most classes of migrant worker. As a result, documented immigration is now dominated by family (including foreign family-members of 'indigenous' residents) and asylum flows. What worker migration persists is now largely accounted for by increasing movements of highly skilled and professional workers (much of which is temporary or transient), and by illegal or clandestine migration (discussed below). According to OECD estimates, seven selected West European countries – Belgium, Germany, Luxembourg, the Netherlands, Norway, Sweden and Switzerland – experienced an inflow of nearly 4 million and an outflow of some 2.5 million foreign nationals between 1985 and 1989, indicating a net immigration of around 1.5 million foreigners during that period.[4] Nevertheless, populations of documented foreign *workers* in Northwestern Europe remained relatively stable during the 1980s, increasing by less than 350,000 between 1980 and 1989 (6% of the total population of foreign workers at the beginning of the decade).[5]

Although the documented migration of workers from 'South' to 'North' has declined, this has not implied a worldwide reduction in levels of international labour migration. Indeed, the number of people working outside their country of origin today is likely to be significantly larger than that of twenty years ago. This increase is due less to rising levels of 'irregular' migration to Western Europe or North America than to the growing importance of so-called 'South/South' flows, i.e. labour migration which is not directed to the most advanced Western industrialized countries. Today, the numbers of international migrants in Western Europe and North America represent around 30% of the estimated 100 million international migrants worldwide. Of the remaining 70 million or so, at least half are accounted for by people moving within the sub-Saharan African region (both 'economic' migrants and refugees), and a quarter by migrants in the Middle East and Southeast Asia.[6] Indeed, contemporary migration patterns suggest that if intensifying pressures to migrate are to translate into an actual increase in migration in the future, labour movement is likely to be characterized more and more by flows within the confines of the 'third world'. It is worth noting, for example, that of the total estimated number of sub-Saharan African migrants living and/or working outside their state of origin, less than 1.5% are currently resident in the European Community.[7] A relative increase in 'South/South' migration will be reinforced by the restrictive stance of the industrialized countries on immigration, and by growing economic and demographic disparities between those countries which are often collectively defined as 'less developed'. This was illustrated most graphically by the sudden expansion of the international migrant labour market in the Arab Gulf following the oil crisis of 1973.

The quadrupling of world oil prices in 1973 led to an economic downturn in the industrialized North, but brought unprecedented economic growth to the world's most important oil-producing states. On the basis of an explosion in export revenues, the Middle East oil-producers opted for a rapid development of their physical and socio-economic infrastructures. This necessitated a supply of workers that could not be satisfied by the indigenous labour force, since the affected populations were both small (with the exception of Iraq) and unsuited to meet the new demand.[8] Within two years of the oil crisis, huge numbers of foreign workers were flowing into the Gulf and Libya. This influx was initially dominated by flows from other Arab countries (Egypt, South Yemen and Jordan), but these were soon joined by rising levels of migration from Asia (particularly from India and Pakistan, and later from Bangladesh, the Philippines, Sri Lanka, Korea and Thailand). This development accompanied a progressive commercialization of the Middle East labour markets, and reflected the great importance of transcontinental migration flows in the world today. Asian countries were able to compete aggressively with Arab sending countries by providing cheaper and more 'regulated' labour, such that between 1975 and 1985 the proportion of Asian workers in the non-national workforce of the Gulf Cooperation Council states had increased from 20% to around 63%. The overall populations of the Arab oil-producing states more than doubled between 1975 and 1985 as a result of immigration.[9]

Those sending states which managed to win a share in the Arab Gulf and Libyan labour markets were not the same countries as those which had previously sent migrants to Western Europe (with the partial exceptions of Pakistan, Bangladesh and Turkey). The reasons for this are complex, and include the fact that many of the traditional sending countries (including the North African states) were geographically, economically, linguistically and/ or politically disadvantaged for competing in the Middle East.

The shift from Arab to Asian labour sources reflected, among other things, the outstanding importance of Asia as a migrant-sending region in the world today. The Philippines, for example, is now one of the largest labour exporters in the world. In the period between 1975 and 1987, over 3 million Filipinos had worked abroad,[10] a figure equal to 5% of the country's population in 1989.[11] Like other sending countries in the region, it has become highly reliant on the ability to export labour. As Manolo Abella observes, 'few developments have had a more profound impact on the economic conditions in a number of ... Asian countries than the overseas migration of labour'. In 1987, emigration represented almost 10% of the total GDP of Pakistan, and 60% of the value of total merchandise exports in Bangladesh.[12]

Although there are small migration flows from Asia to Western Europe, and more substantial flows to North America, most Asian worker migration continues to be to the Middle East oil-producers.[13] There has, however, been a slow-down in the migrant labour markets of the Arab Gulf since the mid-1980s and particularly since the Gulf war, and this has been accompanied by an escalation and diversification of flows within East and Southeast Asia itself. The recent expansion of Asian migrant labour markets reflects both a growth in the volume of trade and capital flows, and a marked variation in rates and patterns of economic and demographic development in the region. Competition among migrant-sending countries to win a share in these new labour markets is fierce. The most successful labour-exporters are the Philippines, Indonesia and Thailand. The main centres of attraction are Japan and the four 'Asian dragons': Hong Kong, Taiwan, the Republic of Korea and Singapore. Malaysia and oil-rich Brunei Darussalam also receive foreign workers. The picture is not straightforward, however, since a number of countries experience high levels of both emigration and immigration (Hong Kong, Korea, Malaysia and Thailand). This reflects the fact that almost no country in the world today can claim to be exclusively a 'sender' or 'receiver' of migrants.

In terms of immigration pressures, the position of Asia's most-developed economies is in many respects more extreme than that of Western Europe's receivers. Japan, for example, has suffered acute labour shortages caused by steep economic growth, negligible population growth (an annual rate of roughly 0.4%) and a rapidly ageing population. Taiwan is experiencing spectacular per capita income growth (around 14% annually) and close to zero unemployment. These countries provide a striking contrast with sending states such as the Philippines, where population growth has been running at an annual rate of nearly 3%[14] (close to world's highest rate), and where, despite emigration, labour force growth is placing severe strains on the absorptive capacity of the national labour market. Pronounced demographic and economic imbalances,[15] combined with shifting patterns of trade and investment,[16] an active promotion of emigration by sending governments and intermediaries (recruitment agents, transnational corporations, etc.), and a failure of both migrant-sending and migrant-receiving countries to adjust their labour markets to cope with their respective demographic problems, have all contributed to the recent acceleration of international labour migration within the region.

In common with the West European immigration countries, the Asian receiving states share a generally negative and restrictive stance towards most kinds of immigration, irrespective of patterns of labour demand. For example, the Japanese government – although relatively open to the immigration of highly skilled workers and professionals – remains committed to keeping its doors shut to other categories of foreign workers. A senior Japanese official recently stated: 'It is our government's policy that we permit the entry and stay of the foreign nationals seeking employment with professional skills, technique or knowledge ... on the other hand, we will not ... allow in principle the entry of unskilled workers and we will maintain our principle of not allowing them at present.'[17] Japan's reasons for preventing the entry of unskilled workers reflect a concern to avoid all the problems that are seen to have plagued Western Europe ever since the full-scale recruitment of foreign labour in the 1960s and 1970s. The same official goes on to state that 'if in the future the question of foreign unskilled labour should be considered ... most careful consideration would be needed, taking into [account] ... the past experience of other developed countries, to work out measures to avoid the problems that other countries have been experiencing from the introduction of foreign labour.'[18] To meet what is a growing demand for unskilled labour in the Japanese economy, the preferred policy is that of offsetting labour shortages with improved efficiency and the use of labour-saving production techniques at home, and encouraging overseas investment and the relocation of labour-intensive operations to labour-surplus (labour-cheap) countries.[19] This is a preference shared – at least theoretically – by the West European states.

In comparison with other receiving countries in the region, Japan's opposition to unskilled worker immigration may be somewhat extreme. Yet, even where unskilled immigration is sanctioned, the preference is for contract-tied temporary migration, and the migration of workers' families is discouraged. All the receiving countries in East and Southeast Asia, like those in Western Europe, are firmly committed to preventing unregulated immigration, as illustrated by the harsh measures implemented by Hong Kong to turn back illegal Chinese immigrants, and by Singapore's recent introduction of mandatory corporal punishment for illegal immigrants, their employers and agents. Nevertheless, undocumented migration is on the increase throughout the region.[20]

'Irregular' or 'undocumented' worker migration

A rise in 'irregular' (illegal) or undocumented migration is an issue of growing concern in the advanced industrialized world. More and more migration is classified as illegal because states have opted to control migration by applying increasingly stringent immigration laws. In addition, and contrary to the restrictionist stance of the industrialized receiving states, an intensification of regional and global economic, demographic, political and social disparities has brought about mounting pressure or potential for international migration. Although restrictive migration policies militate strongly against the direct translation of migration pressures into migration flows, a growth in economic and other inequalities can be expected to give rise to higher migration levels. Where there are fewer and fewer opportunities for legal migration, one can expect more and more migration to take place through 'irregular' channels.

If, as economistic models would suggest, migration is determined predominantly by conditions of supply and demand, or 'push' and 'pull' factors, then illegal migration probably fits the traditional models more closely than other kinds of (international) migration,[21] representing a very direct response to 'push' and 'pull' in which competing state interests play little part.* However, in conjunction with the worldwide increase in illegal migration, there is a growing perception that international movements are determined increasingly by 'push' rather than 'pull' factors,[22] a perception which serves to fuel paranoia in Western Europe about the intensification of migration pressures in surrounding sending states. It is a mistake to think that immigration controls in Western Europe and elsewhere are on the verge of collapse, but it is true that, in determining the shape and composition of migration flows, receiving-state regulation has to some extent been super-seded by supply conditions in sending regions. The increasing importance of such conditions, however, may be due not to a decline in demand from receiving areas but rather to a change in the intervening mechanisms linking the two factors in the migration process. When receiving states attempt to close off old migration channels or prevent the emergence of new ones without eradicating demand, they relinquish a significant degree of control over the pattern and direction of migration flows, since they are no longer in a position to regulate the satisfaction of demand by choosing who should come and where they should come from. As noted in Chapter 7, continuing 'economic' migration into Western Europe is 'demand'- as well as 'supply'- driven. However, the loss of regulative power encourages the perception that immigration has been imposed on receiving states by the countries of North Africa or Eastern Europe.[23]

The dynamics shaping irregular migration are extremely complex, however, and there is considerable evidence that 'irregular' immigration flows themselves generate certain patterns of demand which in turn stimulate further immigration. It is this argument which underpins the view that irregular migration has a distorting effect on receiving labour markets because employers in certain sectors come to rely increasingly on sources of

---

*Note that 'push-pull' models were originally based on movement within countries, i.e. migration that is not influenced by classic forms of migration control.

cheap, flexible and exploitable labour which are not available in the
labour supply. This does not necessarily imply a damaging effect
receiving economy, since many enterprises which depend on irregular
supplies, particularly those in certain labour-sensitive service sectors, would
not exist in the absence of continuing immigration – a point which counters
the view that illegal immigration necessarily displaces indigenous workers.
The fact that the United States and some West European states have at times
turned a blind eye to illegal immigration indicates an implicit recognition of
the economic benefits of undocumented immigration – at least during periods
of economic boom.

Nevertheless, undocumented or irregular immigration is generally viewed
negatively in the West, reflecting concerns which may have little to do with
the objective economic costs or benefits of the phenomenon. As Myron
Weiner observes, 'access rules are not merely the political expression of
economic forces, however important these may be ... economic changes may
induce governments to change their access rules ... but it would be a mistake
to think that the choices governments make are necessarily dictated by
economic considerations'.[24] Since it reflects a lack of control on the part of
the state, anxiety over illegal immigration is often particularly pronounced at
a time when a country's sovereignty seems challenged in wider terms. As
Demetrious Papademetriou argues in relation to the restrictive US Immigration Reform and Control Act of 1986,

> The passage of IRCA was in many respects the US Congress' immi-
> gration response to an ideology of limits. The 1970s and early 1980s
> had given rise to, and had subsequently fuelled, perceptions of ex-
> treme US vulnerability to foreign political and economic events.
> These perceptions had reinforced a US self-image of an eroding
> ability to control its own fate. This self-image, in turn, resulted in a
> 'defensive' approach to immigration policy reform.[25]

Although a general feeling of vulnerability may provide an atmosphere
conducive to a fear of immigration (legal and illegal), the concrete basis of
concern is usually expressed in more tangible terms, such as worries over the
economic and social order or the national identity. Since responses to
'unwanted' immigration are not shaped purely by economic considerations,
they vary considerably from country to country and from region to region,
reflecting differing political traditions and immigration histories, and changing perceptions of national, regional and international economic, political
and social conditions. This is demonstrated clearly in the context of expul-

sions. Weiner observes that 'any country can expel illegals, but such expulsion is obviously politically easier for authoritarian countries than for democracies'.[26] Thus, for example, the Gulf states have scarcely flinched at the prospect of carrying out mass expulsions when political or economic conditions have seemed to demand it (e.g. some 88,000 illegal residents were expelled from Saudi Arabia within a three-month period in 1979, around 18,000 from Kuwait in 1980,[27] and over two million workers were expelled from Saudi Arabia, Iraq and Kuwait in 1990/91). Similarly, one can point to Nigeria's expulsion of two million Ghanaian and other West African illegal immigrants in the early 1980s, Ghana's retaliatory expulsion of 500,000 Nigerians and other aliens, and Algeria's expulsion of some 10,000 nationals of Niger and Mali in the spring of 1986.

The Western democracies face rather different problems from those of the receiving countries in the Middle East or Africa. These include the fact that governments of the Western liberal democracies cannot endorse policies that sanction the formation of an 'immigrant underclass', whatever the actual outcome of the policies pursued. Still less could they tolerate policies of out-and-out segregation and periodic mass expulsion comparable with those practised by the Middle East oil-producing states. Instead – and in common with the Asian receiving states – the Western democracies have looked to enhanced control and enforcement measures to prevent the initial arrival and settlement of undocumented immigrants: border controls, stricter visa regulations, employer and carrier sanctions,* stiff penalties for traffickers, etc. But there are limits to how far these states can take such measures without infringing the rights of legal immigrants and the civil liberties of the population as a whole, and without generating opposition within certain sectors of the national electorate (including immigrant-dependent employers).[28] Furthermore, however harsh they may be, enforcement mechanisms are never likely to prove entirely successful as long as employment opportunities exist in the receiving countries. There will always be some migrants able and willing to surmount legal and procedural barriers if opportunities on the other side are markedly better than those at home. In response to the presence of undocumented immigrant populations, these states have wavered between practising small-scale expulsions and deportations, and carrying out occasional large-scale legalizations[29] and other programmes designed to integrate (previously) undocumented immigrants into mainstream society.

*Penalties for airlines or other carriers transporting passengers lacking necessary documentation or using false documentation.

In spite of these common problems, attitudes and responses to undocumented immigration also differ among these countries. For example, in a recent survey of work on the macroeconomic impact of immigration in OECD countries, Georges Tapinos notes that although immigration is a concern shared by all OECD countries:

> the issues differ on each side of the Atlantic ... [T]he 1990 Act in the US raising entry levels runs counter to the restrictive tendencies expressed by certain currents of opinion. At the same time, the problems of controlling illegal immigration across the Mexican frontier have reinforced the strategy for more open trade and finance which may ultimately reduce the incentive to emigration from Mexico to the United States. Although the free movement of persons is not included in the American–Mexican negotiations, it is an underlying and ongoing concern ... and initial attempts to measure the sectorial and regional effects of a more open policy on employment in the United States are a factor in the negotiations. Europe shows a clearer preference for keeping its frontiers closed. Consequently ... discussion as to the consequences of immigration relates more to the impact of foreigners already in the country than to new entrants.[30]

Western Europe's immigration countries may be seen to face distinct political problems in comparison with the United States, although like the US, receiving states in Western Europe are confronted with growing levels of illegal immigration as a function of a variety of economic and demographic pressures. The number of undocumented foreigners in Western Europe is not known, although some estimates suggest a figure of around 2.6 million. It is thought that at least a million of these are residing and/or working in the new immigration countries of Southern Europe, particularly Italy and Spain.[31] But whereas undocumented immigrant populations in the United States reflect a long history of Hispanic immigration (estimated at between 2 and 3 million after the 'amnesty' of 1987/8, of which some 80% are from Mexico),[32] the receiving states of Southern Europe – which have no comparable history of immigration – are now faced with growing immigrant populations of diverse origins, the greater proportion of which is less than a decade old.

Western Europe is currently experiencing a significant upsurge in xenophobic and anti-immigrant opinion. Although anti-immigrant sentiments are also on the rise in the United States, they have not yet become as powerful in US public opinion as they have in Western Europe. Indeed, it is interesting to note that in the US, elements of the far 'right' – usually associated with an anti-immigration stance in Europe – have at times found themselves in a curious alliance with a variety of other groups opposing legislation designed to restrict immigration. The success of this alliance largely explains the relaxation of US immigration policies in the form of the 1990 Immigration Act, which expanded quotas for certain categories of family and worker immigration.[33] Right-wing support for immigration in the United States stems primarily from an ideology which endorses every aspect of the free market, including that of labour, but it also reflects a belief in the fundamental value of immigration which – despite the potential for a resurgence in American nativism[34] – is still widespread. This attitude has never taken a significant hold in Western Europe, even in those states with a relatively long history of immigration. If one can speak of a country's self-image, that of the United States is based on the idea of a nation built on immigration.[35] Those of the West European immigration states are not, despite the fact that Western Europe now hosts a higher proportion of foreign-born to indigenous population than does the United States. Thus both the United States and Western Europe may be considered 'honeypots' in the contemporary world of international migration, but while this position has on the whole been perceived positively in the United States, it tends to be perceived negatively in Western Europe. It is perhaps for this reason as much as any other that the fear of an impending immigration crisis – so widespread in Western Europe in the early 1990s – was largely absent in the United States.

In addition to differences in the immigration heritage of the two regions, account must be taken of the particular position of Western Europe in relation to the former communist states of Eastern and Central Europe and the ex-Soviet Union. The euphoria with which Western Europe greeted the collapse of the Berlin Wall soon gave way to a sense of anxiety over the region's perceived vulnerability to all potentially adverse developments to the east, including migration. This in turn served to draw attention to longer-standing concerns about immigration from the 'South'. The break-up of the Soviet Union and the outbreak of hostilities in Yugoslavia contributed to this growing sense of insecurity, an unease which was only heightened when the conflict in the Balkans began producing refugee flows across the borders into nearby West European states. The collapse of the Iron Curtain meant that Western Europe could no longer isolate itself from the troubles of its neighbours to the east, and nothing captured this state of affairs more clearly than the arrival of asylum-seekers at its doors.

Asylum flows

Concern over the issue of asylum had been brewing in Western Europe since the numbers of so-called 'spontaneous' (as opposed to 'managed') arrivals of asylum-seekers in the region began increasing in the early to mid-1980s. For example, the numbers of people seeking asylum in the European Community rose from around 70,500 in 1983 to 290,650 in 1988.[36] The reasons for this increase are difficult to pin-point. During the 1960s and 1970s, Western Europe was scarcely touched by the numerous refugee crises which developed in Africa and other parts of the 'third world'. Spontaneous arrivals of asylum-seekers had been rising since the early 1970s, but it was not until the 1980s that numbers began escalating substantially. Improved air transport communications are often cited as one explanation,[37] but it is likely that the well-publicized resettlement of Indochinese refugees in the 1970s was equally important, in that it encouraged new expectations of finding asylum in the West.[38] Probably more significant, however, was the world-wide increase in the global refugee populations, which rose from approximately 10 million to 17 million between 1985 and 1991, or by 70%, excluding those displaced within their own countries. This was the same percentage change as was witnessed in the numbers of asylum-seekers arriving in Western Europe between 1985 and 1988 (an increase of around 120,000).[39]

Nevertheless, the increase in asylum applications in Western Europe during the second half of the 1980s still represented under 5% of the total rise in numbers of refugees worldwide. Rather than flooding to the richer countries of the North, over 90% of the world's 17.6 million refugees (and at least an equal number of internally displaced persons) remain in the 'third world'.[40] Indeed, the highest concentrations of refugees in relation to population occur in some of the world's poorest countries. Thus, for example, in Malawi – a country with a per capita GNP of US$200 – refugees account for over 10% of the national population; and in Guinea (per capita GNP of $480) one in every sixteen residents is a refugee.[41] These figures may be compared with the situation in the European Community, where some 1.3 million applications for asylum were lodged between 1983 and 1989.[42] If around 80% of these asylum-seekers have remained resident in their respective countries of asylum, they represent little more than 0.3% of the total population. In these countries, per capita GNP ranges between US$15,000 and US$33,000.[43]

In the light of these kinds of comparisons, one might question the basis for the widespread concern which has emerged over an apparent 'asylum crisis' in Western Europe during recent years. One could point to the further escalation in asylum applications after 1989, caused by the sudden increase in applications by Central and East Europeans. But rather than amounting to a crisis for the region as a whole, this was principally a problem for the Federal Republic of Germany, which – by virtue of its previously liberal asylum laws and geographical position – received over half the total number of asylum applications lodged in Western Europe during the early 1990s. One can also point to the refugee flows out of the former Yugoslavia. The outbreak of hostilities in the Balkans has faced Europe with a complex refugee crisis of a kind which it had not witnessed since the Second World War. Yet what these developments have triggered is not so much a crisis of numbers as a crisis of policy exacerbated by the increase in numbers. In this respect, the problems in Western Europe cannot be compared very usefully with those faced by a country such as Malawi. Nor, indeed, can the situation in Western Europe be compared directly with that in the United States, Canada or Australia, which – although confronting a number of equivalent problems – have remained more isolated from the European refugee flows of the 1990s.

The roots of today's policy crisis lie to some extent in the orientation of the refugee protection 'regime' which was developed in the West after the Second World War and which remains as the basis of refugee protection in Western Europe today. The central building block of this regime is the 1951 United Nations Convention on the Status of Refugees and its 1967 Protocol,[44] which *inter alia* lay down a universally applicable definition of the 'refugee' and define certain standards of treatment to be accorded to refugees by signatory states. To a great extent, the UN refugee definition reflects the cold-war conditions in which it was formulated.[45] Despite the widespread and large-scale displacement of population in Europe during the Second World War, the United Nations adopted a definition that was applicable to individuals rather than to groups, and one tied to a rather restrictive and subjective idea of 'persecution'. Refugee status became, in essence, a status resulting from a discord between an individual's personal convictions and the tenets of the ruling political system in his or her country of origin – a status which, during the cold war, provided a certain political advantage for Western receiving states when it could be accorded to refugees from the Eastern bloc.[46]

Since the early 1950s, changing social and political conditions throughout the world have given rise to refugee flows of a rather different nature. Nevertheless, the legal definition applied in Western Europe has remained largely unchanged. As observed by James Hathaway,

Refugee law as codified in the 1951 Convention and the 1967 Protocol ... not only continues the original rejection of the notion of comprehensive assistance for all involuntarily displaced persons, but it
allies international law with a series of strategic limitations determined by Western political objectives. It ... defines need in terms
which exclude most refugees from the less developed world ... [and is]
both substantively and procedurally malleable at the instance of state
parties ... [As a result], contemporary international refugee law is
marginal to the protection of most persons coerced to migrate.[47]

Wider definitions were adopted by the Organization of African Unity (OAU)
in 1969 and the Organization of American States (OAS) in 1984 (the
'Cartegena Declaration'[48]). The 1969 OAU Convention on Refugee Problems in Africa begins with the UN definition, then incorporates 'every person
who owing to external aggression, occupation, foreign domination or events
seriously disturbing public order, in either part or whole of his country of
origin or nationality, is compelled to leave his place of habitual residence in
order to seek refuge in another place outside his country of origin or
nationality'.[49] The 1969 OAU Convention thereby facilitated flexible and
pragmatic responses to a wide variety of refugee movements. Such responses
became increasingly important with the emergence of more and more
complex refugee problems in Africa over the following decade.[50]

     Yet it was not until these crises began to touch Western Europe (and the
West as a whole) in the form of 'spontaneous' arrivals of asylum-seekers
from the 'third world' that the limitations of its systems of refugee protection
based on the 1951 UN Convention began to show. With states insisting on
case-by-case determinations, the administrative and financial load increased
signficantly as the numbers rose; and as the majority of asylum-seekers were
eventually allowed to remain on some basis irrespective of whether they were
granted full refugee status, the system appeared to degenerate more and more
into an expensive and cumbersome system of status determination. According to one estimate, the total cost of asylum procedures and refugee protection
in the OECD receiving countries rose from under $1 billion in 1983 to $7
billion in 1990, the latter figure being equal to twelve times the total UN
budget for refugee assistance worldwide, or one-seventh of total development
assistance from the OECD states to the 'third world'.[51] The problem of
definition compounded that of sheer numbers, as observed in 1986 by the
Independent Commission on International Humanitarian Issues (ICIHI):

Attitudes towards the new influx of asylum-seekers and refugees might have been more positive if it had been possible to distinguish them clearly from other immigrant groups. In practice, this has proved a difficult administrative problem ... Governments now classify asylum-seekers as 'de facto' refugees, 'political or economic immigrants', 'externally displaced persons', 'mandate refugees', 'shuttle refugees' and 'refugees in orbit'. Even those who have been granted asylum might find themselves labelled as refugees with 'A' or 'B' status, with 'tolerance status', or with 'exceptional leave to remain'. This confusing list of terms derives partly from the inadequacy of the 1951 Convention and 1967 Protocol ... Many of the asylum-seekers arriving in the developed world left their own country because life had become intolerably dangerous and insecure. But they cannot prove ... that they have a well-founded fear of persecution there.[52]

Most of those arriving in Western Europe during the late 1980s came from countries such as Turkey, Sri Lanka, Somalia, Iran, Ethiopia and Lebanon. These are not necessarily the poorest countries of the world, but all are associated with conflict and/or poor protection of human rights.[53] Many arriving from these states have been in need of protection despite an inability to demonstrate a well-founded and/or personalized fear of persecution. In most cases, some form of protection has been forthcoming; this is reflected in the high frequency of applicants who are granted some other kind of humanitarian status such as 'de facto refugee' or 'refugee B' status (e.g. 94% of applicants in Norway, 92% in Sweden, 50% in Switzerland and 59% in the United Kingdom in 1991). Nevertheless, because most of the countries of origin are economically poor in relation to the receiving countries of Western Europe, and because the majority have not been accorded full refugee status on the basis of the 1951 UN Convention, politicians have found it easy to justify the introduction of restrictive measures by arguing that the majority of the asylum-seekers are 'economic migrants' or 'bogus' refugees using asylum procedures to gain entry to the West.[54]

Both the problems of financial and administrative load and the blurring of categories were compounded by the increase in asylum applications from Central and East Europeans after 1989. Given that these asylum-seekers came from newly democratized states which had been deemed 'safe' by the receiving states, their arrival had the effect of further strengthening the perception that the majority of asylum-seekers arriving in Western Europe were voluntary or economic migrants 'abusing' asylum systems as a means of side-stepping restrictive immigration controls. As a consequence, what humanitarian concern remained to offset the real or perceived costs of refugee protection was considerably eroded, and pressure increased for more restrictive asylum policies to be introduced.[55] Germany responded to its own particular problems by amending its Constitution in July 1993 to do away with the unqualified right of asylum in Germany. This paved the way for new policies to restrict admissions and facilitate expulsions or transfers of asylum-seekers, particularly to the new migrant-'transit' countries of Central and Eastern Europe. Indeed – as discussed in Chapter 7 – new restrictive measures have been or are in the process of being introduced throughout Western Europe, including visa requirements for nationals of states generating refugees, the summary rejection of so-called 'manifestly unfounded' applications at the border, and the detention of asylum-seekers.[56] As a result, the numbers of asylum applications lodged in and/or considered by most West European countries stabilized or fell during 1993–4 (including Germany). Such measures have come under harsh criticism from humanitarian organizations and other non-governmental interest groups on the grounds that they impinge on *bona fide* refugees as much as – or more than – other categories of asylum-seekers. Thus Western Europe's 'asylum crisis' has been partly a crisis of principles, with restrictive measures causing 'serious concern to those who believe in an international humanitarian order' as 'humanitarian principles are threatened and basic standards of refugee protection lowered in the West'.[57] Moreover, the restriction of access to asylum in Western Europe has transferred much of the pressure onto Central and East European migrant-'transit' states which are less well-equipped to cope, whether in political, financial or institutional terms.

Taken on their own, West European responses to the Yugoslav refugee crisis might be seen in some respects to bode well for the future development of refugee protection in Western Europe. Rather than applying cumbersome case-by-case determination procedures, receiving states have tended to respond more flexibly by granting 'temporary protection' on a group basis – reflecting a recognition that the strict refugee definition and procedures based on the 1951 Convention may not be the most useful instrument to apply in situations of mass displacement. Moreover, the crisis has forced states to consider how 'solutions' to refugee movements can be related more closely to the causes, and thus to conditions of peace and security and human rights in the countries of origin. As stated recently by the UN High Commissioner for Refugees, 'the growing scale and complexity of the problem, as well as the changed international context, make clear the inadequacy of asylum as the whole response'.[58] Thus the increasing interest in a 'comprehensive response' based on a recognition of people's 'right to stay' (flight-prevention, creation of 'safe areas', etc.) and 'right to return' – in addition to their right to flee (asylum) – should be regarded positively. Yet the success of any response in which the stress is placed on prevention, temporary protection and eventual return is entirely contingent upon a range of often highly unpredictable political factors in the countries of origin, and upon the varying capacity and will of the international community to act. Current developments in the former Yugoslavia indicate above all the uncertainty of success in preventing or resolving the complex refugee-generating crises of the kind which are likely to dominate in the post-cold war world. Against the backdrop of a general restriction of asylum systems in Western Europe, initiatives in respect of refugees from the former Yugoslavia – including the creation of 'safe areas' in Bosnia–Herzegovina and 'temporary protection' for those outside – can be looked at primarily in terms of a weakening of support for the principle of asylum in Western Europe in the absence of any clear or reliable alternatives.

As the following chapter demonstrates, refugees are not a new phenomenon. Throughout history people have been forced to flee, whether by war, persecution or natural disaster. However, there have never been so many refugees in the world as there are today. The world's population of displaced persons (both internally and externally displaced) is now estimated to exceed 30 million. This is primarily a tragedy for the poorer and less stable parts of the world in which these populations are (and will continue to be) concentrated. Yet – as the current Rwandan crisis indicates – it is also a tragedy from which the countries of Western Europe cannot isolate themselves. If there is a refugee crisis facing Western Europe today, it is arguably principally one of conscience; for whatever success is achieved in terms of prevention, people will continue to be forced to move, and many will continue to seek protection in Western Europe. Thus if refugee protection is to survive as a central principle and basis for policy, asylum will have to supported as an integral component of the West European refugee policy.

Chapter 3

From Babylon to Berlin: A Historical Overview

No society is static, and the history of Europe, like that of every continent, has been marked by significant migratory movements at every stage. Even after the close of the so-called 'great migration period' which followed the collapse of the Roman Empire, the ethnic map of Europe continued to be transformed by periodic conquests and migratory movements. As Eugene Kulischer observed, by AD 900, 'Europe had entered the "sedentary" era. Yet at that time, not one German was in Berlin, not one Russian in Moscow, not one Hungarian in Budapest ... Constantinople existed ... but the only Turks there were a few slaves and mercenaries.'[1]

Patterns of forced and voluntary migration of the contemporary era are in many respects mirrored in the migratory movements of the past. Forced expulsion as a means of conflict resolution can be traced back at least as far as Old Testament times, as illustrated in the biblical record of the Jews' Babylonian exile. Even during the period of absolutist monarchical rule in Europe, when movement of population was severely curtailed, periodic large-scale forced migrations took place that were not unlike those of the modern era. Although the particular dynamics of every migratory movement are complex and unique, in so far as migration is patterned by the interrelation of social, economic and political change and the efforts of rulers and governments to exercise control over populations, general processes of migration can be seen to have remained fundamentally similar over centuries of societal transformation in Europe. As expressed by the same writer, 'the modern age did not so much invent new forms of migration as alter drastically the means and conditions of the old forms'.[2]

The changes in the 'means and conditions' of migration that have taken place in Europe are inextricably bound up with the economic and political transformation of the state: the expansion of state control, shifts in the relationship between subject or citizen and the state, and changing relations between states. In so far as the freedom to move is determined by political structures controlling any given community or population, the particular pattern of migration that takes place at any one time cannot be understood without reference to the nature of a ruler's or government's control over the migratory process. Furthermore, conditions underlying an original desire to migrate can themselves be related back to the political structures in question and the political, economic and social relations that exist between sending and receiving areas. Migration patterns between states must therefore be related to developments within and among the states which condition the desire, freedom and means of individuals to migrate. In cases of forced migration it can be demonstrated that, although certain fundamental determinants of involuntary movement can be traced back to the time of Nebuchadnezzar,[3] the scale and scope of and responses to refugee movements have changed with the development of the state, the emergence of the 'nation-state', and the expansion of state control over populations.

The aim of this chapter is to trace the overall trends in international migration that have taken place in Europe since the emergence of sovereign and state in Europe after the thirteenth century. It is hoped that aspects of continuity and of change in international migration patterns can be identified, and that, in so doing, some light will be shed on current trends and responses to migration.

The mercantilist era: emigration control and forced expulsion

The expansion of monarchical power after the thirteenth century, the decline of the concept of a universal but non-territorial community of Christendom in Europe and the emergence of state sovereign control over distinct subject communities gave rise to the first strictly 'interstate' migrations in Europe.[4] With the expansion of monarchical power and the emergence of absolutist rule that took place in Europe during the fifteenth and sixteenth centuries came what Adam Smith termed the 'mercantilist' order.[5] As the sovereign gained control over the economy and foreign trade, there emerged ideas of state strategic and economic interests. Because a large population was considered an economic and military asset, rulers did all they could to prevent subjects from travelling abroad. Therefore, just as a large proportion of Europe's population had been tied to a particular landlord and locality under the preceding feudal system, so the new order bound the people to a particular monarch and his territory. As noted by Alan Dowty, 'mercantilism in the service of absolutism – the combination of national economic calculation with the habits of authoritarian rule – produced a strikingly modern system of emigration control.'[6] Unlike today, however, because population was considered a valuable resource the rulers generally welcomed immigration and showed little hostility to in-migration of peoples of diverse ethnic origins.

Although not greatly worried by the ethnic make-up of subject populations, the monarchs of this period were concerned with questions of integration, and sought to consolidate their power by promoting identification with their rule. Their power rested on religion, and so Christianity became the prime instrument of integration. These efforts to render populations more religiously homogeneous gave rise to large-scale migratory movements. Just as authoritarian regimes of the twentieth century have resorted to expulsions of minority groups in the interests of national consolidation, so thousands of non-Christians and 'heretics' were periodically expelled or forced to flee as a result of the totalitarian claims of the Christian rulers of this period. According to one estimate, over one million people were forced to move within Europe between 1492 and 1713.[7]

One of the first large-scale expulsions of this period was that of the Sephardic Jews from Spain in 1492. As noted by Kulischer, since the time of the First Crusade the 'persecution of Jews [had become] a permanent part of the social and political life of Christian Europe.'[8] Towards the end of the thirteenth century Jews had been expelled from England, and in the fourteenth century they suffered expulsions from France and periodic banishment from German feudal domains. Similarly, the efforts of the Spanish monarchy during the fifteenth century to convert the Spanish Jewish population to Catholicism proved largely unsuccessful. The powerful position of the Jewish community in the Spanish economy was considered a threat to the crown and, following the implementation of a series of anti-Jewish measures, a decree was issued in 1492 ordering the Jews to convert or leave. Of the some quarter of a million Jews who had been practising their religion openly in Spain, about 200,000 fled. The largest group settled in the Ottoman Empire,[9] others eventually found refuge in the Netherlands and England.[10] This served as a precedent for the expulsion of the Moorish Muslim community from the Iberian Peninsula in 1609 after the failure of Philip II to enforce cultural and linguistic assimilation. Most fled to North Africa.

It was not only non-Christians who fled or suffered expulsions during this period. Towards the end of the sixteenth century, for example, Philip II forced roughly 175,000 Protestants out of the Spanish Lowlands.[11] Most of these subsequently settled in the northern provinces of the Netherlands when the regions gained independence in 1609. At least 200,000 Huguenots fled France after 1685 when Louis XIV revoked the Edict of Nantes which had granted Protestants freedom of worship since 1598.[12] The English use of the term 'refugee' was first used to denote this group. Migration movements also resulted from religious conflicts in England and Germany. Periodic flights of Catholics and Protestants from the German states continued until 1555 when the Peace of Augsburg instituted the general right of the sovereign to decide the faith of his subjects. Significant movement between German states followed as people sought freedom to practise their religion. Oliver Cromwell's campaign against the Irish Catholics in the mid-seventeenth century caused many to flee to France and Spain, while others, resisting deportation to Western Ireland, were sent as indentured plantation labour to Barbados.[13] State campaigns against religious and political dissent also gave rise to refugee movements from the Habsburg lands, such as the flight of about 150,000 Protestants from Bohemia after the Catholic counter-reformation issued a total ban on Protestantism.[14]

It was during this period that the New World began to be opened up. From the fifteenth up to the eighteenth century, over two million Europeans left to settle in the Americas.[15] Yet a much larger migration process was also taking place at that time which linked the two continents. As Kingsley Davis noted, 'for the first time, the world began to be one migratory network dominated by a single group of technologically advanced and culturally similar states'.[16] Davis was referring to the forced movement of up to ten million slaves from West Africa to Europe and the New World which started at the beginning of the sixteenth century with Spain sending slaves to Haiti, Cuba and Jamaica, and which expanded into a worldwide trading network during the seventeenth and eighteenth centuries.[17] The slave trade must be understood in the context of developments in the more advanced European economies of the time. During the early period of colonization, new territories were seen to have immense potential value, to be exploited for luxuries and precious metals, and subsequently for the production of crops (particularly those areas which could be accessed relatively easily: the Caribbean, the Gulf of Mexico, and the coasts of North and South America). Manpower was needed for crop production, and, since a concern to maintain European population levels still prevailed, labour was sought elsewhere. Because the demand for labour in the colonies exceeded that within Europe, most of the slaves were sent to the New World.

Slave imports were prohibited by Britain, the USA and Denmark during the first decade of the nineteenth century, and slavery abolished altogether in the British Empire in 1833. The demand for plantation labour did not disappear with the changes in the law, however. Plantation owners in the Caribbean and the Indian Ocean found a substitute supply in the form of indentured labour drawn largely from landless Asian populations, particularly from India, Southern China and Java. This system was later extended to supply plantations in Southern and Eastern Africa and Southeast Asia, and continued until the beginning of this century. Kingsley Davis has estimated that as many as 16.8 million Indians left under this system, of whom about 4.4 million never returned.[18] The Atlantic slave trade and the subsequent 'coolie' migration together constituted one of the largest involuntary migratory movements to have taken place in history.

The 'new migration epoch'

Towards the end of the seventeenth century the basis of the monarchs' power came under threat from theorists such as John Locke espousing ideas of the natural rights and the social contract. These thoughts were later expanded by the Enlightenment thinkers, who stressed individual liberty and restraint of state power. These ideas found expression in the French Revolution and 1791 French Constitution, which stipulated the 'freedom of everyone to go, to stay, or to leave, without being halted or arrested unless in accordance with procedures established by the Constitution'.[19] The development of individual social and political freedom at this time was inextricably linked to developments in the economic sphere. The advent of a market economy in Europe was reflected in the emergence of the liberal *laissez-faire* economic thinking of theorists such as Adam Smith, which stressed the importance of individual economic action and the withdrawal of state control over production and consumption.[20] Human mobility was argued to be essential for the proper functioning of the market, as expressed in Frank Knight's typification of the market economy when he asserted that there be 'no exercise of constraint over any individual by another individual or "society"; each controls his own activities with a view to results that accrue to him individually ... [There must be] complete absence of physical obstacles to the making, execution, and changing of plans at will; that is, there must be "perfect mobility".'[21]

Contemporaneous with the rise of market capitalism was the emergence of industrial forms of production, and, in the words of the economic historian Karl Polanyi,

The more complicated industrial production became, the more numerous were the elements of industry the supply of which had to be
safeguarded. Three of these, of course, were of outstanding importance: *labour*, land and money ... they would have to be organized for
sale on the market – in other words, as commodities. The extension of
the market mechanism to the elements of industry ... was the inevitable consequence of the introduction of the factory system in a commercial society.[22]

This social, economic and political transformation of European society was
accompanied by a steady rise in population growth, and for the first time
governments began to be concerned about the danger of overpopulation.
Malthus published his famous treatise on population growth in 1798[23] which
drew attention to the high birth-rate of the time and saw widespread famine
as inevitable if nothing could be done to reduce the rate of population growth.
Although not initially, Malthus subsequently came to support emigration as
a mechanism which might alleviate population pressures in certain areas.
More explicit support for emigration came from Adam Smith, who criticized
mercantilist (exploitative) colonial policy, and argued that the New World
economies would be more valuable to Europe if encouraged to develop into
equal trading partners.[24] The following decade witnessed mounting demographic, social, political and economic pressures for the increased movement
of individuals within and across state borders.

Aristide Zolberg points to the 'demographic, industrial and democratic
revolutions', which took place from the second half of the eighteenth century
into the first few decades of the nineteenth century, as heralding a transition
to a 'new migration epoch' characterized by a shift from emigration control
to a positive encouragement of emigration.[25] Over the eight years preceding
Malthus's publication, over 700,000 British citizens had emigrated to North
America.[26] By the late 1820s, legal controls hindering exit had been removed
from most countries in Europe, and, with a waning in refugee movements,
voluntary migration to the New World began to dominate European
transnational migrations. For European governments, the benefits of emigration in terms of defusing social tensions that resulted from population
increase and from religious conflict played a significant part in this shift in
policy. Within ten years of passing an act designed to curb emigration,[27] the
British government was supporting emigration to the British colonies.
Inspired both by concern over increasing pauperism in England and by a

desire to direct flows of emigrants to British possessions overseas rather than to America, the British government conducted a series of experiments in state-supported emigration between 1815 and 1826 designed to encourage members of the Irish and other poor communities to leave.[28] In 1827 Britain established an immigration service in Canada.[29] In fact, these experiments had limited success when compared with the rising levels of independent voluntary migration to the United States. France, which was undergoing only a slow process of industrialization, was to prove an exception through continued concern over population deficit, and was thus the only state in Northwest Europe to maintain restrictions on exit throughout the nineteenth century. By the mid-nineteenth century, France was second only to the USA as a country of immigration.[30]

The migration dynamic at this time seems to have been provided largely by the 'push' factor of population growth and by sectoral social and economic dislocation caused by the industrial revolution in Northwest Europe. As noted by Frank Thistlethwaite, 'nineteenth century migration may have been powerfully attracted to the New World but acquired momentum within Europe itself ... waves of migration surging across the Americas were formed by impulses which were local'.[31] Nevertheless, the migration dynamic must be seen as a complex two-way process – a process intimately bound to the dynamics of the so-called 'Atlantic Economy'. The basis of this economy was the exploitation of the grasslands of North America by means of European capital and labour, described by Thistlethwaite as 'not merely a condition of international trade, but one in which there was such freedom of movement for the factors of production, that we can hardly distinguish the two principal countries concerned ... as two separate, closed economies ... emigrants were essential to its operation.'[32]

The subsequent development of the American economy into a trading partner not only created opportunities for European migrants, but also opened up lines of communication which increased the ability and willingness of potential emigrants to make the journey. By 1915 about 52 million Europeans had emigrated, roughly 34 million of whom left for the United States.[33] The numbers who left during this period equalled approximately one-fifth of the total population of emigration countries at the beginning of the nineteenth century.[34] However, the emigration flow did little to stem population growth in Europe. With an overall population increase in Europe from 194 million in 1840 to 463 million in 1930,[35] the only European country that suffered depopulation as a result of migration was Ireland. Ireland experienced extremely high levels of emigration over the years following the Great Famine. Between 1847 and 1854 over 1.6 million people migrated overseas.[36]

As the migration flow out of Europe continued through the nineteenth century, an increasing proportion of those leaving came from the less-developed areas of Southern and Eastern Europe. This marked the beginnings of a new pattern in international migration flows. Whereas transcontinental flows had previously been characterized by movement from the more developed areas of Europe to the underdeveloped regions of the New World and colonies, the new pattern that was emerging was one dominated by movements out of less-developed areas.[37] This was a pattern which had shaped movements within European states in the form of rural-to-urban migration since the beginnings of industrial development, and towards the end of the nineteenth century had started to characterize migration flows within the United States itself. It is also, of course, the pattern which dominates migration throughout the world today. Thistlethwaite wrote that 'the new immigration can be thought of as rural-to-urban migration which happened to be transoceanic rather than local in character'.[38]

This shift can be explained in part by the fact that as the countries of Northwestern Europe developed further, birth rates fell, social welfare was improved, and the pressure to emigrate declined. Meanwhile, uneven development in the more 'peripheral' European states was beginning to result in the same kinds of pressures that had initially spurred emigration from the 'core' countries of Northwest Europe. In the industrializing regions of the New World, '"areas of concentration" replaced the "great open spaces" as magnets of migration'.[39] Greater numbers of migrants returned home than had previously done so, and in this respect transoceanic migration increasingly resembled the pattern of temporary international labour migration which was becoming a dominant pattern of intra-European migration. As with international migration in the twentieth century, improved transoceanic lines of communication and lower transport costs reinforced this trend.

Towards the end of the nineteenth century, migratory movements within Europe began to exceed the flow to the Americas. During the last two decades before the turn of the century, Germany, England, Scandinavia, France and Switzerland were experiencing net inflows of population as the 'push' factors driving emigration began to decline. With a shift towards heavy industry, the most advanced European economies turned increasingly to foreign labour to satisfy manpower needs which could not be met by the immediate internal labour pool. By 1880 Germany had passed its emigration peak and was attracting workers from Poland. France, which had been experiencing net inflows of population by the mid-nineteenth century, began actively recruiting foreign labour. By 1911 the number of foreign workers in France had reached over one million (Italian, Belgian, Spanish and Polish).[40] Britain continued to depend on Irish labour which, already by the mid-nineteenth century, made up roughly one-quarter of the urban industrial population of England and Scotland.[41] Generally these migrants came from a rural background and filled unskilled positions at the lower end of the labour spectrum. Their work was usually considered temporary, to be taken up or disposed of as dictated by demand. The seasonal nature of much of this migration was made possible by the relatively short distances to be travelled. Nevertheless, just as with later international labour migrations, many workers settled.

From free movement to immigration control and involuntary migration
Alan Dowty writes of the late nineteenth/early twentieth century as the 'closest approximation to an open world in modern times'. Yet at the same as the world had been opening up to free movement in and out of states, the nature of the state in Europe had been changing as it expanded to take on roles affecting all levels of social, economic and political life. With this transformation emerged a deepening national consciousness – nationalism with the concomitant appeal for 'one nation, one state'. Just as the mercantilist rulers of the Middle Ages were troubled by questions of religious integration, so European societies of the late nineteenth and twentieth centuries became increasingly concerned with the problem of integration based on national/ ethnic identity. As noted by Ernest Gellner: 'Industrial society presupposes a mobile population with a shared literate culture ... The state supervises the transmission of that culture ... It is hostile to deep ... culturally marked chasms between its own sub-groups'.[42] While a new relationship was emerging between citizen and state through developments such as the introduction of state education and widening political representation, technological-industrial advances were rendering the centralizing and growing state apparatus increasingly equipped for internal control and external intervention.

Although the nineteenth century had witnessed numerous refugee movements (for example, those resulting from the suppression of the Italian uprisings in 1820–21 and 1833, and the counter-revolutionary upheavals of 1848), Michael Marrus argues that a high proportion of those who sought asylum abroad during this period in many ways resembled exiles rather than refugees. The numbers involved were relatively small and, since most were wealthy enough to travel, most had the means to support themselves until they felt they could return home. According to Marrus, 'so long as the refugees remained few in number and so long as they seemed relatively innocuous guests in the ... countries that were willing to accept them, nothing changed'.[43] Few had any trouble finding refuge. The largest numbers who remained in Europe went to Switzerland or London, which for a time was known as the 'great exile centre of Europe'.

The completion of Italy's unification in 1861 and the proclamation of a German Empire in 1870 contributed to the growth in nationalist sentiment in nineteenth-century Europe. Yet the ideal of the nation-state could never be easily realized, and the presence of minority populations posed a substantial challenge to the integrity of many of Europe's new-style nation-states. Efforts to consolidate new nation-states and conflicts over the internal social and political order of both new and old states began to emerge as the dominant refugee-generating processes in Europe – forces which are as strong today as they were a century ago. Furthermore, the forces giving rise to the flight of many refugees began working to reduce asylum-seekers' chances of finding a safe haven. As expressed by Hannah Arendt, 'Those whom the persecutor had singled out as scum of the earth – Jews, Trotskyites, etc. – actually were received as scum of the earth everywhere; those whom persecution had called undesirable became the "indésirables" of Europe',[44] a statement which, it is worth noting, could describe equally well the situation of many refugees in Europe today.

The nature of refugee movements in Europe began to change with the wars of German unification (1864–71). The nationalist nature of these wars created movement of groups in and out of areas under Bismarckian rule, including 80,000 Germans who were forced to leave France in 1870 and the flight of large numbers of Poles out of the German Reich.[45] These movements were followed two decades later by a much larger refugee flow as Jews began fleeing a series of pogroms in Russia, Austrian Poland, Romania, the Baltics and the Ukraine. Many fled a combination of political discrimination, economic hardship and social disorder, adding to the more generalized emigration out of Eastern and Central Europe, which was being driven by depressed agricultural conditions and overpopulation. The majority travelled to the USA, making use of improved and cheaper transatlantic transport communications. Between 1881 and 1914 over 2.25 million Jews emigrated to the United States[46] and roughly 120,000 settled in Britain.[47]

Liberal immigration policies began to come under question in the receiving countries. The United States was already facing problems in its efforts to return so-called 'coolie' labour migrants to China.[48] The mounting numbers of arrivals from outside Northwest Europe and the influx of Jewish refugees accelerated moves towards immigration control. Although strong pro-immigrationist sentiment persisted within certain sectors of the industrial and business community, the US economy had by this time developed to the point where its dependence on European capital and labour was declining and the state could begin exercising a degree of selective control over who should be allowed to settle. In 1892, a judgment in a US court included the statement that 'It is an accepted maxim of international law, that every sovereign nation has the power, as inherent in sovereignty, and essential to its self-preservation, to forbid the entrance of foreigners within its dominions, or to admit them only in such cases and upon such conditions as it may see fit to prescribe.'[49]

In 1896, the US Congress approved a bill imposing a literacy requirement on immigrants in an attempt to reduce entry of foreigners from less-developed parts of Europe and the Far East. This was followed in 1903 with the passing of an Immigration Law which included provisions for head taxes on immigrants and listed certain categories of prohibited immigrants.[50] A Congress report of 1911 recommended the prohibition of immigration from much of Asia.[51] Similar provisions were introduced in Canada and Australia.[52]

While most Jewish refugees continued to leave Europe for America, European asylum countries could afford to maintain relatively liberal immigration policies. At an international conference held in 1898, Britain, Belgium and Switzerland stated their commitment to existing liberal asylum and immigration policies.[53] However, by the end of the nineteenth century anti-Semitism was widespread in Europe, and with the closing of the American safety-valve it was not long before demands for more restrictive policies began to be heard in these countries. In Britain, growing concern over the numbers of Jewish arrivals generated support for the 1905 Aliens Act designed to limit entry of unwanted immigrants.[54] The shift towards stricter immigration controls in Europe was hastened by the outbreak of war in 1914, as marked by the widespread imposition of passport controls during the first year of conflict. By 1919, systematic immigration regulations and alien control measures were the norm and the 'open world' of the nineteenth century had come to an end.

From the Balkan wars to the Second World War: a new refugee era

A series of new refugee crises emerged with the political upheavals of the first two decades of the twentieth century and the eruption of regional and international conflicts in Europe. As observed by Zolberg et al., refugee flows of the early twentieth century were caused principally by multi-ethnic states 'adopting a mononational formula', which entailed 'some form of exclusion, either extreme segregation or expulsion' of 'unwanted' minorities. Interactions among a number of states 'striving to achieve this monistic objective' tended 'to invite mutual hostility and endless attempts at unmixing nationalities'.[55] With the decline of Ottoman control in the Balkans during the decades preceding the First World War, there arose an increase in nationalist activity and a series of refugee movements dominated by flows of Muslims to the South and Christians to the North. The first large-scale movements took place during the Balkan wars of 1912–13 and included the exodus of some 177,000 Muslims into Turkey and about 70,000 Greeks out of Western Thrace.[56] Struggling to introduce an element of control into the inflow of refugees, Bulgaria reached a population exchange agreement with Turkey in 1913,[57] which resulted in the transfer of roughly 50,000 people from each side. This agreement served as a precedent for much larger population exchanges which took place between Greece and Bulgaria and Greece and Turkey in the mid-1920s. The exchange negotiated between Greece and the new Turkish Republic at the Lausanne Convention of 1923[58] provided for 'a compulsory exchange of Turkish nationals of the Greek orthodox religion in Turkish territory and of Greek nationals of the Muslim religion established in Greek territory',[59] and resulted in the forced transfer of roughly 1.5 million people.[60] Large as these population movements were, they were generally confined to the Balkan region and involved a 'readjustment' of the ethnic map of the area to suit the new nation-states. Unlike today, refugee flows in the Balkans had little effect on the rest of Europe.

A new kind of refugee challenge was soon to appear on the European continent posed by what Hannah Arendt described as 'the most symptomatic group in contemporary politics':[61] refugees for whom no state was willing to accept responsibility. The flight of Russian refugees from persecution, famine, or the upheavals of revolution and civil war in the Soviet Union created one of the first groups of 'stateless' people. Although the main thrust of refugee flows took place within what was or had been tsarist territory, many managed to escape abroad. By 1922 at least three-quarters of a million Russians (including large numbers of Jews) had fled the Soviet Union.[62]

While the Soviet government was stripping émigrés of their citizenship, the USA and the European receiving states demonstrated increasing reluctance to extend protection to Russian refugees. In 1921 the International Red Cross Committee appealed to the Council of the League of Nations to take action. Later that year the High Commission on Behalf of the League in Connection with the Problem of Russian Refugees in Europe was established,[63] its main function being to deal with questions of legal status, including (subsequently) the provision of travel documents for denaturalized refugees who had no means of identification. In the mid-1920s, the Soviet Union adopted a no-exit policy which, in the words of one writer, 'immobilized what was at that time probably the largest pool of potential emigrants in the world'.[64]

The Russian emigration was only the first of a series of refugee problems that arose in Europe over the following two decades to which the League of Nations was called upon to respond. The post-First World War peace settlements were intended to satisfy European national aspirations as far as possible, yet with the dissolution of three multinational empires, it was inevitable that groups would emerge who could not assume the nationality of a successor state.[65] In the early 1920s the League Council was requested to extend its services to help the million or so Armenian,[66] Assyrian, Assyro-Chaldean and Kurdish refugees who were fleeing persecution or had been expelled from the newly independent Turkish Republic. According to Zolberg et al., there were as many as 9.5 million refugees in Europe in 1926.[67]

At a time when the grip of nationalist and protectionist sentiments was strengthening throughout Europe and all states were attempting to reduce flows of immigrants, the League proved relatively impotent in its efforts to ensure protection for these refugees. As with its previous efforts to assist Russian refugees, its success was limited to legal rather than humanitarian assistance. The US immigration report of 1911,[68] which had expressed alarm over the 'alien invasion', laid the foundation for a restrictive US national origins quota system, which was first enacted as a temporary measure in 1921 and was made permanent in 1924.[69] The numbers of Europeans to be admitted by the United States was severely curtailed, especially in respect of those from Southern and Eastern Europe. By the 1930s nearly every country of Northwest Europe had followed suit with the introduction of discriminatory immigration policies designed to keep out all but a few self-supporting immigrants.[70]

The problems facing the League in its efforts to encourage protection of refugees became all the more apparent during the Great Depression, when

Europe faced the new refugee crisis of thousands of 'non-Aryans' fleeing systematic harassment and persecution in Nazi Germany. By the end of 1937 roughly 165,000 German Jews had emigrated.[71] The conditions of economic depression that prevailed throughout Europe at the time made governments increasingly nervous about the possibility of mass refugee influxes. The League of Nations proved reluctant to lean too heavily on Germany or on receiving states at that time, and sought a compromise in the establishment of the High Commission for Refugees Coming from Germany, which was to work independently of the League in the coordination of relief operations in member states. At an intergovernmental conference held at Evian in 1938, all participants – fearful of a massive Jewish emigration from Poland, Hungary and Romania[72] – stated that they could not accept any additional refugees. Even France, despite not yet having to face large numbers of refugees from the Spanish civil war, was reported as being 'saturated with refugees'.[73] The same year saw the German annexation of Austria, the absorption of Sudetenland (increasing the numbers of Jews and gypsies resident within areas under the control of the German Reich) and the November 'Kristallnacht' (a night remembered for the destruction of synagogues and widespread violence against Jews). The number of refugees displaced by the German Reich doubled between the beginning of 1938 and the middle of 1939.[74] By this time, the United Kingdom had fixed quotas on the numbers of Jews allowed to settle in Palestine, and the outbreak of war in September 1939 reinforced the general reluctance to receive refugees from Germany. Hitler had originally favoured mass emigration as a means of ridding Germany of its unwanted minority populations, but as receiving countries tightened up their immigration controls the effectiveness of this solution came into question. The Nazi policy of encouraging emigration was eventually superseded by a policy of institutionalized genocide.

Millions of people were displaced during the war itself, including 100,000 French Alsatians forcibly moved from Alsace-Lorraine to areas under Vichy control following the German invasion of France,[75] and forced transfers of people to labour and concentration camps from other areas falling under German occupation. The Soviet occupation of Eastern Poland in the winter of 1939/40 led to one of a series of collective deportations and population transfers carried out by Stalin as roughly 1.5 million Poles and Jewish refugees were sent to the Soviet interior.[76] This was followed in 1940 with the forced movement of up to 0.5 million Finns,[77] and in 1941/2 with the deportation of about 61,000 Latvians, Lithuanians and Estonians into Soviet

Asia and Siberia after the 1941 invasion of the Baltic states,[78] and the movement of over 0.5 million Volga Germans. Huge numbers of civilians were forced to move throughout Europe as they were evacuated or fled areas suffering aerial bombardment. The advance of German forces into France generated one of the greatest upheavals of the war as up to a quarter of the entire French population moved South.[79] One estimate puts the number of people forced to move within Europe during the war at roughly 30 million.[80]

At the end of the war there were approximately 14 million 'displaced persons' who would need to be repatriated or resettled.[81] The aim of the Western Allies was to repatriate as many as possible as quickly as possible – a task to be carried out primarily by the military institutions. Soon after the war had ended, nearly a quarter of the population of the former German Reich was made up of refugees. In 1946 the International Refugee Organization (IRO) was established by the United Nations in response to the problem of the 'last million' refugees who could not be repatriated.[82] The establishment of the IRO marked the beginning of a recognition among governments that the refugee problem was not one that would disappear with the end of the war. In 1949 the United Nations General Assembly adopted a resolution to create the office of the United Nations High Commissioner for Refugees, which was to have a wider mandate than the IRO and, although initially set up with a life-span of only three years, was to become a more permanent fixture. The UNHCR statute was adopted a year later and included a universal definition of the refugee* and the obligation for the UNHCR to seek 'permanent solutions' to refugee problems. In 1951 the United Nations adopted the Convention Relating to the Status of Refugees, which bound signatory states to minimum standards of protection for refugees, including the undertaking not to return refugees to a country where they might suffer persecution. The Convention limited application of the refugee definition to those who acquired such status 'as a result of events occurring before 1 January 1951', and included the optional geographical limitation permitting states to limit their obligations to refugees resulting from events occurring in Europe prior to the critical date.[83] These temporal and geographical restrictions reflected a recognition that new refugee crises were likely to occur in the future and that these might not be confined to Europe,[84] and constituted an attempt by party states to limit their obligations vis-à-vis future refugees.[85]

*A person who is outside his or her country of origin and unable or unwilling to avail him/ herself of its protection owing to a well-founded fear of being persecuted on the grounds of his or her race, religion, nationality or political opinion.

Immediately following the war, over 14 million Germans were expelled from Eastern Europe in accordance with a protocol agreed to at Potsdam in 1945. Article 13 of the protocol stated that: 'The Three Governments ... recognise that the transfer to Germany of German populations, or elements thereof, will have to be undertaken'[86] – a resolution introduced partly in response to the expulsions already being carried out by Poland, Czechoslovakia, Romania, Yugoslavia and Bulgaria. As a result of these expulsions, only about 2.5 million ethnic Germans remained in Eastern Europe outside Germany and the Soviet Union. In the same year, an agreement reached at Yalta sanctioned the forced repatriation of Soviet prisoners of war by Britain and the United States. Over 2 million were sent back before the operation was halted as a result of concern within the British Foreign Office over the fate of returnees.[87]

These postwar repatriations did not mark the end of large-scale population movements within Europe; the emerging cold war and the division of Europe started to produce new waves of refugees. Shortly after the war, up to one million Poles and roughly 400,000 Finns fled areas annexed by the Soviet Union, and between 1949 and 1952 over 170,000 ethnic Turks were forced out of Bulgaria. In 1956 at least 200,000 Hungarians fled after the crushing of the Budapest revolution, and in 1968 about the same number of people left Czechoslovakia following the Soviet invasion. The largest flow out of the Eastern bloc during the 1950s was created by the exodus of some 3.5 million Germans from areas under Soviet control into West Germany. This flow represented about 20% of the East German population and began to bring about a serious labour shortage. It was, as Alan Dowty noted, 'easier, and more natural, for [the citizens of Eastern Europe] ... to contemplate crossing a border in response to economic or political pressures, especially in East Germany, bordered as it [was] ... by a state of the same culture and language ... The threat of manpower loss was therefore quite real, and it came at a time when these regimes could least afford it.'[88]

During the 1950s, the communist regimes of Eastern and Central Europe began to implement the kind of emigration controls which had been in place in the Soviet Union since the 1920s. Emigration not only threatened the labour markets of these states, but also constituted a challenge to the ideological foundations of the new regimes. Emigration came to be seen in several countries as a crime against the state. By introducing measures such as restrictions in the issue of passports and access to foreign currency, exit was made virtually impossible for all but a small minority of the population.

Through instituting policies promoting population growth and curtailment of emigration, the communist regimes of Eastern and Central Europe began to resemble those of classical mercantilism.

The East German authorities failed to control the numbers of people leaving, and on 13 August 1961 resorted to sealing the border between East and West Berlin with a barrier that was to become the Berlin Wall. Emigration from the GDR was cut down significantly as a result.* In general, the Eastern bloc countries succeeded in reducing emigration to a trickle of refugees during the 1960s and 1970s.† Just as the economic or strategic value of refugees in the fifteenth century facilitated their reception in countries of refuge, so the political value of refugees from communism ensured a welcome in the West in the cold-war conditions that followed the Second World War. Most were accepted without question and granted what may be termed 'presumptive refugee status', made easier by the limited numbers involved and the fact that 'ancient cultural and ethnic affinities between populations of receiving countries and European refugees made their reception and integration relatively smooth'.[89] In the United States a series of acts were passed after the war which resulted in an American conception of refugees virtually tied to refugees from communism.[90] The USA admitted a total of about 400,000 European refugees over the three decades following the war.

Just as the absolutist monarchs attempted forced assimilation of certain religious minorities or practised periodic expulsions of groups deemed unassimilable, so communist governments of twentieth-century Europe demonstrated a concern to integrate populations at least on ideological grounds and at times allowed the emigration of sizeable numbers of members of certain minority groups, particularly those with a 'homeland' or strong ties elsewhere. For example, in 1970 Poland, having sought the voluntary emigration of ethnic Germans since the expulsions that followed the Second World War, reached an agreement with the Federal Republic of Germany designed to expedite the emigration of the remaining German population. Three years before this, Poland had tried to rid itself of the Jewish community that had remained within its borders since the war. Approximately 25,000 out of a population of 30,000 emigrated, most to Israel and the United States. The most significant emigration from Bulgaria was that of ethnic Turks fleeing

*Of the some 840,000 East German migrants lost to the West after 1961, about a quarter left in 1989.
†Except Yugoslavia, which exported labour to Western Europe throughout this period.

Bulgarian policies of forced assimilation. Although the Soviet Union had adhered to strict policies preventing emigration since the 1920s, it did allow the emigration of members of certain minority groups which, because of their strong links with the United States or Germany, were conspicuous in terms of East/West relations: the Russian Jews, ethnic Germans and Armenians.

It was not only refugees that moved overseas following the Second World War; there was a general increase in voluntary transcontinental migration from Western Europe to North America and white-controlled Common-wealth countries. Although the USA reaffirmed quantitive immigration limitations and reduced ethnic selection criteria with the 1952 Walter-McCarren Act, in practice a more liberal attitude to European immigration developed during the 1950s and 1960s. When European immigration re-sumed, it continually exceeded annual quota figures by four times or more (particularly in the case of emigration from South European states). This migration was motivated largely by the initially slow postwar recovery of the West European economies or (in the cases of Ireland, Portugal, Italy and Greece) relative underdevelopment. As postwar reconstruction took off in Europe, however, the pressures to emigrate from Northwestern countries began to wane, declining rapidly during the 1960s. Nevertheless, many continued to migrate to Australia, which was gradually reducing immigration restrictions for all European groups and providing financial assistance for large numbers of Northwest Europeans wishing to migrate.

The dominant pattern of migration which was to emerge after the Second World War linking Western Europe with other continents of the world, was, however, that of migration into, rather than out of, Northwestern Europe. Economic recovery not only reduced the pressure to emigrate, but brought with it a new demand for labour which could not be satisfied by the indigenous labour force, or, in many cases, by the labour forces of contiguous states. The postwar years signalled a new era of labour migration for Western Europe which was to have a fundamental social and political impact on European societies of a sort that was hardly recognized at the time, and which, indeed, is still poorly understood today.

Chapter 4

Immigration Policy in Postwar Europe

The implementation of the postwar Marshall Plan for Europe was followed by rapid economic recovery and over two decades of sustained economic growth in all the most industrialized states of Northwestern Europe. This paved the way for a transformation in the structure of interregional and international migration patterns as these states progressively extended the scope of their labour markets to fuel economic reconstruction and development. The pattern of international labour migration that arose in Europe during the 1950s and 1960s can be seen in some respects as a revival and expansion of pre-First World War labour migration patterns. Yet whereas European labour migration flows of the late-nineteenth and twentieth centuries were largely restricted to localized regions and to movements between neighbouring countries, those of the postwar era took place within increasingly broader zones – from contiguous labour pools on to more distant countries, such as those bordering the Mediterranean and the former colonies.[1]

By the early 1960s all the highly industrialized countries of Northwestern Europe were experiencing sectoral labour shortages and had become labour importers. Although the form, dynamics and rationale of in-migration differed from one receiving country to the next, certain common trends can be identified over the four and a half decades following the war. This period can be roughly divided into three phases according to the general thrust of immigration policies predominating at the time: (1) 1945 to 1973, policies facilitating or encouraging large-scale labour immigration; (2) 1973 into the 1980s, introduction of policies designed to halt all further labour immigration; (3) 1980s and 1990s, strengthening of restrictive immigration policies and increasing preoccupation with illegal immigration and asylum-seekers. The past decade has also witnessed new efforts to achieve a degree of harmonization in West European immigration policies, as discussed in Chapter 7. Although much of the ensuing discussion is relevant to the majority of Europe's traditional receiving states, reference to national policies is restricted to the three European countries with the greatest number of immigrants in the 1960s and 1970s, comparisons between which illustrate both common trends and points of divergence: France, the Federal Republic of Germany and the United Kingdom.[2]

Open doors? 1945–73

Although the underlying factors generating high levels of immigration were on the whole similar for all Europe's receiving states during the period 1945–73, it was perhaps at this time that the particular policies pursued by each country manifested the greatest diversity. What states shared in common was a demand for manpower, initially connected with the drive for economic recovery in the years immediately following the war, and subsequently linked to sectoral labour shortages caused by rapid economic growth. As the economies of Northwest Europe revived and expanded, employers in certain sectors of heavy industry, in the new and growing service sectors, and – in the cases of France and West Germany – in agriculture, found it increasingly difficult to attract indigenous labour. Explicit recognition of this demand by governments and state authorities in France and in West Germany resulted in state policies designed to facilitate and encourage in-migration of workers from less-developed countries with a surplus of manpower.

Nowhere was the link between economic development and labour needs made so explicit as in France, where the 'population deficit' persisted as a concern of primary national importance. In 1946 the Commissariat Général du Plan de Modernisation et d'Equipement issued a statement to the effect that 'the population problem is the number one problem in the whole of French economic policy'.[3] Government estimates for the levels of immigration needed to stand the country on its feet again ranged from one to five million.[4] Already in 1945 a ministerial order had been issued calling for the creation of the Office National d'Immigration (ONI), charged with organizing and facilitating large-scale immigration.[5] As noted by one writer, 'in the spring of 1946, a vast immigration programme appeared to be on the point of taking place, in a bold national recovery policy in which demographic needs would be happily reconciled with economic necessities'.[6]

The large numbers of displaced persons requiring resettlement in the years immediately following the war was seen by some as a potentially useful labour pool. Indeed, West Germany felt no need to look abroad for labour when faced with the task of settling millions of German refugees and expellees from East and Central Europe.[7] Furthermore, migration from East to West Germany served as a major source of manpower up until the erection of the Berlin Wall in 1961.[8] Although the French government was reluctant to authorize any immigration from Germany,[9] agreements were reached with the International Refugee Organization on resettlement of refugees, and an accord was signed in 1947 with the allies which foresaw the possibility of turning German prisoners of war into free workers.[10] In the same year the UK government passed the 1947 Polish Resettlement Act providing for a coordinated effort to integrate over 100,000 Poles who had served in the Allied Forces.[11] This was followed shortly after by the promotion of European Voluntary Worker schemes, aimed at recruiting displaced persons and prisoners of war from the continent for one-year contracts to work in, for example, hospitals, agriculture, coal mining, textiles and construction where labour shortages were already being felt.[12] Yet for France and the UK, projects of this sort proved relatively unsuccessful, since the numbers of workers that had been hoped for never materialized.

It was also in 1947 that France redefined Algeria's status as a colony with the 'statut organique de l'Algérie' (organic status of Algeria), which conferred French citizenship on all Algerians and confirmed the principle of free movement between Algeria and the metropole. In 1947 roughly 65,000 Algerians migrated to France,[13] and by 1949 the figure had reached 265,000.[14] Although this immigration was doubtless seen to be of economic benefit, the French government, ONI and the Ministry of Population were concerned that policy should be aimed at a large-scale immigration most 'suitable' for cultural 'adaptation' and 'assimilation',[15] favouring, therefore, European immigration over immigration from North Africa. The then director of ONI later stated the aim as having been to avoid 'the formation of colonies that could not be assimilated on the national territory'.[16] France was already looking towards Italy as a potential large-scale supplier of labour, entering into a series of accords with the Italian government designed to facilitate an in-migration of Italian labour and to ensure a degree of state control over the direction of flows and sectoral/geographical distribution of workers.[17] The agreement reached in November 1946 had envisaged the immigration of over 200,000 Italians over the following year. However, only 49,000 were registered by ONI.[18] Disappointed with these figures, the French government sought a new agreement with Germany, which included the establishment of an ONI mission there in July 1950.[19] A further accord was signed with Italy in March 1951, followed three years later by a recruitment agreement with Greece.[20]

Britain, having traditionally favoured free movement of capital and labour within the empire, and being anxious to maintain close links with the 'Old' and expanding 'New' Commonwealth (note Britain's withdrawal from India in 1947), passed a Nationality Act in 1948 which reaffirmed the principle of free movement within the Empire and Commonwealth by stating that all colonial and Commonwealth citizens were British subjects. As such, they were free to hold a British passport and could enter Britain to find work, to settle and to bring families without being subject to immigration controls. Once here, Commonwealth immigrants could exercise full citizenship rights, including the right to vote. Although the primary rationale behind the Nationality Act was one of foreign policy (maintaining influence in the Empire and the Commonwealth) rather than labour market considerations, the same year saw the government's establishment of a working party on Employment in the United Kingdom of Surplus Colonial Labour, which was charged with investigating the 'possibilities of employing in the United Kingdom surplus manpower of certain colonial territories in order to assist the manpower situation in this country and to relieve unemployment in these colonial territories'.[21] In fact the working party concluded that, in view of the probable discrimination which would be directed towards 'coloured' workers, large-scale immigration from the colonies should be discouraged.[22] The following year the Royal Commission on Population published a report which stated that: 'A systematic immigration policy could only be welcomed without reserve if the migrants were of good human stock and not prevented by religion or race from intermarrying with the host population and becoming merged with it.'[23]

Despite these misgivings, colonial immigration was already underway with the first arrivals from the West Indies in 1948.[24] Although Britain never formulated an explicit labour recruitment policy, labour shortages did appear over the next decade, particularly in regions with expanding industries and in sectors where working conditions were unattractive to the indigenous labour force.[25] These labour demands were not being met by Irish immigration, and, since no other European labour pool was easily accessible by Britain,[26] significant flows from the colonies and the Commonwealth soon developed which were fuelled by 'push' factors in the sending regions (relative poverty, unemployment, etc.) as well as by the 'pull' of labour demand in Britain. This flow was also certainly accelerated by a drop in West Indian migration to the United States following the passage of the US 1952 Walter-McCarren Act, which restricted Caribbean migration to the USA to a hundred per year. As noted by Stuart Hall, 'this piece of legislation diverted interest back to the United Kingdom which, in addition to being the head of the Commonwealth, was also the only major industrial country to which large-scale migration from the Caribbean was possible'.[27] The latter was manifested most clearly when certain state employers (e.g. London Transport[28] and the National Health Service) began to recruit directly from the West Indies. Flows from the Caribbean were soon followed by high levels of immigration from the Indian sub-continent and – to a lesser extent – from Africa, Malaysia and Hong Kong. Between the census years of 1951 and 1961, the enumerated population of West Indian origin in Britain had increased from 15,300 to 171,800, that of Indian origin from 30,800 to 81,400, and that of Pakistani origin from 5,000 to 24,900.[29]

Whereas immigration flows into the UK developed outside any system of state control because no such system had been implemented, immigration into France took on an increasingly anarchic character because the state structures established to regulate flows proved too rigid to respond to the growing demand for labour.[30] Moreover, as in Britain, colonial immigration did not fall within the mandate of state regulatory institutions. Immigration into France was at that time dominated by flows from Italy and – subsequently – from the Iberian peninsula (and, in the north, from Belgium), much of which was seasonal, serving manpower needs in agriculture brought about by large-scale rural to urban migration of the French population. Whether migration was temporary or more permanent, it suited employers and migrants to by-pass the heavily bureaucratic state mechanisms which had been designed to regulate and channel flows. In this respect, economic necessity began to take precedence over demographic concerns, resulting in an increasing perception of migrants as an economic commodity and a progressive abandonment of the original aim to ensure 'permanent settlement and integration of foreigners into French society'.[31]

West Germany only began to experience labour shortages in the mid- to late 1950s. Following consultations among the Federal government, the Federal Employment Agency, employers and labour unions, the Federal Republic reached a bilateral labour recruitment agreement with Italy in 1955. This was to serve as a precedent for a series of later agreements reached during the 1960s with less-developed states in Europe and further afield. In

1960 similar agreements were reached with Greece and Spain. The impetus for large-scale labour recruitment strengthened after the erection of the Berlin Wall in 1961 and the resulting loss of access to East German labour. By 1968 Germany had established extensive labour recruitment programmes not only with Italy, Spain and Greece, but also with Morocco, Turkey, Portugal, Tunisia and Yugoslavia.[32] The recruitment arrangements established by Germany did not amount only to formal legal arrangements between the contracting states, but extended to comprehensive programmes which included the setting up of German recruitment commissions within the territory of the sending states concerned. The intention was to regulate flows in such a way that would benefit employers at the same time as protecting the German labour market: German employers notified the nearest Employment Office of their manpower needs, and the Employment Office, having checked that no German workers were available to fill the vacancies, informed the Federal Labour Office of the demand, which in turn contacted the recruitment commission offices set up in the sending states.

Constrained neither by the kinds of foreign policy concerns impinging on France and Britain as a result of their imperial history, nor by the demographic considerations which had troubled France for so long, the Federal Republic was free to practise a 'qualified' immigration policy, indeed a labour recruitment policy deemed explicitly not to be an immigration policy at all. Throughout the 1960s, the economic primacy of Germany's 'in-migration' policies was never questioned. The Aliens Act of 1965[33] intended immigrant labour to be 'a manoeuvrable resource ... for solving ... economic problems'.[34] The system of residence and work permits established by the 1965 Act was based on the intention to create a 'rotation' of workers. Workers in this *Gastarbeiter* or 'guestworker' category should stay in the Federal Republic for a limited period for the purposes of employment and then return to be replaced by new recruits according to need, thereby ensuring a match in supply and demand in the labour market. Residence permits were valid for periods ranging from two to five years and were granted on the basis of possession of a work permit, which in turn was dependent on employment guarantees. Underlying the development of this policy was a consensus among both sending and receiving states that all would benefit economically – the migrants because of the earnings and training that would accrue during the period spent in Germany, the Federal Republic because of labour supply, and the sending state because of the potential for unemployment relief, capital transfers and the eventual return of skilled workers.

Yet, just as the state structures set up in France to regulate immigration proved too rigid to cope with employer demands, so Germany's 'rotation' model proved inefficient in its attempt to balance the manpower needs of employers, despite the fact that the bulk of Germany's immigrants did enter through the official channels. The basic flaw in the German recruitment policies was the notion that temporary workers should fill what were essentially permanent jobs. Rotation of workers conflicted with employers' concern for continuity in a trained workforce. Under pressure from the business and industrial sectors, the system of rotation effectively gave way to one of permanent immigration. A large number of immigrants themselves, often not wanting to return after only a few years, were able to renew residence and work permits with the backing of their employers. Gradually it became clear that most of Germany's foreign workers would not leave. During the recession of 1967, lower numbers than might have been expected returned to the country of origin, despite unemployment within immigrant communities.[35] The pattern of Italian migration, characterized by relatively high levels of return migration when conditions in Italy began to improve,[36] hints at the fact that the migrants' decision to stay or return depended (and depends today) as much on perceptions of conditions in the country of origin as on conditions in the host country.

The series of agreements with sending countries sought by the French government during the early 1960s proved even less successful in regulating migration flows than those instituted by Germany. As noted above, the French authorities had begun to lose control over immigration soon after the regulatory institutions had been put in place. This trend continued into the mid- to late 1960s as immigration rates accelerated and migration sources diversified. Towards the end of the decade most migration to France was spontaneous, and the role of the Office National d'Immigration had been reduced to one of *a posteriori* regularization of immigrants who had already entered and established themselves.[37] Declining Italian immigration was being replaced by Spanish, then Portuguese, and, from the early 1960s, Tunisian, Moroccan, Yugoslav and a resurgence of Algerian immigration.[38] As observed by one writer, 'it is a question of an immigration that is for the most part uncontrolled, characterized by the great variety of countries of origin and the legal (or illegal) routes through which they entered the country – unorganized, lacking in any sense of security, deprived of political rights, poorly integrated into workers' organizations, and mainly apolitical'.[39]

The agreements reached with the sending countries (Morocco, Tunisia and Portugal in 1963, and Yugoslavia and Turkey in 1965) constituted an attempt to fill the institutional and juridical vacuum alluded to above. The French government's new desire to rationalize and streamline immigration was evident in the fact that the Evian Accords, signed between France and Algeria in 1962[40] guaranteeing freedom of movement between the two countries, were followed only two years later by an agreement designed to limit Algerian immigration according to the needs of the labour market.[41] This attempt was not successful, and two further Franco-Algerian accords were signed, in 1968 and in 1971, aimed at restricting Algerian immigration to an annual contingent of 35,000 and 25,000 respectively (with only temporary rights of entry).[42] These agreements, together with the establishment of a new governmental office, La Direction de la Population et des Migrations, in 1966, reflected the growing recognition of the need for a new and coherent immigration policy. Nevertheless, the Minister for Social Affairs still felt justified in stating in 1966 that 'illegal immigration itself is not pointless, for if we were to stick to the strict application of the international rules and accords, we would perhaps end up with a shortage of manpower'.[43]

By the early 1970s, the situations in which France, Germany and Britain, and indeed all the labour-importing countries of Northwestern Europe, found themselves vis-à-vis immigration were very similar despite having implemented different immigration policies over the preceding two decades. All had experienced large-scale migration inflows over which direct government control had been limited. All were having to face up to the fact that the majority of immigrants – particularly those from outside Europe – were not destined to return to their countries of origin when and if demand for their labour declined. In this respect (whether it had been intended or not) postwar immigration had not been a temporary economic phenomenon, but was, as Wihtol de Wenden observed, permanent, structural, and socially and politically significant.

Closing doors? The 1970s and 1980s
The oil crisis of 1973 marked a turning-point in postwar immigration policies in Europe. As economic recession set in, European labour-importing states one by one[44] introduced measures designed to close their doors to any further influx of workers from outside their regional economic groupings (European Economic Community, European Free Trade Association). By this time,

foreigners constituted at least 16% of the total population of Switzerland, 5% in the Federal Republic, 6.5% in France, 7.5% in Britain (foreign-born including Irish), 7% in Belgium and 2% in the Netherlands.[45] In every case a significant proportion of these foreign populations had migrated from outside Europe.

Although the economic recession was – and still is – given by governments and many observers as the reason or justification behind the immigration 'stop' of 1973/4, there are clear signs that concern over the social and political costs associated with these large immigrant populations had been growing for several years before the clamp-down, and that this anxiety might have had more than a little to do with decisions to suspend any further labour immigration. In a special report published by the Organization for Economic Cooperation and Development (OECD), prompted by the halt on immigration, correspondents noted the social tensions in countries apparently 'saturated' with migrants, but argued that there was very little competition between indigenous and immigrant labour in the job market and therefore that nationals of the host countries would not substitute for foreign workers. In a further report the following year it was suggested that decisions taken by governments to restrict immigration levels should be seen as 'the result of essentially political considerations', since 'the social and political drawbacks of immigration now seem to have become greater than the economic advantages'.[46]

Indeed, in the United Kingdom it would have been difficult to claim that restrictive measures had been introduced for any other than social and political reasons. Having never couched immigration policy in terms of economic necessity, British leaders had tended to be rather reticent on the subject of immigrants' economic contribution to the country,* and discussion on immigration had been dominated by anxiety about the social repercussions of 'coloured' immigration since the first arrivals from the colonies.[47] Preoccupation with the social and political costs of Commonwealth immigration led to comparatively early moves towards the introduction of legislative immigration controls. The first of these was enacted in 1962 with the Commonwealth Immigrants Act, which aimed to regulate migration flows through a system of employment vouchers.[48] These were granted liberally until the 1964 general election in which immigration figured as an issue of

---

*Note that economic growth during the 1950s and 1960s had been slower in Britain than in other Northwest European states.

central concern. In a review of the post-electoral situation in Britain, Enoch Powell, the Conservative Party Spokesman on Defence, stated that 'immigration was, and is, an issue. In my constituency it has for years been question number one, into which discussion of every other political topic – housing, health, benefits, employment – promptly turns ... Only if substantial further addition to our population is now prevented will it be possible to assimilate the immigrants already here, which in turn is the only way to avoid the evils of a colour question.'[49] Although Enoch Powell was marginalized in British politics for his extreme views,[50] this very point was to be repeated continually by policy-makers over the following two decades, not only in Britain, but in every European state that was host to immigrant populations, and was to form one of the bases for immigration control policies from the early 1970s onwards. At the time of the introduction of Britain's second Commonwealth Immigrants Act (1968) the then Prime Minister, Harold Wilson, stated that: 'We shall remain subject to ... risks of continuing tensions and stimulation of prejudice unless we amend the law so that the public in this country is confident that immigration is being effectively controlled. Only in such an atmosphere can good race relations be fostered'.[51] The British government enacted its first race relations legislation in 1965.[52]

Whereas other countries were able to implement a halt on labour recruitment as a measure to restrict immigration, in Britain immigrants were on the whole British subjects exercising their citizenship rights, and thus, if immigration was to be controlled, the government was bound to introduce legislation involving a redefinition of these rights. The question of citizenship and the right to enter the United Kingdom was raised most graphically in 1967 when the Kenyan government announced its intention to expel the Kenyan Asian population, most of whom had opted for UK and colonies rather than Kenyan citizenship when offered the choice after independence in 1962.[53] During the two months before the 1968 Commonwealth Immigrants Act came into force, 12,823 Asians entered the United Kingdom. By restricting right of entry into Britain to passport holders who could claim a close connection with the UK, the Act effectively extended immigration controls both to this group[54] and to all non-patrial UK passport holders. This legislation came in for criticism on the grounds that it favoured immigration from the 'Old' Commonwealth and was designed to limit 'coloured' immigration from the New Commonwealth. Both the 1962 and 1968 Acts were succeeded in 1971 by the Immigration Act,[55] which replaced all previous immigration legislation with a single statute introducing provisions for control of admission and stay of Commonwealth citizens and foreign nationals. Free movement for Irish nationals and the 1968 distinction between patrials and non-patrials were preserved. Provisions were also included for the introduction of visa requirements for nationals of particular foreign or Commonwealth countries as might be required.

It was not until the late 1960s that concern over the social impacts of immigration began to figure prominently in French political discourse. By the early 1970s, however, the question of integration of foreigners was coming to the fore. Anxiety began to be expressed over a range of issues including immigrants' housing and working conditions, the risks of xenophobic reactions among host communities, and the possibility that immigrants were a drain on public spending, hindering modernization of industrial structures and damaging general working conditions. This heightened concern over the social implications of immigration was reflected in the so-called 'Marcellin-Fontanet' circulars of 1972, issued by the Ministers of the Interior and of Employment. These called for restrictions on regularization of immigrants, confining the granting of residence permits to those who could produce evidence of employment and adequate accommodation.[56] Two subsequent circulars were issued the same year designed to limit regularization of illegal immigrants by stipulating that regularizations would be restricted to those who had entered France before a specific date.[57] The summer of 1973 witnessed an explosion of racial tension in Marseille directed primarily against Algerian immigrants, prompting the Algerian government to announce its intention to suspend all further emigration to France. President Georges Pompidou responded to the trouble in Marseille with an official condemnation of racism. During the months leading up to the 1974 election, the immigration debate had become public and politicized, and although consensus on the issue was limited, it was in the early summer of that year, following the election of Valéry Giscard d'Estaing to the presidency, that the decision was taken to halt all further immigration.[58] A new office of Secretary of State for Immigrant Workers was created. This post was filled by Paul Dijoud, who issued a circular on 5 July suspending worker immigration, followed by a second on 19 July implementing a stop on 'secondary' family immigration.

Concern over the social aspects of immigration and a reordering of priorities in favour of integration of foreigners and away from recruitment was also evident in West Germany at the very beginning of the 1970s. By 1971, the German Federal government had already begun restricting entry of

workers to those processed by the German Commissions stationed in the
sending countries, and in June 1973 the government published a new 'Action
Programme on Employment of Foreigners' which indicated a new awareness
of the integration problem (and of rising unemployment, particularly within
immigrant groups). Anxious to cut down foreign worker inflows, but not
wanting to abrogate the agreements entered into with the sending countries,
the government introduced domestic measures designed to discourage employers from seeking to take on any more foreigners, including stricter
supervision of housing supplied by employers, higher fees to be paid for each
recruited worker, and penalties for employment of illegal immigrants.
Mandatory rotation was deemed unacceptable, in line with the government's
new intention to ensure successful integration of all foreigners who did not
wish to return voluntarily. Only a few months after announcing this policy,
the government decided that it was necessary to implement a complete stop
on all further recruitment activities from non-EC states.[59] The reorientation
of policy towards integration of 'foreigners' (cf. 'immigrants') amounted to
a tacit recognition that (although it had not been intended) the Federal
Republic had become an immigration country. However, despite continued
immigration ever since the time of the first recruitment agreements, this has
never been acknowledged officially, as reflected in a recent government
document: 'The fact that aliens stay here for a long time or permanently does
not mean that the Federal Republic of Germany has become an "immigration
country".'[60]

In the interests of achieving the integration of foreigners, and in accordance with various international legal instruments dealing with human rights,[61]
the 1973 stop on immigration throughout Northwestern Europe generally did
not extend to family members and dependants of immigrants already resident
in the host countries. Many might have agreed with Enoch Powell when he
stated that 'It can be no part of any policy that existing families should be kept
divided, but there are two directions in which families can be reunited, and
if our former and present immigration laws have brought about the division
of families ... we ought to be prepared to arrange for them to be reunited in
their countries of origin.' Yet no European democracy would have been
prepared to embark on a programme of comprehensive forced repatriations,
and although there were early signs of hesitation on the part of governments
over the extent to which family reunification should be facilitated,[62] by the
late 1970s immigration had resumed relatively high levels in all the prior
labour-importing countries as more and more immigrants resident before

1973/4 began bringing in their families.* The emphasis remained, nevertheless, on restriction and control. In July 1978 the British Home Secretary observed that 'subject to commitments to United Kingdom passport holders under the special voucher scheme ... and to those arising out of the Immigration Act 1971 and from our membership of the EEC, "there will be no further major primary immigration in the foreseeable future"'. In respect of family reunification he stated that 'The great majority of those who qualify for settlement now do so by virtue of their family relationship with someone already settled here ... subject to the requirement ... that the sponsor ... must be able to support and accommodate them without recourse to public funds ... the Government acknowledges a clear commitment to them.'[63] Most countries attached conditions to the entry of family members, most notably, as mentioned here, proof of adequate funds and accommodation on the part of the sponsor.[64]

Despite continuing family immigration, migration inflows during the 1970s and into the 1980s did not lead to a marked increase in total stocks of foreign population in Europe's main receiving countries, in-migration being balanced by voluntary return migration, particularly to the European sending states. The changes that took place over the decade after 1973 were more structural than numerical. Thus, although the total legally resident alien population of Germany increased by only 5.7% between 1974 and 1984,[65] the proportion of immigrants of non-European origin was increasing while that of southern Europeans was declining. As noted in the 1985 OECD report, 'the OECD immigrant populations are changing in favour of populations from increasingly physically and culturally distant lands'.[66] This shift was accompanied by a significant feminization of immigrant populations as well as a decrease in the average age.[67] These changes created the impression that immigration levels were increasing at a much higher rate than they actually were.[68]

The 1970s and 1980s witnessed an overall convergence in the immigration policies of West European states, following the rather disparate approaches of the preceding two decades,† all professing a commitment to strict

---

*Family immigration had been increasing as immigrant communities became more settled, but it was not until after the labour immigration stop of the early 1970s that family immigration came to dominate immigration flows.
†Note that Italy, Spain, Portugal and Greece began introducing immigration policies in line with those of states farther north as they started experiencing significant immigration flows from the mid-1980s onwards.

controls on primary immigration from outside the EC (/EFTA) and regulated family (secondary) immigration in the interests of the integration of foreign populations. Indeed, as noted below, even the traditional sending states of Southern Europe had, by the late 1980s, introduced immigration legislation comparable to that operating elsewhere in Western Europe, since there was not only declining emigration and increasing return migration to these countries, but also a significant increase in immigration, much of which derived from countries outside Europe which had previously dominated migration to the major receiving states of the 1960s and 1970s. This convergence in European policies was reflected at the international level, where tentative moves had been made towards international cooperation and harmonization on the issue of immigration. In October 1974, Paul Dijoud (French Secretary of State for Immigrant Workers) stated that 'Europe ... must strive to reach a common definition of objectives and to organize a model of cooperation with the countries, in which immigration will find its true place'.[69]

Prior international instruments dealing with migrant workers included: the 1949 International Labour Organization (ILO) Convention concerning Migration for Employment (Revised), setting out modest provisions for recruitment, conditions of work, etc.; the accompanying Migration for Employment Recommendation (Revised), which recommended a general duty to facilitate movement of manpower from areas of labour surplus to those of labour deficiency (about which few states had many reservations at the time); the 1955 European Convention on Establishment, which was to regulate nearly all legal questions affecting aliens permanently resident in a European state but which attracted very few ratifications; and the European Social Charter, signed in 1961, which dealt with the rights of migrant workers and their families, but only applied to nationals of Contracting States. Two further instruments were established in the mid-1970s which reflected both the desire to create a cohesive international or European 'migration regime' and the highly restrictive climate which prevailed at the time. The ILO Migrant Workers (Supplementary Provisions) Convention of 1975, which dealt with 'migrations in abusive conditions and the promotion of equality of opportunity and treatment of migrant workers', began with a preamble stating the 'need to avoid excessive and uncontrolled or unassisted increase of migratory movements'.[70] The European Convention on the Legal Status of Migrant Workers included provisions for equal treatment of migrants, but was very limited in its scope, extending minimal protection only to nationals of signatory states in situations of permanent paid employment. As noted by Richard Plender, the fact that 'only five States ... ratified this Convention, which imposes such modest obligations, illustrates with pellucid clarity the reserve with which most West European States have treated migration for employment since the date when it was opened for signature'.[71] Similarly, the United Nations' International Convention on the Protection of the Rights of all Migrant Workers and Members of their Families, adopted by the General Assembly of the UN on 18 December 1990, has not received the broad support of West European states in terms of ratification. This Convention – which *inter alia* sets down certain minimum standards of treatment for illegal, as well as legal, immigrants – still requires 20 ratifications to enter into force.

By the late 1970s, the preoccupation of receiving states with finding solutions to the 'immigration problem' was extending beyond simple immigration control to an increasing interest in positive encouragement of return migration. In June 1977, France introduced a programme of financial incentives to induce immigrants to leave. Over the following year, roughly 45,000 immigrants returned to their country of origin – nowhere near the officially declared target of 200,000.[72] Furthermore, it seems that most returns were largely autonomous, being as a result of individual decisions based on an evaluation of opportunities in the country of origin, rather than being related to the government programme. This was evident in the fact that most of those making use of the assistance were Spaniards and Portuguese – groups that the authorities might have been most willing to keep. In September 1980 France entered into an agreement to encourage the resettlement of Algerian workers that involved financial assistance from France and help in housing and employment from Algeria (reflecting a shift towards seeking cooperation with countries of origin).[73] In Germany, the aim of encouraging returns was made clear in February 1982 in the government's consolidation of the basic tenets of its policy on aliens (restriction, encouragement of repatriation, integration), and in July decisions were taken that translated this objective into a clear policy, including financial incentives for returns and measures taken in the field of development. These decisions were reaffirmed the following year in an Act of 28 November 1983 to Promote the Preparedness of Foreign Workers to Return.[74] No return policies introduced during the late 1970s and early 1980s had any significant impact on migration trends.

Aware that efforts to return migrants would not provide a solution to the immigration problem, receiving states continued to focus attention on immigration control. In Germany, recommendations were issued by the Federal government in December 1981 on 'urgent measures dictated by social responsibility to control subsequent immigration of dependants (in particular, lowering the maximum age of children who immigrate subsequently to 16 years and limitation of subsequent immigration of spouses joining aliens of the second generation)'. In December of the following year, visa requirements were introduced for aliens from non-EC member states intending to stay longer than three months on German territory.[75] In France, controls had been progressively strengthened over the three years leading up to the 1981 elections, the most notable policy developments being ever more stringent entry conditions (for all non-EC immigrants), improved expulsion powers introduced by Lionel Stoleru (Secretary of State for Manual Labour) and beginning in 1977, and the 'Loi Bonnet' of spring 1979, based on the measures implemented by Stoleru but designed to introduce a degree of clarity and coherence into what had become 'un véritable labyrinthe administratif'.[76] In Britain, 1981 saw the passing of the British Nationality Act, which further defined different categories of British citizenship and connected rights, reflecting a 'wish to divest itself of remaining obligations to the imperial status of British subjects'.[77]

Both as a concomitant of the restrictive climate which prevailed at the time, and as a partial consequence of the restrictive policies in place (policies which closed off many channels for legal immigration), illegal immigration and the growth in arrivals of asylum-seekers, as discussed in Chapter 2, began to emerge as the primary policy concerns for the 1980s. In France, 'la lutte contre l'immigration clandestine' (the fight against illegal imigration) was a phrase quoted over and over again in policy statements from the beginning of that decade. The two central tenets of the new, more liberal, approach to immigration adopted in France after the socialist victory in the presidential and legislative elections of 1981 were expressed as (1) the restriction of any new immigration and the fight against illegal immigration, and (2) the improvement of the living and working conditions of those already resident in France. A circular was issued in August of that year which stipulated that all foreigners in France in an irregular situation could be regularized if able to prove that they were in France before 1 January 1981;[78] employers could regularize their position before 1 January 1982. It was stated that thereafter no regularizations would take place, and that control of borders and sanctioning of employers of illegal immigrants would be strictly applied.[79]

Illegal immigration has never proved to be as significant a factor for Britain as for other countries in Western Europe. Nevertheless, the Home Secretary affirmed in 1978 the government's determination 'to take firm action to prevent evasion and abuse of the immigration control', noting that 'the prevention and detection of attempted evasion and abuse of the control ... is one of the main features of the Government's immigration policy ... The system is open to abuse at four points: at the entry clearance stage, or at the port of entry (on the basis of false documents or statements), or by clandestine illegal immigration, or by overstaying in this country by people originally properly admitted on a temporary basis.'[80] The methods of illegal or clandestine entry listed here would apply to all receiving states, although in the case of Britain overstaying accounts for the bulk of illegal immigration (difficult to monitor in a country which relies on checks on entry rather than post-entry internal controls).[81]

Germany's growing preoccupation with undocumented immigration during the 1980s was reflected in the adoption of a range of new laws, policies and procedures beginning with the Act to Control Illegal Employment, passed in January 1982, and followed in 1985 by the Recruitment Promotion Act, and in 1990 by the Act Amending the Aliens Law. Together, these Acts contain regulations on the imprisonment, fining or expulsion of illegal immigrants, employer sanctions, and sanctions imposed on transport companies caught transporting foreigners not in possession of the requisite documentation[82] – the kind of measures in place or considered throughout Western Europe during the 1980s and early 1990s.

By the late 1980s, the new immigration states of Southern Europe were also becoming seriously concerned about rising levels of 'unwanted' immigration. Italy, for example, passed its first immigration legislation in December 1986 (law no. 943), which included a legalization programme for clandestine workers and set out general principles for the regulation of the conditions of non-EC workers. This was followed in 1989/90 by the so-called 'Martelli Law' (law no. 39), which allowed for a second wave of regularizations, established annual quotas for the number of immigrants to be admitted, introduced severe sanctions for employers and traffickers encouraging illegal immigration, and introduced new powers for the expulsion of immigrants violating immigration laws.[83] On balance, however, such measures have not had any great success. Despite the regularizations and strengthened efforts to prevent illegal immigration, an estimated 25% of Italy's one million-plus immigrants are present illegally; of these, an estimated 60% have been resident in Italy for less than four years.[84] Law no. 39 also embodied Italy's first comprehensive legislation for dealing with asylum applications. This included, importantly, the abolition of the geographical limitation which had previously precluded refugees from outside Europe applying for asylum in Italy – a limitation which had almost certainly resulted in large numbers of would-be asylum-seekers entering Italy as undocumented immigrants.

The early 1990s: shifting priorities or more of the same?

Although governments were increasingly concerned about undocumented immigration and asylum inflows during the 1980s, it was not until the end of the decade that these concerns became a primary political issue in the region. The emergence of widespread anxiety over a looming immigration 'crisis' in Western Europe can be traced back principally to the dramatic events which took place in Europe in 1989. Within the space of just a few months, over a million people surged across the borders from east to west, signalling the collapse of the Eastern bloc and, with it, the collapse of the barrier that had separated the populations of Eastern and Western Europe for over three decades. This exodus gave rise to a sense of vulnerability to uncontrolled population movements that had not been felt in Western Europe since the Second World War. The entire European geopolitical and economic map had undergone a sudden transformation, and in the wake of this transformation emerged, it seemed, the prospect of a massive influx of migrants fuelled by economic and political instability to the east. America would not provide the 'safety-valve' that it had done earlier in the century, and in this respect the new migration from east to west was to be a European problem requiring European responses.

This anxiety brought about a partial reappraisal of migration policy in Western Europe. 'Action to address the root-causes' soon became a central phrase in the European political vocabulary as traditional forms of immigration control, such as border controls and visa regimes, suddenly appeared insufficient to cope with the perceived crisis ahead. The Conclusions and Resolutions adopted at the Fourth Council of Europe Conference of European Ministers Responsible for Migration Affairs in September 1991 included a resolve to develop and strengthen bilateral and multilateral cooperation aimed at reaching a better economic balance between countries of origin and host countries: programmes of productive investment in the emigration regions were to be encouraged, and the possibilities of the Social

Development Fund of the Council of Europe were to be used to promote job creation in the disadvantaged regions of European countries.[85] Adopted within the framework of the Council of Europe, this Resolution envisaged cooperation extending beyond the confines of the European Community, to include not only other receiving states in Western Europe, but also the new sending – and, in some cases, receiving – countries of the former Eastern bloc.

Concern has not been restricted to developments on the European continent, however. Fears of potential mass 'East/West' migration served to draw attention to longer-standing concerns over so-called 'South/North' migration, particularly from North Africa. The same Resolution notes the continuing pressure for migration into European countries as a result of enormous economic, social and demographic imbalances between different parts of the world. This concern was echoed in the EC's Declaration on Principles Governing External Aspects of Migration Policy issued at the Edinburgh European Council in December 1992, and which called *inter alia* for policies to promote:

> the preservation of peace and the termination of armed conflicts; full respect for human rights; the creation of democratic societies and adequate social conditions; a liberal trade policy, which should improve economic conditions in the countries of emigration [and] coordination of action in the fields of foreign policy, [and] economic cooperation.[86]

The mass influx of 'economic' migrants from the East which many feared during the earliest stages of transition in Eastern and Central Europe and the former Soviet Union failed to materialize. Indeed, of all documented movements which took place from East to West between 1989 and 1991, the great majority involved members of particular ethnic groups with strong ties in the West (Jews, ethnic Germans, Greeks, and Armenians) – groups with a history of emigration which substantially pre-dated the revolutions of 1989 and 1990.

It was not long, however, before fears of uncontrolled 'economic' migration from the East were subsumed by fears of mass movements caused by political instability in the former Eastern bloc countries. The first politically generated movements which accompanied the collapse of communism did not stir up serious concerns because of the predominant euphoria of that time, and because the specific conditions which gave rise to this migration were relatively short-lived. However, subsequent refugee movements within the former Eastern bloc have been caused by more intractable problems of inter-ethnic and inter-communal tension and conflict – problems of the sort that gave rise to much of the migration in Europe during the first half of this century. Of these, the crisis unfolding in the former Yugoslavia has been the most visible, taking place in an area of critical geopolitical importance, and – unlike the population movements in the Balkans earlier in the century – giving rise to substantial refugee flows directly into the neighbouring countries of Western Europe.

The widespread anxiety over immigration which developed during the early 1990s can therefore be largely attributed to the general climate of insecurity in Europe following the end of the cold war, coupled with a real decline in control over immigration flows in Western Europe. Additional factors contributed to this concern, however. First, as discussed in Chapter 7, the member states of the European Community were by then endeavouring to harmonize their immigration and asylum policies in anticipation of the implementation of the Single Market. The difficulty of achieving swift and effective harmonization, combined with the evident failure to achieve complete control over migration flows, drew attention to all aspects of the issue, particularly in the media.

Second, the early 1990s witnessed a significant upsurge in anti-immigrant and xenophobic attitudes throughout much of Western Europe – an upsurge which has 'fed on alarmist pronouncements about the danger of an invasion'.[87] In Germany, asylum-seekers and other immigrants came under vicious attack from elements of newly emergent extreme right-wing movements. Although, as argued by the German government, xenophobia based on racism and fanatic nationalism may exist only within 'an infinitely small proportion of the population',[88] so-called 'reservations'[89] towards foreigners are widespread[90] and have resulted in growing support for political parties often extolling extreme anti-immigrant policies. As discussed in Chapter 6, failure to integrate existing immigrant communities can be seen simultaneously as a cause and an effect of this development. A report drawn up on behalf of the European Commission in 1990, for example, noted that 'the failure of integration policies is likely to stimulate the reawakening or development of sentiments based on fear of the foreigner, but, at the same time, a collective feeling of mistrust towards foreigners may ... affect some specific, important elements of the integration of immigrants, such as access to housing or schooling.'[91]

Thus mounting concerns surrounding all aspects of immigration and refugee flows coalesced to render migration a highly sensitive political issue in Western Europe. Whereas previously immigration has primarily been the concern of labour and immigration ministries, it now engages the heads of states, cabinets and ministries involved in defence, internal security and foreign policy.[92] At the same time, the issue has become more politicized at the local and national levels as politicians have attempted to respond to or exploit rising anxiety over the issue among the public at large.

Thus a new urgency has entered the policy debate in recent years. However, this has not brought about a significant shift in the direction of West European immigration policies. Indeed, if anything, the new sense of urgency is resulting in a further entrenchment of old forms of control and apparently little in the way of new policy initiatives. Today's principal concerns regarding migration into Western Europe centre around the three issues of external migration pressure, immigration control and – against the background of widespread hostility towards immigrants – immigrant integration. Only calls for action to combat external migration pressure represent any significant departure from the policies of the past. Immigration control and immigrant integration have formed the primary pillars of migration policy in Western Europe ever since the immigration clamp-down of the early 1970s. Moreover, as discussed in the Conclusion, although the new emphasis on tackling migration pressure is ever-present in the rhetoric, as yet almost nothing has emerged in terms of clear policy objectives in this area. Important though it is for the future development of migration policy in Western Europe, the harmonization process is, in essence, one of shifting traditional national control measures to the supranational level to suit a strengthening supranational grouping. The emphasis is still on negative actions such as tighter border controls and stricter visa regimes, and action still tends to be ruled by short-term objectives and short-term concerns. And underlying all policy measures is a largely negative attitude towards immigration which has changed very little over the past two decades. Receiving states in Western Europe continue to see themselves as non-immigration countries despite the fact that some have been receiving substantial numbers of foreign immigrants for over a century.

Chapter 5

The Sending Countries

Traditionally, as Papademetriou points out, labour-surplus countries have seen 'the opportunity for emigration of their un- and underemployed workers as an unqualified blessing ... The coincidence of interests between labour-scarce and labour-surplus societies gave rise to a buoyant, almost reckless enthusiasm for both organised and spontaneous migratory flows.'[1] But the economic benefits of emigration are by no means certain. Indeed, according to the ILO, the effects may be negative in the aggregate: 'The worst but not the most unlikely effect is that emigration breeds the emigrating subproletariat of tomorrow. Clearly, the sending countries do not profit as much from emigration ... [as] the receiving countries.'[2]

When looking at questions of policy in international migration, there has been a tendency for observers to focus on the role of receiving states and thus fail to take full notice of the importance of sending countries' emigration policies. This bias has been attributed to the assumption that the international labour market is largely controlled by labour-receiving countries.[3] The result has been an implicit neglect of the part played by sending countries in influencing, and to a varying extent controlling, migration flows. The building of the Berlin Wall in 1961, and the subsequent separation of the East and West European labour markets, provides perhaps the most graphic example of the influence of sending countries (or potential sending countries) over international labour flows. Although the no-exit policies pursued by the Eastern bloc countries were exceptional, a number of postwar sending states did develop emigration policies which reflected domestic labour market or national development interests, and all, to a greater or lesser extent, exerted influence over migration flows.

The huge variation in causes, impacts and responses to migration in different sending countries and regions means that generalization is extremely difficult.[4] Nevertheless, certain central questions relating to migrant-sending countries have been raised repeatedly over the past three decades. Attention has focused particularly on the macroeconomic impact of emigration on these countries. Although a full consideration of this issue falls well beyond the scope of this discussion, it is hoped that by looking at policies pursued by certain sending states since the early 1960s some indication can be given of the most important questions raised in this context. This chapter centres on the main postwar labour-sending countries which are still significant in the context of current (and future) migration flows into Western Europe. The discussion is therefore limited to the non-European sending states of the Mediterranean basin (Turkey and the North African states).*

Promotion of emigration

As noted in Chapter 4, the postwar economic boom in Northwestern Europe was accompanied by a progressive expansion of labour markets in the industrialized states to incorporate workers not only from less-developed European countries (Italy, Spain, Portugal, Ireland, etc.), but also from non-European countries, including the colonies and former colonies. According to some observers, this development marked the start of 'the progressive disappearance of national boundaries for labour and [the] transformation [of labour] into a structural component of the international political economy'.[5] For the sending countries, it signified their 'penetration by, and incorporation into, the world economy',[6] an incorporation based on ties of dependency between the less-developed and the more-developed economies of the world.[7] However, although their position in relation to the industrialized migrant-receiving countries was undoubtedly unequal, a number of existing or potential sending countries looked very positively on the idea of emigration. Labour export appeared to be a solution to many ills, particularly employment and balance-of-payments problems which – although in some cases linked directly to national development programmes – were seen to be hampering further economic progress. Encouraged by the high demand for labour in Northwestern Europe, a number of countries began implementing policies aimed specifically at encouraging the emigration of workers.

*Excepting the former Yugoslavia which, while obviously of primary importance in current migration flows, is now giving rise to flows of an entirely different nature. Note also that the countries listed were not the major postwar labour-sending countries for the UK.

In Turkey, for example, development planning during the 1960s and 1970s stressed rapid industrialization on the basis of large-scale capital-intensive industries. This programme was not expected to lead to extensive job-creation (at least in the short term), and it implied a reliance on other countries for the import of raw materials, semi-manufactured goods and technology. Emigration of workers was seen as an instant solution to Turkey's growing unemployment problem and worsening balance-of-payments position. Promotion of emigration was stated as an explicit policy objective in Turkey's first three five-year plans. Throughout the 1960s and early 1970s, 'the emphasis was on maximising the outflow of individuals and the consequent inflow of hard currency – little else had such high priority'.[8]

Turkey entered into bilateral labour recruitment agreements with the Federal Republic of Germany in 1961, with Austria, Belgium and the Netherlands in 1964, with France in 1965, and with Sweden in 1967.[9] These agreements, although covering a range of issues, such as workers' pensions, health, identity cards, etc., were primarily concerned with matching labour supply in Turkey with demand in the recruiting country. The 1965 Franco-Turkish accord, for example, began as follows:

> The French government and the Turkish government, being desirous of organizing in their mutual interest the recruitment of Turkish workers, have hereby agreed as follows:
> *Art. 1*: The French government will periodically inform the Turkish government about any of its manpower needs that would be suitable for Turkish workers. This information will, in particular, provide exact details of requirements regarding age, specializations, professional aptitudes and health. The Turkish government will provide the French government with as precise details as possible on the number, age and qualifications of Turkish workers desirous of working in France.[10]

The recruitment of workers required a high degree of cooperation between Turkey and the recruiting country. Although the recruiting government and employers had the final say in selection, the Turkish Employment Service (TES) played an active role and maintained a monopoly over the registration of potential migrants throughout the recruitment period. By 1974 there were close to one million Turkish workers resident in Northwestern Europe, of whom roughly 800,000 had migrated through the TES.[11]

The North African sending states also came to support emigration, reaching a whole series of bilateral labour-exchange agreements with the European labour recruiters during the course of the 1960s. Both Tunisia and Morocco signed agreements with France in 1963, and although that between Tunisia and France was not implemented until 1969, both Tunisia and Morocco were soon actively promoting emigration through their national development plans in an effort to reduce the growing pressures of un- and underemployment. The Office of Professional Training and Employment[12] in Tunisia performed a similar role to Turkey's TES, being responsible for finding new markets for Tunisian emigrant labour, and for selecting candidates; by 1972, at least 75% of Tunisian departures passed through official channels.[13] Morocco similarly created a Central Emigration Service so as to introduce more effective coordination of emigration. However, beyond policy statements supporting labour export, the Moroccan authorities achieved little more than the negotiation of labour agreements with the European receiving countries. The Moroccan position was thus largely one of *laissez-faire*.

The Algerian government's attitude towards emigration, at least during the second half of the 1960s, mirrored that of Turkey. Algerian support for emigration was, in fact, hesitant during the first few years after independence, but the overthrow of Ben Bella, the Algerian Republic's first president, by Colonel Houari Boumédienne in 1965 ushered in a new phase of development which favoured the rapid expansion of high-technology, capital-intensive, heavy industries. This programme implied a neglect of agricultural development and the creation of relatively few jobs in relation to the capital invested. Labour export was seen as a 'vital safety valve'[14] to relieve the social and economic pressures of unemployment and underemployment.

However, Algeria was in a rather different position from Turkey and the other North African states in terms of its negotiating position. The primary destination for Algerian migrants was, of course, France – as it was for Tunisia and Morocco. However, in the case of Algeria (in contrast to Tunisia and Morocco), labour migration to France dated back to the First World War, when Algerians were recruited to work in French munitions factories, mines and armed services, and by 1962 migration had become 'a massive, structural, permanent feature' of both the Algerian and the French economies.[15] By virtue of its oil and gas resources and close integration with the French economy, Algeria, as compared with other sending states, was in a peculiarly strong position to negotiate labour export agreements with the French government. Although the labour agreements reached between the two countries after 1962 seemed to reflect French interests more than those of Algeria,[16] the latter's negotiating position can be seen to have strengthened during this period such that, by 1973, Algeria was able to impose a unilateral freeze on all further labour emigration before France introduced immigration restrictions. The reasons for this action were almost certainly political, reflecting, among other things, Algeria's concern to sever all obvious links with its colonial past in the lead up to the Algiers 'non-aligned' summit. The decision to stop emigration was facilitated, however, by Algeria's improved economic position following the nationalization of the oil industry in 1971. Algeria was no longer so reliant on remittances from labour export,[17] and, it was argued, was in a better position to create employment at home. This view was reflected in the 1976 National Charter, which stated that: 'Because of the development of the country, workers no longer need to emigrate to find a job. Moreover ... the Revolution has created for each Algerian the obligation [to make] his contribution to the common task of national reconstruction.'[18]

Nevertheless, on balance, the sending countries were disadvantaged in the bilateral recruitment negotiations of the 1960s because the volume, composition and timing of migration flows were determined more by labour demand than by supply. This was observed by Adler in the context of the 1964 Franco-Algerian 'Nekhache–Grandval' Agreement (named after the negotiatiors). He noted that although in principle labour migration was to be regulated according to availability of labour in Algeria as well as to demand in France, Algerian labour supply was in effect 'infinitely elastic', and thus France could decide more or less unilaterally how many Algerian workers to admit.[19]

The weaker position of the labour-sending countries became more obvious with the halt on recruitment in 1973/4. The unilateral decision by the receiving countries to discontinue recruitment not only removed labour export promotion from the sending countries' choice of policy options (at least as regards export to Europe), but also faced the sending countries with the prospect of a sudden flood of returning migrants. This was a scenario for which they were ill-prepared and over which they would have little control. In fact the massive returns that some had feared never materialized, indicating, among other things, an inherent weakness in the receiving countries' position vis-à-vis control of immigrant labour. None the less, the policy changes introduced by the receiving states in the early 1970s, and the resulting fluctuations in migration flows, caused sufficient concern among sending countries to prompt the ILO to call for a Programme of Action encouraging agreements which would make 'migration movements, remittances and returns ... a predictable and continuous part of sending-country development programmes'.[20]

Since the sending countries were no longer in a position to negotiate labour transfers with the European receiving states after 1973, their attention shifted to the questions of return migration, of the status and treatment of migrants and their families in the receiving countries, and of remittances.

From labour emigration to return migration and family migration

The fact that two recessions (in 1966/7 and that following the 1973 oil crisis) and the recruitment stop had not resulted in a wholesale return of migrants was a cause of considerable concern in Western Europe, and led to a growing interest in proposals to encourage (or force) return migration in the mid- to late 1970s. The policies subsequently introduced were motivated by the domestic political interests of the receiving states concerned (France and West Germany). This development was not entirely divorced from the concerns of the sending states, however.

An interest in return migration after 1973 might appear to be a departure by the sending states from the labour export policies of the 1960s and early 1970s. However, because the sending states hoped to benefit from a constant and continuing inflow of migrants' remittances and soon the return of skilled and motivated emigrants, their primary interest was in 'temporary but long-term' migration[21] rather than permanent emigration (cf. receiving-country interest in temporary but short-term migration). Despite the widely held belief that labour emigration would provide a cheap mechanism for training workers, concern about the potential skill-drain effect of emigration was apparent within the sending countries even before any labour agreements had been signed. In Tunisia, for example – a country which had no tradition of emigration before independence in 1956 – emigration was initially discouraged so as to protect against the loss of skilled workers, and it was only when unemployment began to present itself as a serious problem that the position of the Tunisian government shifted to a positive encouragement of emigration.[22] The attitudes of the sending countries varied a great deal during the 1960s, but all were concerned to safeguard domestic labour markets while reaping maximum benefit from emigration. The 1973/4 recruitment halt forced a reordering of priorities in sending states' migration policies, but did not result in a total break from the interests pursued during the period of labour recruitment.

During the 1960s and early 1970s, the concern of sending countries to protect and/or improve skill levels within the domestic labour market was commonly reflected in policies and procedures designed explicitly to manipulate the composition of migration flows. As already noted, the TES in Turkey, the OFPE/OTTEEFP in Tunisia, and the Office National Algérien de Main-d'Oeuvre (National Algerian Manpower Office) were all directly involved in the recruitment process, and all at one stage or another introduced selection procedures which favoured the emigration of certain groups over others. The Turkish government, for example, introduced restrictions on the emigration of coal miners following production losses resulting from the emigration of skilled workers from the Zonguldak mining area;[23] by the late 1960s, the TES was favouring unskilled applicants from the less-developed areas of Turkey.[24]

In Algeria, administered and controlled departure of emigrants was emphasized from the very beginning, reflecting in part an ambivalence towards policies which implied dependence on France. As early as 1964, Algeria was attempting to regulate emigration through the operation of a work permit scheme (ONAMO permits), which enabled the authorities to encourage emigration from particular areas and thus diversify the sources of migration. This, it was hoped, would ensure that returning migrants would settle in areas in which their new skills would be needed. It is also possible that this policy was motivated by a concern to reduce the proportion of migrants from the (Berber) Kabylia region. The Algerian government was not unaware of the potential political dangers associated with a predominantly Berber expatriate community in France. By the early 1970s, the emphasis of Algerian emigration policy had shifted away from a concern with overall numbers (note the contingency negotiations of the 1960s) towards an interest in the qualitative nature of migration flows. Adler notes that, although numbers of emigrants dominated the Franco-Algerian negotiations in 1964, attention had turned more to questions of training by 1968, and by 1973 'qualitative questions completely overshadowed quantitative ones'. The nationalization of the oil industry in 1971 not only reduced Algeria's reliance on emigration, but also enabled the government to plan a programme of rapid industrialization. This threw Algeria's shortage of skilled workers into sharp relief, and planners began to think more seriously about the possibility of using the pool of skilled Algerian labour currently in France.

The Algerian government maintained stricter control over emigration than the governments of either Morocco or Tunisia.[25] The efforts made by the

OTTEEFP in Tunisia to control the composition of emigrant flows came rather late in the day and had very little impact. In as far as Morocco had an emigration policy,[26] it was designed more to remove barriers to emigration than to regulate it. The 1968–72 Moroccan Development Plan recommended the reorganization of the Central Emigration Service (SCE) to ensure more effective coordination, but emigration continued to follow patterns which had developed independently of government control.[27] Even in Turkey, despite the stated policy aims, control over worker emigration was limited. According to Rinus Penninx, the priority to be accorded to candidates from underdeveloped regions of the country remained a gesture rather than an influential policy line, reflecting a 'general negligence of the phenomenon of uneven regional development' in Turkish state planning.[28]

The degree of skill-drain experienced by the sending states during the 1960s and early 1970s, and the implications of this for the economies of those countries, varied considerably. The fact that the loss of skilled workers was often sectorally and/or geographically very localized meant that the overall impact on one particular country was (and is) difficult to gauge. However, it is clear that, in general, emigration did not result in any significant return of skilled and motivated workers to the sending regions, and in fact often resulted in substantial skill losses. For example, of the 800,000 emigrants who left Turkey through the TES, approximately one-third were skilled or qualified. Roughly 17% of Turkey's population of men aged between 20 and 35, up to 40% of all carpenters, masons and miners, and between 5% and 10% of Turkish plumbers and electricians departed during the peak years of labour emigration between 1967 and 1973.[29] Most Turkish emigrants, including those who migrated with skills, were employed in unskilled positions in Germany. Thus, in terms of occupation, emigration resulted in downward mobility for many, and little or no upward mobility for the majority. It is likely that those who received training and/or occupied skilled or qualified positions in Europe were (and are) less likely to return to Turkey than those who remained in unskilled jobs.[30]

As already noted, sending countries' interest in promoting return migration was founded on an interest in the reinsertion of skilled and enterprising emigrants. By 1974, Turkey, Tunisia and Algeria had all formulated policies to encourage workers to return.[31] In Algeria, the emphasis was on skilled industrial workers; in Tunisia, it was on migrants who might establish themselves as small merchants or businessmen; and in Turkey, on a combination of these. Priorities reflected broader development interests in each country. Moroccan policy during the early 1970s was unique in that labour export continued to be promoted in official development plans (including the 1973–7 National Plan). The 1978–80 Three Year Plan, while not encouraging labour emigration, made no provision for return migration.[32]

Algeria's first comprehensive return policy was introduced in 1977 with the establishment of the *Service de Réinsertion* (at the same time as the French government introduced a programme of financial incentives to encourage migrants to return). The Algerian government also put pressure on France to improve training facilities for Algerian immigrants, and the *Amicale des Algériens en Europe** actively encouraged the *Sociétés Nationales* in Algeria to recruit from the emigrant community in France. Despite these efforts, and the 1974–7 Four Year Development Plan which stressed job-creation, relatively few skilled emigrants were attracted back. Labour market conditions in Algeria in the late 1970s were not sufficiently attractive to encourage the reinsertion of substantial numbers of emigrants.† In 1980, Algeria entered into an agreement with France to cooperate in a three-year programme to encourage migrant resettlement. The provisions included repatriation allowances, training opportunities and enterprise loans for returning migrants. Again, the response was very limited.[33] Despite high levels of unemployment and underemployment, Algeria continued to suffer skill shortages, and eventually resorted to importing skilled workers from advanced industrial economies (including France) and from Asia (the Philippines and Indonesia).

The varied impact of the skill-drain on sending countries is reflected in the fact that, despite a high level of skill emigration and low rates of return migration, Turkey did not seem to suffer from the kinds of skill shortages experienced in Algeria. Suzanne Paine wrote in 1974 that the Turkish economy had 'certainly lost some scarce skilled manpower, but this does not as yet seem to have been accompanied by serious output losses'.[34] According to Adler, this may be explained by the increasing use of sophisticated and modern technology in Turkish factories, which led to a decline in the demand for the traditional artisan skills lost through emigration (carpenters, masons, etc.).[35] The Turkish government was none the less keen to promote return migration, particularly of emigrants returning with savings to set up small and medium-sized enterprises, since it was hoped that this would stimulate job-creation and development in the areas to which they returned. In 1962 the

---

*The government-backed organization set up to promote the interests of Algerian migrants.
†Although there was some success in certain areas experiencing labour shortages, e.g. Oran.

Turkish government established a Village Development Cooperatives scheme (VDC) to promote rural development. The TES gave priority to VDC members in selecting emigrants in the hope that these migrants would channel resources into the cooperatives and eventually return with knowledge and skills to expand the cooperatives' activities.[36] In 1972, Turkey reached an agreement with West Germany under which German funds would be made available to returning migrants wishing to set up small businesses in Turkey (on the condition that the migrants participated in training programmes in both Germany and Turkey[37]). However, according to Werner and König, this programme proved too costly and complicated to work effectively.[38] In no sending country did efforts to encourage return migration prove particularly successful.[39]

The 1973 halt on recruitment in Europe marked the beginning of a declining trend in return migration to all the non-European sending states. Indeed in some areas the recruitment stop signalled a sudden upsurge in emigration as migrants hurried to bring their families to Europe before any further restrictions were imposed. The restrictions on family immigration introduced by the French and West German governments during the 1970s and early 1980s posed a dilemma for the sending countries. All had turned their attention to the treatment of their nationals in the recruitment countries, and were concerned to see an improvement in migrants' living and working conditions. It is worth noting, for example, that the Algerian government's stated reason for suspending emigration in 1973 was the failure of the French government to protect Algerians from racist attacks.[40] Restricting family reunion conflicted with the sending countries' concern for the social and economic rights of migrants in the receiving countries. On the other hand, support for family migration conflicted with the sending countries' primary interest in maximizing remittance flows (and promoting return migration). Family migration implied two developments which were considered to have a direct bearing on remittances: (1) it suggested permanent settlement and thus a shift in migrants' orientation away from the country of origin; and (2) it indicated an increase in the amount of migrants' earnings being spent in the receiving country (family consumption) and thus less being sent back in the form of remittances. Adler notes, for example, that the Algerian authorities were undecided on the issue of family migration: on the one hand, they were annoyed by French efforts to restrict family immigration, but on the other, they were concerned about the dangers associated with family migration. The slowdown in Algerian family migration which took place in the late 1960s can be partly attributed to restrictions imposed by the Algerian government.[41] It is likely that much louder protest would have been voiced by the sending states over receiving states' restriction of family migration had it not been for the overarching concern to protect remittance flows.

A number of governments attempted to compensate for the effects of family migration by introducing or strengthening indirect measures to 'maintain the umbilical cord between motherland and emigrants'.[42] Some governments have been more successful in this regard than others. The *Amicale des Algériens en Europe* dates back to the Ben Bella government in Algeria, and from the beginning it actively tried to shape migrants' social, cultural and political life outside Algeria.[43] Yugoslav cultural associations performed a similar function. Turkey, on the other hand, never succeeded in institutionalizing state interests within emigrant communities.[44] King Hassan's concern to maintain the link between the Moroccan emigrant population and their 'mother country' was reflected in his explicit opposition to emigrants' integration into West European society, a stance which has softened only in recent years.

Remittances

Writing about Turkey in 1982, Rinus Penninx observed that 'the effort of the national government is mainly directed to one aim: to attract as much hard currency from Turkish migrants in Europe as possible'.[45] In 1973, remittances from migrant workers represented 64% of Turkish exported goods and services.[46] Although this proportion has fallen since that time (to 27% in 1982 and 17% in 1989[47]), the total sums involved have increased.* Remittances returned through official channels† totalled over US$2 billion in 1980 and over US$3 billion in 1990.[48] Workers' remittances in 1989 (just over US$3 billion) offset roughly 75% of Turkey's visible trade deficit.[49] Comparable figures apply in the cases of Algeria, Morocco, Tunisia and Yugoslavia. It should be noted, however, that remittances tend to fluctuate from year to year, and in the case of countries that have only a small share in the labour markets of the Middle East oil producers (e.g. Algeria, Morocco, Tunisia), their value may decline as links with emigrant communities in Europe weaken.

In terms of their actual value, the overall sums involved in remittance transfers may be somewhat misleading. One reason for this is that government control over how remittances are used, for example whether the money

---

*Owing in part to the export of labour to the Middle East.

†A considerable proportion of migrants' savings tend to be remitted through unofficial channels, since exchange rates are often more favourable. Thus actual figures can be assumed to be significantly higher than those quoted from official sources.

is invested (e.g. in state bank accounts) or channelled into immediate consumption, is usually limited. As observed by Penninx, 'migration on the national level seems to be a fortune, but it is paid in small change and it seems to yield little profit'.[50] There has been a long-standing debate over the overall benefits of remittances and their impact on economic development. Although remittances have often been seen as the litmus test of a successful emigration policy, considerable costs associated with their inflow have also been identified. It has been argued, for example, that (1) dependence on remittances is self-reinforcing and increases dependency on labour importers; (2) remittances are unreliable and susceptible to sudden swings; and (3) they distort and sometimes damage the development process by increasing income differentials or – since they tend to be channelled into consumption rather than productive investment – by generating or reinforcing inflation.[51] Ismail Serageldin et al. come to this conclusion in their 1983 study of manpower and international migration in the Middle East and North Africa,

> Remittances are the most tangible benefit from labor migration, yet evaluating their effect on the economy is difficult ... They are not by any means unambiguously beneficial or, on the contrary, deleterious in their impact. Remittances appear to cause demand-led inflation [and there] ... is evidence of changes in consumption patterns [which are] ... to the detriment of indigenous agriculture and domestic industries. This is a perfect example of the difficulty of evaluating the impact of migration on economic development and the impact of remittances in particular on these capital-poor economies. Overall, migration for employment ... cannot be seen as having accelerated economic growth among the labor-supplying countries as a whole.[52]

Nevertheless, remittances continue to represent an essential source of foreign currency for most sending countries, as is reflected in the range of policies introduced to encourage migrants to send back their savings. In Turkey, for example, preferential exchange rates for remittances were introduced in the early 1960s. In the face of strong inflation and the constant devaluation of the Turkish lira, this measure failed to make an appreciable impact on remittance flows, and new measures were introduced after 1973 when remittances began to decline. These included a foreign exchange deposit programme, whereby migrants were allowed to open foreign currency accounts in Turkey. Paying premium interest rates,[53] these accounts attracted some US$4 billion between 1979 and 1988.[54] As well as trying to maximize remittance flows, the Turkish government also sought to channel foreign currency into productive invest-

ment. Thus, for example, migrants returning with cars, trucks and professional equipment, or those wishing to secure loans for homes, farms and
businesses, were required to open foreign currency savings accounts with the
Turkish Central Bank. However, Turkey has not succeeded in developing an
effective policy on the investment of migrant transfers, and non-productive
personal investment continues to dominate over the productive investment of
remittances. The same could generally be said of remittance transfers to the
North African sending states, although the importance of remittances for
supporting local economies and infrastructure development in certain regions
of Tunisia and Morocco should not be underestimated.[55] Remittance transfers to Algeria have declined substantially over the past decade, reflecting
both (i) the relative lack of importance attached to remittances by the Algerian
government (and thus the lack of policies to attract them) because of Algeria's
ability to rely on hydrocarbon exports for foreign currency; and (ii) the
increasing economic and political instability of the country, which has
dissuaded emigrants from sending or investing their savings there. Remittances have, however, become increasingly important for the balance of
payments in Tunisia and Morocco. They now represent Morocco's number
one source of foreign-currency receipts following the fall in world phosphate
prices; and – since the depreciation of the Tunisian dinar in 1986[56] – Tunisia's
third most important source after energy exports and tourism, offsetting its
loss of earnings from the decline of its textile industry and now more or less
covering its external debt repayments.

Redirection of emigration flows?
Despite a growing recognition of the costs associated with large-scale
emigration, labour export still constituted an important element of the
development programmes in many sending states when the European receiving countries closed their labour markets in the early 1970s. In this respect,
the 1973 recruitment halt resulted in an 'emigration crisis'[57] for a number of
sending countries. Emigration to Europe had failed to have a significant or
lasting impact on un- or underemployment in any of the non-European
sending states, and thus problems of labour surplus were as, if not more,
critical in the early 1970s as they had been a decade before. All sending states
turned to domestic development strategies to substitute for labour export
(Algeria particularly), but some also looked to redirecting migration flows to
new destinations (Tunisia, Morocco and Turkey, and also Portugal and
Yugoslavia). The rapid expansion of the economies of the Middle East oil-

producing states after 1973, and the resulting acute labour shortages, raised hopes in a number of sending countries of a new market for labour exports.

By the late 1960s Tunisia had already diversified emigrant destinations to include Libya. Although migration to Libya proved very vulnerable to fluctuating political relations between the two countries,[58] by 1974 Tunisian workers migrating to Libya outnumbered those leaving for France. Libya remains an important destination for Tunisian emigrant workers, but the statistics indicate that they stay only a comparatively short time before returning home.[59] Moreover, emigration to Libya increasingly involves skilled workers and is not accompanied by family emigration; thus the Libyan labour market cannot be said to have replaced the employment opportunities previously provided by the European labour markets. Morocco also sought to redirect migrant flows after 1973, but migration to Libya was prevented by poor political relations between the two states after Colonel Muammar Qadhafi came to power in 1969. By contrast, relations between Libya and Turkey were good during the 1970s, and in 1975 an agreement was signed for the transfer to Libya of 10,000 skilled Turkish workers.[60] According to one estimate, there were some 84,000 Turks resident there by 1982.[61]

By the mid- to late 1970s, acute labour shortages had appeared in the oil-rich Gulf states. In 1976, Morocco signed an agreement with Saudi Arabia for the transfer of 50–100,000 Moroccan workers, and, in the same year, some 300 Tunisian workers left for Saudi Arabia under direct contract. However, this did not mark the beginnings of a substantial transfer of labour between North Africa and the Gulf; by 1981 there were no more than 700 Tunisians working in Saudi Arabia, and only 650 North Africans were living in Kuwait.

Turkey was far more successful in exporting labour to the Middle East than either Morocco or Tunisia, thanks largely to the success of Turkish companies in winning construction contracts in the region. Turkish migration to the Middle East accelerated so rapidly during the first half of the 1980s that by 1985 movement to Arab countries accounted for over 90% of all departures recorded by the Turkish Labour Office,[62] and the number of Turkish workers living in Libya and Saudi Arabia exceeded the figures for Turks working in France, the Netherlands, Belgium and Switzerland (roughly 177,000 and 135,400 respectively).[63]

However, even in the case of Turkey, the Middle East oil-producing countries have not provided a replacement market for labour previously directed towards Western Europe. Although the foreign currency receipts from contracts in the Middle East are enormous, the numbers of workers involved in emigration to the oil-producing countries do not compare with the figures for migration to West Germany and other European receiving states two decades earlier. Moreover, this new migration is qualitatively very different from previous flows. Migrants to the Middle East are predominantly skilled men drawn from the less-developed areas of Turkey (carpenters, builders, mechanics, engineers, etc.), who are recruited for specific contracts. They are attracted by the opportunity of saving relatively large amounts of money over a short duration; and they generally migrate without their families and return at the end of the contract or on completion of a particular project (usually one to three years). The incentive to remain abroad for long periods is weaker than that in Europe in the past, since living and working conditions experienced on project sites are usually very harsh.

For Turkey, migration to the Middle East has proved financially advantageous, but it has not been on a scale sufficient to provide a solution to long-term employment problems. For Morocco and Tunisia, prospects for substantial labour transfers to the Gulf remain slim. Even if major new labour export opportunities were to present themselves in the future, the experiences of the 1960s and early 1970s indicate that resumed large-scale emigration of workers would not have a significant impact on the deeper structural economic problems currently faced by these countries. Indeed, changes in the international labour market over the past decade are such that future demand for migrant workers is likely to be increasingly for skilled and qualified workers whom the sending countries can ill-afford to lose.[64]

Because official access to external labour markets is now extremely limited for the sending countries of the Mediterranean basin, debates over the advantages and disadvantages of emigration have become less and less relevant for policy-makers in the labour-sending countries. To some extent, however, the migration policies of both sending and receiving countries defy the facts, for, despite an official clamp-down on immigration throughout Western Europe, undocumented worker migration from these countries continues at substantial levels. Although the actual numbers are unknown, estimates of the size of foreign populations in the new immigration countries of Southern Europe (Italy, Spain, Portugal and Greece) provide some indication of the scale. In 1990, a Council of Europe report[65] estimated that there were some 1.3 to 1.5 million undocumented immigrants in these four countries.[66] Although these populations are very mixed, North Africans appear to be the dominant group, particularly in Italy. In view of the intensification of migration pressures – measured in terms of under- and unemployment, relative poverty, population growth and, particularly in Algeria, political instability[67] – it is possible that the rate of migration out of the Maghreb will increase between now and the end of the decade, whether it be documented family emigration, undocumented 'economic' emigration or, in the case of Algeria, more politically motivated emigration. It should be noted, however, that the trends differ considerably from one country to another. Thus, for example, Tunisian emigration has stabilized with an increase in rates of return, while Moroccan emigration has accelerated appreciably over the past decade relative to both Tunisian and Algerian emigration. The current political and economic crisis in Algeria makes prediction of future migration trends there very difficult, but all the indicators point to intensifying emigration pressures and the growing potential for sudden refugee-type movements out of the country into Europe, Morocco and Tunisia. It should also be remembered, however, that intensifying 'emigration pressures' do not always translate directly into increased emigration rates, as actual migration trends are dependent on a number of factors including immigration controls in the receiving countries.

New questions have emerged over recent years which are connected to concerns in Western Europe over 'irregular' or undocumented immigration. The central issue is no longer that of how emigration might be promoted to benefit the economies of the sending countries, but rather how to tackle fundamental economic and demographic problems in sending countries which give rise to unregulated migration into Western Europe. As argued by Bimal Ghosh,

> In the light of contemporary economic realities it is not difficult to agree that migration is no short-cut to enduring development. The very magnitude of the problem of development, or the absence of it, measured in terms, for example, of unemployment, underemployment and absolute poverty in the labour-sending developing countries, should drive home the point. When they are juxtaposed against the relevant migration statistics such as the annual outflow of migrants from developing countries (roughly 0.4 per cent of the labour force) ... the absurdity of looking to migration as a short-cut to effective development becomes even more clear.[68]

Thus, at the level of rhetoric, the emphasis is now increasingly placed on development to prevent migration, rather than on migration to spur development. The relationship between migration and development, however, is complex in the extreme, and understanding of it still wholly inadequate for the planning of policy measures which could possibly have any substantial short-term impact on migration trends. In the meantime, there appears to be a widening gap opening up between the reality of migration trends and the rationale of receiving states' policies which are founded almost entirely on concepts of prevention, restriction and control. There is, in this context, a growing need for policy-makers on both sides of the Mediterranean to incorporate the existence and persistence of migration into their respective migration policies, since without an explicit recognition of the reality, little can be done towards minimizing the disruptive effects or maximizing the potential benefits of migration for both sending and receiving countries. If policies were to develop in this way, many of the arguments which guided those of the Mediterranean sending states during the period of labour recruitment might once again resurface, for planners might begin to approach migration (as before) as an instrument and not merely as an object of policy. This should not, however, be seen as an instrument capable of solving all the problems of underdevelopment in today's sending countries, but rather one which could be factored positively into the development process. As argued recently by Reginald Appleyard,

> What is needed is an *active* policy with respect to international migration and not just passive *ad hoc* reaction to events as they materialise. A comprehensive development strategy in which international migration is assigned a specific role, represents the most promising direction.[69]

Chapter 6

Immigrant Minorities in Europe Today

A recognition of the potential social and political impacts of postwar immigration, and its expression as a central policy issue in European immigration states, appeared in the main as a reaction to a process that had been under way for two decades or more and that was to a large extent irreversible. Labour immigration of the 1950s and 1960s had given rise to the *de facto* permanent settlement of large foreign populations. These were often distinctive in terms of culture, language, religion and/or ethnic group. They posed a new, and in many respects unprecedented, challenge to the concept of the European 'nation-state' based on a common cultural, racial and linguistic identity. By the early 1970s, all governments were turning their attention towards the question of integration: those immigrants who could not be expected or persuaded to return to their country of origin would have to be incorporated into the fabric of the host society. Indeed, 'the integration of immigrants into the social system ... had become inevitable'[1] since long-term institutionalized segregation would have threatened the future social and political stability of the new welfare democracies.

Despite a common concern over the integration of immigrants, diverse approaches to the problem have been adopted by the various host countries (and by different institutions within those countries). These reflect the different socio-political structures of the receiving states (e.g. degree of centralization and state intervention in social affairs), contrasting immigration experiences, and differing interpretations or expectations of processes of integration. 'Integration' is a rather vague term which can be used to denote a varying range of processes across the spectrum, from social and cultural assimilation of minorities to the preservation of distinct minority identities. Some countries have at times leant towards 'assimilate or return' policies (such as France and the FRG), while others (the Netherlands, Sweden and Britain) have opted for policies promoting 'multiculturalism' or supporting recognition of a 'multiracial society'.

Attitudes and policies adopted towards immigrant minorities have also differed according to the identities of the groups concerned (e.g. European versus African, Christian versus Muslim), and have varied over time and according to the 'maturity' of different immigration flows and the particular aspects of the immigration history (e.g. permanent colonial immigration versus 'temporary' recruited labour). The picture is complicated further by the fact that integration – to the extent that it is accomplished – is never a straightforward one-way process, but one based on the dynamic interactive relationships which develop between immigrants and the state, and between immigrant and receiving communities. Not only have receiving states and communities responded to immigrant populations in different ways, but immigrant groups themselves have adopted a great variety of strategies and demonstrated widely contrasting responses to their situation as minorities, in turn influencing the reactions and responses of the majority population. The nature of the integration process varies not only from country to country and from group to group, but from one region, town or locality to another, and from one sub-group, family or individual to another. For this reason, generalizations on the subject should be treated with a degree of caution.

Considerable variation is also apparent in the terminology used to describe minorities of immigrant origin; this is indicative of the specific socio-political, historical and legal background to the immigration phenomenon in each receiving country. As discussed below, the terminology is significant inasmuch as it reflects a lot about the attitudes which have shaped the reception and integration of immigrant groups and the bases of immigrant minority status in receiving countries. For example, in Britain and the Netherlands it is usual to talk of 'ethnic minorities', in Germany of 'foreigners', 'aliens' or 'foreign co-citizens',[2] and in France of 'immigrants' or 'populations of foreign origin'. To some extent these terms reflect objective differences in citizenship laws (as discussed below), but they are also indicative of the degree to which immigrant minorities are identified as a 'class apart'.[3] It should be noted that these terms are generally used to denote immigrant groups whose integration is perceived as a problem, and are therefore not usually applied to immigrant minority communities of West European and/or pre-Second World War origins (e.g. Irish residents in Britain or Italians in France).

For the purposes of this discussion, the term 'immigrant minorities' or 'immigrant groups' is used to denote minorities of immigrant origin. However, the term is used very loosely, as it is becoming increasingly misleading to use the label 'immigrant', given that these communities now include a growing contingent of second- and third-generation members who have been born and brought up in their country of residence.

Although much of the ensuing discussion is relevant to Western Europe as a whole, reference to national policies is restricted to France, the Federal Republic of Germany, the United Kingdom, the Netherlands and – as one of southern Europe's 'new' immigration countries – Italy. Not only do these five countries figure significantly in Western Europe's postwar immigration history, but comparisons between them illustrate important points of divergence in the development of their integration policies.

The first section of this chapter is devoted to a brief quantification and breakdown of the different immigrant minorities in Western Europe, focusing on France, the Federal Republic of Germany, the United Kingdom (the countries with the largest immigrant minorities) and Italy. More detailed information on the size and distribution of immigrant groups is provided in Table 6.1. The subsequent three sections consider, respectively, integration as a policy issue, immigrant minorities' social and economic rights and opportunities, and the issues of citizenship and political rights. Immigrant integration in Italy is not discussed in these sections because this country has only recently started tackling immigrant minority integration as a policy issue.

Europe's immigrant minority population

Statistical data on immigration, emigration and foreign populations are generally very unsatisfactory. Not only are statistics frequently defective, with undocumented immigrants excluded, but different countries depend on different methods of data collection, use different defining categories, and carry out censuses and other surveys at different times.[4] This makes cross-country comparison and data compilation extremely difficult. Furthermore, data from separate sources within one country often disagree. For example, estimates of the numbers of 'foreigners' in France issued by different ministries can vary by as much as one million.[5] The situation is further complicated by the fact that distinctions between nationals and foreigners are blurred because different citizenship and nationality laws

Sheet 1 wks.

Table 6.1: Foreign population by nationality: major recruitment countries and major immigrant groups in the early 1980s and 1990s (in thousands)

Nationality	Belgium		France		'Host' country Germany		Netherlands		UK		Switzerland	
	1981	1991	1982	1990	1980	1991	1980	1991	1984	1991	1980	1991
Italy	277	240	340	253	618	560	21	17	83	86	421	377
Ireland	1	2.5	—	—	—	—	—	—	491	469	—	—
Spain	58	51	327	216	180	135	23	17	25	30	97	115
Portugal	11	18	767	650	112	93	9	9	10[a]	20	11	101
Greece	21	21	—	—	298	337	4	5	—	—	9	8
Turkey	66	89	122	198	1462	1780	139	215	—	—	38	69.5
Yugoslavia	6	6.5	63	52.5	632	775	14	15	—	—	44	171
Algeria	11	11	805	614	5[b]	9	—	—	—	—	—	—
Morocco	110	146	441	573	36	75	83	164	—	—	—	—
Tunisia	7	6.5	191	206	23	27	2	3	—	—	—	—
Poland	—	—	65	47	88[c]	271	—	—	—	—	—	5
New C'wealth & E/W Africa	—	—	—	—	—	—	—	—	442	373	—	—
Other countries	318	330.5	593	787.5	1000	1820	225	287	698	772	273	253.5
Total	886	922	3714	3597	4453	5882	521	732	1601	1750	893	1100
of which EC	594	555	1595	1312	1494[d]	1487	171	176	701[e]	740	701	760

(a) Less than 10,000; (b) figure for 1982; (c) figure for 1983; (d) figure for 1982; (e) figure for 1983.

Source: SOPEMI (OECD Continuous Reporting System on Migration), *SOPEMI 1993 (Annual Report). Trends in International Migration*, OECD, Paris, 1994.

operate in different countries. Especially in Britain and France, but also in the Netherlands, substantial proportions of immigrant or immigrant-origin minority populations are not classified as 'foreigners' in the statistics because they entered with citizenship of the host country, naturalized to host-country citizenship, or were granted citizenship at the time of their birth within the territory of the host country.[6] As noted in a recent resumé of the population of immigrant origin in France:

> According to a study ... based on the 1990 census, the number of people in France of immigrant origin is about 6.1 million, including French children and children of mixed couples ... [However] the reality is more complex. In 1990 there were 3.6 million foreigners and 4.19 million immigrants in France. A foreigner is not necessarily an immigrant and vice versa. Included in the category 'immigrants' are foreigners (69%) and people born abroad who subsequently acquired French citizenship (31%, or about 100,000 each year). On the other hand, most foreigners (79%) are immigrants because they were born abroad, but the category of 'foreigners' also includes those born in France (21%) who, strictly speaking, are not immigrants.[7]

To exclude immigrants and descendants of immigrants who are nationals of a receiving state from cross-country comparisons means to exclude a large number of people who could be considered to fall within the broad category of 'immigrant minorities'.*

Perhaps the most useful cross-country immigration and immigrant population statistics are those compiled by the OECD Continuous Reporting System on Migration (SOPEMI)[8] and those compiled by the Statistical Office of the European Communities (Eurostat),[9] which aim for the greatest possible comparative consistency. However, both rely on state-specific official statistical sources and are therefore subject to all the inaccuracies referred to above. According to Eurostat, there were between 13 and 14 million foreigners resident in the twelve EC member states in 1991 out of a total population of 329 million (excluding additional population of the former

---

*In Germany the majority of immigrants and descendants of immigrants do not possess German citizenship, but numbers of immigrant naturalizations have increased substantially over recent years. This is due principally to citizenship applications from immigrants from Central and Eastern Europe who have been able to prove their 'ethnic German' origins. See OECD, *SOPEMI 1993 (Annual Report). Trends in International Migration*, OECD, Paris, 1994, p. 50.

GDR). 'Foreigners' (defined as such and legally resident) thus account for about 4% of the total population. However, this figure includes EC citizens resident in another member state. The population of legally resident 'third-country nationals' (non-EC citizens) was estimated at close to 9 million in 1991, or less than 3% of the total. For Western Europe as a whole, over one million non-EC/non-EFTA nationals may be added if account is taken of foreign populations in Switzerland, Sweden, Norway and Austria.[10] Of the 9 million non-EC citizens living in the European Community in 1991, some 2 million or so came from advanced industrialized countries (EFTA countries, USA, Canada, Australia, Japan, etc.).[11] Thus the legally resident foreign population of the EC, excluding EC nationals and nationals of other advanced industrialized countries, can be estimated on the basis of these data to have amounted to some 7 million.

In all cases the figures quoted can be assumed to be below the actual numbers owing to the presence of statistically 'invisible' groups, including undocumented immigrants (e.g. clandestine immigrants and seasonal workers) as well as those possessing 'host'-country citizenship. There are no reliable figures for numbers of undocumented immigrants in Europe. In 1990, a Council of Europe report estimated that there were some 1.3 to 1.5 million non-nationals in an undocumented or irregular situation in the 'new' immigration countries of Southern Europe (Italy, Spain, Portugal and Greece), making a total non-national population of roughly 2.7 million in these countries.[12] More recent ILO estimates are more modest: 600,000 undocumented immigrants in Italy, 300,000 in Spain, 200,000 in France and 650,000 in Germany, and a total of 2.6 million in Western Europe as a whole.[13] These figures include clandestine immigrants, seasonal workers and asylum-seekers whose applications for asylum have been refused but who have not left the country.

The majority of non-EC immigrants and their descendants live in France (roughly 2.3 million non-EC foreign nationals in 1990*), Germany (some 4.4 million non-EC foreign nationals in 1991) and Britain (just over one million, excluding those with British citizenship).[14] The origins of immigrant minority populations in France and Germany reflect the fact that the majority of non-EC nationals resident in the European Community come from Mediterranean countries,† most notably Turkey (24.4%), Algeria (10.3%), Yugoslavia

---

*Note that this figure excludes immigrants and descendants of immigrants who are French citizens and who do not have dual nationality.

†Not reflected in the composition of Britain's ethnic minorities, since the majority of non-EC immigrants in the UK came from the New Commonwealth.

(8.6%) and Morocco (9.7%).[15] Thus in Germany, Turks form the largest contingent (over 1.7 million), followed by nationals of the former Yugoslavia (over 770,000, excluding refugees who have entered since 1991).[16] In France, Algerians form the largest non-EC immigrant group (614,000 Algerian nationals in 1990[17]), and the population of Moroccan nationality exceeds 570,000.

Exclusion of EC nationals from the statistics hides the fact that both France and Germany have substantial minority populations originating in Mediterranean countries that are now within the European Community: in France, the largest 'foreign' minority (i.e. measured in terms of foreign nationality) is that of Portuguese origin, numbering about 650,000, and Spaniards and Italians together account for almost half a million. Italians constitute the third-largest immigrant group in Germany (over 550,000), followed by roughly 330,000 Greeks. Exclusion of EC nationals also masks the fact that the Irish constitute the largest foreign group by nationality in the UK (469,000 Irish nationals in 1991).[18]

At least in so far as the largest minorities are concerned, the profile of immigrant groups in Germany broadly reflects the recruitment policies of the 1950s and 1960s, while that of France reflects past colonial links and geographical position vis-à-vis the European sending states.[19] The profile of ethnic minorities of immigrant origin in the United Kingdom is very different from those of continental European receiving states since – apart from the Irish minority – it is dominated by populations of New Commonwealth origin.[20] As noted above, the most appropriate quantification of immigrant-origin minority groups in the UK is by ethnic identity rather than by nationality. According to the 1991 census, 5.5% of people living in Great Britain identify themselves as belonging to a non-white ethnic group (roughly 2.7 million).[21] Of these, just over half are of Indian (31%), Pakistani (17%) or Bangladeshi descent (3%); roughly 19% are of West Indian origin;[22] the remainder includes those of mixed ethnic origin (11%), and the smaller categories of Chinese, African or Arab descent (each around 3–4%).[23] Ethnic minorities in Britain reflect past colonial ties more clearly than in any other receiving country.

Although in Italy the presence of large immigrant groups is a very recent phenomenon, the country's postwar immigration history does none the less date back several decades. This history is reflected in a very complex immigrant or immigrant-origin population. The longer-established immigrant groups in Italy include Eritreans who first began entering in the early 1960s, often as domestic workers accompanying Italian families returning from the former colony – a flow which took on a more political and spontaneous character as it continued throughout the 1970s. Somali immigration also dates back to the early post-independence years, although all migration from sub-Saharan Africa was generally very limited until the 1980s. During that decade, increasing numbers of (predominantly) single men began migrating from a number of African countries.[24] Other immigrant groups dating back to the 1970s or early 1980s include Filipinos and Sinhalese (predominantly female domestic workers*), South Americans (many of whom entered as refugees or exiles, some of Italian descent), Chinese (dating back to the interwar period) and Tamils (refugees fleeing violence in Sri Lanka). Italy is also host to large numbers of immigrants from Lebanon, Iran, Iraq, India, Pakistan and Poland. North Africans (Algerians, Moroccans, Tunisians, plus Egyptians), however, constitute the largest immigrant contingent in Italy. Although dating back to the early 1970s, this group has only taken on significant dimensions since the mid-1980s (reflecting, in part, a redirection of migration flows towards Italy following the introduction of tighter immigration controls by other European countries). In a survey carried out in 1991, almost 60% of immigrants interviewed had been in Italy for no more than three years, and over 30% had arrived in the twelve months prior to March 1990.[25] Although traditionally a sending country, Italy is now an immigration country. Net migration of Italians has largely stabilized, with emigration of Italians in 1989 (estimated at 49,400) balancing numbers returning (49,100).[26] One estimate put the number of foreigners resident in Italy in 1990 at roughly one million[27] (just under 2% of the total population). This was almost double the number registered by the Ministry of the Interior and about three times the number recorded in the municipal records offices.

Demographic trends

As noted in Chapter 4, the clamp-down on immigration in the early 1970s had the general effect of stabilizing and consolidating immigrant populations in all the main postwar receiving states, although the impact of the new immigration controls and changes in the economic climate differed from one immigrant group to another. In Germany, for example, the Italian, Greek, Spanish, Portuguese and Yugoslav populations decreased in the decade after 1973, while the Turkish immigrant population increased by roughly 150%.[28] The overall percentage of foreigners in the total population of Germany

---

*Many of whom have been in Italy for ten years or more and can be considered 'immigrants'.

increased by only about one per cent during the same period. With worker immigration suspended, family migration accounted for almost all immigration flows after 1973. This was indicative of the fact that immigrants who remained in Germany had settled more or less permanently. France also experienced an increase in non-European immigrants in relation to numbers of European immigrants, although this pattern was not entirely clear-cut: the number of Italian and Spanish immigrants in France declined significantly between 1975 and 1982, while the Portuguese immigrant population increased slightly.[29]

In Britain, the West Indian population was already well established by the early 1970s; the inflow had started earlier and had included a high proportion of women and children from the beginning. Immigration during the 1970s was dominated by family migration from the Indian subcontinent, since initial inflows from India, Pakistan and Bangladesh had characteristically been of men migrating individually. Thus, whereas the population of West Indian ethnic origin increased by only 9% between 1971 and 1976 (and subsequently decreased by 6% between 1981 and 1988*), the Pakistani/ Bangladeshi and Indian ethnic group populations increased by 44% and 27% respectively during this period. This trend continued into the 1980s, particularly in the case of the Pakistani minority, which expanded by 144% between 1981 and 1988 (from 284,000 to 479,000).[30] The entry of some 100,000 East African Asians during the 1970s further boosted Britain's Asian population.

Of course, the growth in immigrant populations in all the receiving states since the early 1970s is due not only to continuing immigration, but also to a natural increase within these populations. As a consequence of family reunion, immigrant populations became progressively balanced in terms of age and sex. This resulted in a substantial rise in fertility rates and thus a growth in the so-called 'second generation' of immigrant groups. The fertility component as a factor in the development of the size of immigrant minorities has become more and more significant relative to immigration rates over the past decade. Whereas fertility rates among most European host populations have declined to near or below the replacement threshold (2.1),[31] those within immigrant populations tend to be higher (e.g. 6.19 for Tunisian women who arrived in France after 1975).[32] For this reason, and because of the overall younger age profiles of immigrant populations,† immigrant minority

*Owing primarily to an excess of births over deaths.
†At least during the first few decades of settlement, owing to low numbers of persons falling into the older age-group categories, as well as being due to higher numbers of children.

populations have become particularly important in the lowest age-groups. For example, 17% of all children born in the Federal Republic of Germany in 1974 had foreign parents.[33]

Fertility rates, however, vary considerably from one nationality group to another, and within nationality groups from one country to another,[34] reflecting a range of factors such as fertility rates in the country of origin, length of settlement in the receiving country and rates of female participation in the labour force. For example, the fertility rate among the Italian immigrant population in France was 1.74 (below the replacement threshold) in 1982, whereas that of the Moroccan community was 5.23.[35] The overall trend among immigrant groups is one of declining fertility over time, often converging with or even dropping below the fertility rate of the population as a whole.[36]

According to Eurostat, the total population of the European Community rose by 1.647 million in 1989, and by 2 million in 1990, half to two-thirds of which was attributable to net migration and one-third to a half due to a surplus of births over deaths.[37] A 1990 Eurostat report observes that net migration into the Community 'was higher than ever before, and for the first time, too, net migration was the main component of population growth', but that 'this exceptional situation results from the upheavals in Eastern Europe in 1989'.[38] The overall increase for the Community as a whole therefore masks considerable differences between member states. The Federal Republic of Germany experienced an inflow of approximately one million immigrants in 1989, predominantly from Eastern and Central Europe and including some 344,000 *Ubersiedler* (Germans from the GDR) and 377,000 *Aussiedler* (persons of German ethnic origin from outside the Federal Republic or the GDR),[39] and thus immigration accounted for a much greater part of the country's population growth than did natural increase. On the other hand, population growth in France during the same year was predominantly due to natural increase rather than to immigration. In 1989, population grew by 984,000 or 1.58% in the Federal Republic; by 287,000 or 0.51% in France (50,000 attributed to net immigration); by 183,000 or 0.32% in the UK (64,000 as a result of net immigration); and by 65,800 or 1.1% in Italy (36,000 as a result of net immigration). The populations of Spain and the Republic of Ireland declined by an estimated 13,600 and 42,500 respectively.[40] It is worth noting that net migration was negative for Britain during much of the 1980s despite inflows of foreign population (e.g. a net loss through migration of 21,000 in 1988). This is indicative of the downward trend in net immigration rates for all the postwar receiving states during the mid-1980s. Immigration rates did increase substantially during the early 1990s; this was attributable principally to an upturn in labour inflows (including skilled immigration and clandestine immigration from Central and Eastern Europe and non-EC Mediterranean countries) and to the increase in numbers of asylum-seekers (including refugees from the former Yugoslavia and asylum-seekers from Eastern Europe).[41] Yet, according to the most recent OECD *SOPEMI* report:

> with the exception of Germany [and] Sweden ... 1992 and the first part of 1993 seem to mark a turning point in migration, characterised by low growth or a fall in arrivals of new immigrants and asylum seekers for which there are various reasons. Perhaps slower economic growth and persistent unemployment mean that OECD countries have less need for fresh immigrant labour ... Or perhaps it is merely a cyclical downturn unlikely to have a fundamental effect on the acceleration of international migration or the independent behaviour of certain migratory flows such as family reunification.[42]

The report goes on to note that 'past experience shows that it is impossible to predict the scale and direction of future migratory flows; thus, it would seem premature to suggest that the trend has been definitively reversed.'[43] Nevertheless, it can be concluded that, in general, all the major European migrant-receiving states succeeded in stabilizing the growth of their immigrant populations between 1973 and the late 1980s. Indeed, it may be suggested that considerably more was achieved in the field of immigration control than was accomplished in efforts to ensure the successful integration of immigrant groups.

Integration as a policy issue
By the mid-1970s, all of Europe's receiving states had introduced policies geared towards the integration of immigrant minorities. Until then there had been little open recognition of the potential social and political impacts of immigration, and virtually nothing in the way of long-term planning for the integration of immigrants. Indeed, even after the importance of integration had gained explicit recognition, the tendency was for policies to be adopted in a piecemeal and reactive way, in response to specific problems, rather than through the formulation of comprehensive and far-sighted strategies.

This was particularly apparent in the 'guestworker' countries (West Germany, Switzerland and, to a lesser extent, the Netherlands), where the emphasis on return of workers and *de facto* institutionalized segregation of foreign workers during the 1950s and 1960s meant that recognition of a need for full integration of immigrants was slow to develop.

Those countries which were more open to accepting the fact of immigrant settlement (including the United Kingdom and France) demonstrated a concern for integration or responded to integration-related issues rather earlier. Nevertheless, even in Britain, the issue took some time to reach the national political agenda. Indeed, politicians on both the left and the right were reluctant to discuss the issue openly during the 1950s, as they were concerned not to strain their relations with the new Commonwealth governments. Moreover, because most immigrants entered independently with full civic and political rights, special measures on behalf of immigrant minorities were not initially considered particularly necessary or appropriate. The first race relations legislation passed in Britain (the 1965 Race Relations Act) was limited in scope (outlawing discrimination in public places) and could not have been expected to make a substantial impact on the position of immigrants in British society.[44]

Similarly in France, the assumption prevailed for a long time that immigrants' welfare could be sufficiently protected through the formal guarantee of legal rights deriving from the Constitution and the operation of state institutions applicable to French society as a whole. State action on behalf of immigrants was initially restricted to attempts to tackle the problem of immigrant housing, and then only in connection with efforts to eliminate the infamous immigrant *bidonvilles* (slum shanty towns)[45] that had grown up around Paris and other large French cities during the 1950s.

The differences in approaches to integration that were manifest between states in the 1960s were also apparent during the 1970s, despite the new and universal expressions of concern over the issue which arose in conjunction with the immigration clamp-down of 1973/4.

The United Kingdom
The British experience of postwar immigration differed significantly from that of other states in Western Europe, as the majority of migrants to Britain were colonial immigrants entering the country as British subjects with full citizenship rights.[46]

As in France, the imperial legacy profoundly influenced the reception of immigrants in British society and their subsequent integration. Zig Layton-

Henry notes that the 'feeling and behaviour of native white British people ... towards Afro-Caribbean and Asian migrant workers, and their images of them, were influenced by the knowledge that these migrants had been subject peoples of the British empire'; the migrants in turn 'knew that they had been badly treated in the past', but hoped that their contribution to the war effort would bring a better future, 'so great was their confidence in British institutions and especially British notions of justice and fair play'. Their disappointment on meeting discrimination in Britain was therefore all the greater, he argues, and the history of slavery and racism 'provided powerful explanations for failure'.[47] Ever since it has been an issue for national debate in Britain, the immigration issue has been dominated by the race question. Layton-Henry observes that 'an "immigrant" in popular discourse came to mean a non-white person ... Such descriptions, setting non-whites apart from the rest of the population, were never applied to ... Irish, Italians or Poles, and showed the depth of racial prejudice and the political potential of the issue'.[48]

Although the British political elite has never been entirely free of racial prejudice, all the main political parties expressed a commitment to the elimination of racial disadvantage in a multiracial society. However, fearing a backlash from the white population (particularly the white working class), policy-makers were wary of instituting any programmes aimed explicitly at improving the social and economic status of immigrants. The emphasis at national level has therefore been on the promotion of equal opportunities through enforceable anti-discrimination legislation rather than on the creation of positive programmes to benefit ethnic minorities.[49] This attitude was expressed by the Home Secretary when he introduced the second reading of the 1968 Race Relations Bill:

> The Bill is concerned with equal rights, equal responsibilities and equal opportunities and it is therefore a Bill for the whole nation and not just minority groups ... Its purpose is to protect society as a whole against actions which will lead to social disruption and to prevent the emergence of a class of second-class citizens.[50]

The term 'integration', when used in the UK, has generally been defined 'not as a flattening process of assimilation but as equal opportunity, accompanied by cultural diversity, in an atmosphere of mutual tolerance'.[51] More recently, British policy has been defined as being directed towards shaping society so that all 'can participate freely and fully in the economic, social and public life of the nation while having the freedom to maintain their own religious and cultural identity'.[52] Where housing and employment conditions and the education of minorities have been the specific objects of policy, these have tended to be at the local authority level. Yet where central government has addressed these matters, it has generally been in terms that avoid the singling-out of ethnic minorities (e.g. through general 'urban renewal' or 'youth opportunity' programmes).

By the mid-1970s it was apparent that discrimination against ethnic minorities was still widespread, particularly in the fields of housing and employment, and that it could not be combatted effectively on the basis of the two existing race relations acts. In 1976 a new bill was passed which outlawed indirect as well as direct discrimination in all areas of public life, and which established the Commission for Racial Equality (CRE) as the institution responsible for ensuring its enforcement (replacing the Race Relations Board and Community Relations Commission).

The 1976 Race Relations Act and the CRE remain the backbone of British policy aimed at promoting the integration of ethnic minorities. The CRE has far greater powers of investigation and enforcement than its predecessors,[53] and is charged with working towards the elimination of discrimination and working to promote equality of opportunity and good relations between persons of different racial groups. Although it has had some degree of success, the CRE has generally failed to live up to expectations. A survey carried out in 1984/5 revealed that over 30% of employers discriminated directly against black job applicants, indicating 'a level of discrimination on racial grounds that is widespread, serious and persistent over time'.[54] The CRE has argued that:

> the prejudices and hostility which showed in crude outbursts and
> exclusive practices may now hide behind less inelegant expression and
> more covert behaviour ... [therefore] it is too complacent to comfort
> ourselves that we have seen off the most blatant forms of racism when
> we witness the scale of harassment on housing estates and in schools
> or the neo-fascist desecration of Jewish cemeteries.[55]

British policy has sometimes been described as multicultural because of the relative space allowed for minority cultural autonomy, and because a number of local authorities have adopted a more active multicultural line than central government, particularly in the field of education. However, Britain has never adopted an explicitly multicultural policy at national level; national government has tended to favour a more hands-off approach to cultural matters.

France

The French and West German approaches to integration have contrasted significantly with Britain's emphasis on anti-discrimination and recognition of a multiracial society. In France it is the issue of culture, rather than race, that has dominated debates on the issue.

On the basis of an extensive study of the position of immigrants in Lyon in the 1970s, Grillo observed that 'since the French Revolution the problem of how to handle *étrangeté* ... has been a significant one in the development of a French social order', and he goes on to suggest that 'Britain allows more room for, and pays greater attention to, independent immigrant representation, just as it allows more room for cultural autonomy ... the French state is engaged in a much closer monitoring and control of its citizens than we like to believe occurs in Britain ... There is a contrast here between two traditions of nation and state that tempers the way in which each country handles its constituent minorities.'[56] In fact, as discussed in Chapter 4, the French state had little control over the immigration process during the first two decades of immigration, and although the *'assimilation'* of immigrants was expressed as an ultimate goal, it was assumed or hoped that this would come about automatically if immigrants were forced to address existing traditional French institutions. Until the late 1960s the only effective organizations set up to deal with immigrant issues were those created informally on a local and voluntary basis.

The state only started to involve itself directly with immigrants' welfare in the 1960s with the creation of institutional housing specifically for immigrants – *cités de transit* and *foyers-hôtels* – and the resettlement of certain groups in normal social housing. However, in the years leading up to the halt on labour immigration of 1974, concern began to be expressed at state level over a whole range of immigrant issues (employment conditions, inter-ethnic relations, etc.). With the creation of a new office of Secretary of State for Immigrant Workers in 1974, a machinery was set in motion to place all immigrant affairs – welfare, housing, employment, education, training, cultural expression – under the control of the state. Rather than relying on general measures to ensure equal opportunity, the French state embarked on a programme of direct *'insertion'*[57] of immigrants into French society. This policy was based on the insistence on a direct and unified identification with the French state which precluded the recognition of minorities.

Yet, in the very restrictive climate of the 1970s, *insertion* was pursued in tandem with the contradictory aim of encouraging certain immigrant groups to return to their countries of origin, an objective which could only be carried out by maintaining a sense of insecurity among immigrant groups and

which, paradoxically, encouraged policies promoting immigrants' maintenance of their own culture (as in West Germany, see below). Patrick Weil and
John Crowley observe that 'the right for non-European immigrants to retain
their own culture ... could be seen as preparing them to leave France ... and to
make their deportation easier than if they were already mixed in French
society.'[58] This approach had little impact on rates of return, but, as Philip
Ogden notes, did prove 'an effective way of souring the political atmosphere'.[59]

Those groups that were deemed 'least assimilable' – North Africans and
to some extent Portuguese – suffered the brunt of a state policy that was based
largely on the notion of 'assimilate or return'. Speaking at a meeting in Lyon
in 1975, Paul Dijoud (Secretary of State for Immigrant Workers) stated that
there must be 'justice, assimilation, integration, living together'; but he added
that, although half of the some 4 million immigrants in France rarely posed
problems, if nothing were done about the other half 'we might have an *îlot de
blocage social*, which might lead to the same situation as with the blacks in
the United States'.[60] This policy stance reinforced ideas of 'cultural distance'
and 'desirable' and 'undesirable' immigrants which persist to a large extent
today, particularly in respect of Algerians.[61] Indeed, immigration has increasingly been perceived as a problem of the Arab presence in France.[62]

On coming to power in 1981, the new socialist government promised to
replace the discriminatory and assimilationist policies of the past with a more
open recognition and acceptance of the reality of immigrant settlement and
the cultural heterogeneity that it implied. A more liberal approach of
'*intégration*' was adopted in an attempt to ease growing interethnic tensions
in French society, with policies that emphasized the right to live and work in
France without having to assimilate and without discrimination in employment and housing.[63] The policies of return and arbitrary expulsion of
immigrants were discarded in the interests of creating a feeling of security
within immigrant communities, as security was considered to be a prerequi-
site for successful integration: foreign nationals were granted rights of
political association (though not the right to vote); most were granted a ten-
year renewable residence permit which guaranteed their right to settle in
France;[64] and the status of over 150,000 undocumented immigrants was
regularized. The Chirac government of 1986–8 would, no doubt, have
brought about a further reversal of policy had it remained in power for longer,
but the more liberal stance dominated into the early 1990s.

As in the past, the government saw the integration of immigrants as the
direct responsibility of the state. This view is reflected in the plethora of state
institutions created to deal with the immigrant issue. In 1989 and 1990 alone,

measures taken at state level included the setting up of an Interministerial Committee for Integration,[65] the reinstatement of the National Council for Immigrant Populations, the creation of a Council for Reflection on Islam in France, and the issuing of countless ministerial circulars on the subject of social integration (housing, urban development, education, etc.).[66] However, the government was still reluctant to formulate policy on the basis of an institutional recognition of immigrant minorities *qua* minorities. The continuing emphasis on individuals as targets of policy was articulated in a report issued in 1991 by the *Haut Conseil à l'Intégration* which aims to define integration policy in France. It states that:

> The *Haut Conseil* does not deny the existence of minorities in France, as elsewhere. It thinks, however, that the traditional principles of equality, recognition of individual rights and non-discrimination better assure individual freedom and opportunity in the country as a whole than the institutional recognition of minorities, which would necessarily be discriminatory ... An integration policy stresses similarities and convergences in the equality of rights and obligations ... in order to bind the different ethnic and cultural elements of our society together and give each person, whatever his or her origin, the opportunity to live in that society, whose rules he or she has accepted, and become a constituent element of that society.[67]

The liberal approach of the 1980s has come under attack from the centre-right parties now in power. In response to growing anxieties in French society about continuing immigration, and under pressure from Jean-Marie Le Pen's *Front National*, the new government has picked up where the Chirac government of 1986–8 left off by introducing new laws both to strengthen immigration control and reduce security of residence in a number of areas,[68] and to restrict naturalization for 'second-generation' immigrants.[69] The politicization of the migration issue has encouraged the development of increasingly defensive and restrictive policies, with the social aspects of integration becoming overshadowed by or conflated with broader immigration concerns – concerns which are in turn discussed more and more in terms of security and which are associated with a range of social and political ills, including terrorism, 'delinquents, drugs ... and violence'.[70]

Although the principle of non-discrimination is written into the French Constitution, no anti-discrimination machinery has been introduced comparable to that operating in Britain.[71]

The Federal Republic of Germany

The French authorities had been forced to consider the issue of immigrants' welfare relatively early on because of problems that arose in connection with housing shortages. West Germany was also faced with a considerable housing shortage in the decades following the Second World War, but this did not initially affect immigrants because employers in Germany were bound to provide accommodation for all foreign workers. Immigrants were housed in workers' hostels or barracks, often on-site, and were effectively segregated from the general population and from the German housing market. This, coupled with the notion that foreign workers would eventually return, meant that for the first two decades of immigration there was no pressure or incentive for the state to consider questions of integration. It was only with the increase in family immigration towards the end of the 1960s, which resulted in a progressive movement of immigrants into the general housing markets and which raised questions related to the status of workers' families, that German policy-makers began to concern themselves with the social aspects of immigration.

The first official attempts to develop a policy framework geared towards integration appeared in the form of the 1973 Action Programme for the Employment of Immigrant Labour, aimed primarily at housing and education for immigrants, and in the creation in 1975 of a committee responsible for formulating guidelines for an immigration policy. This committee issued a report which called for priority to be given to the social over the economic aspects of immigration, while at the same time demanding stronger promotion of return migration.[72] The emphasis was less on 'assimilate or return' than on 'temporary integration and return', reflecting a reluctance to accept that a large proportion of immigrants were 'here for good'.[73] As in France, the interest in preserving an element of mobility (and therefore preparedness to return) within immigrant groups was translated into policies which kept immigrants in 'a state of dependence and insecurity'.[74] The 1965 Aliens Act did not include a right of residence, even for those who had been in the Federal Republic for over ten years, but instead stated that 'a residence permit may be granted if it does not harm the interests of the German Federal Republic'.[75] The Act also stated that foreigners enjoy all basic rights, 'except the basic rights of freedom of assembly, freedom of association, freedom of movement and free choice of occupation, place of work and place of education, and protection from extradition abroad'.[76] The law linked residence permits to work permits, and allowed considerable administrative discretion in their issue and renewal. In accordance with a decree issued in 1973, foreign workers' family members were to be issued residence permits without work permits, although this was rescinded in 1979.

The first official report representing an attempt to come to terms fully with the presence of immigrant minorities in the Federal Republic was that published in 1979 by Heinz Kuhn, the federal ombudsman for foreign workers and their families. Kuhn stated that:

> future policy towards foreign employees and their families living in the FRG must be based on the assumption that a development has taken place which can no longer be reversed and that the majority of those concerned are no longer guestworkers but immigrants, for whom return to their countries of origin is for various reasons no longer a viable option.[77]

He recommended a series of measures designed to ensure a more secure legal status and greater opportunities for foreigners, including the restriction of arbitrary powers in the policing of foreigners and the introduction of their right to vote in local elections after eight to ten years' residence. In the same year, a list of guidelines were drawn up by the Coordination Committee on Foreign Workers, which stressed in particular the need to concentrate on the social integration of the second and third generations. This recommendation implied a writing-off of the first immigrant generation, an attitude which persists in many respects today.[78] The generally progressive tone of these two reports, however, was not reproduced in government policy for over a decade. As in France, the restrictive climate in respect of immigrants intensified in the lead-up to the 1982 national elections, with politicians talking more and more in terms of 'assimilate or return'[79] – sentiments that were directed primarily at Turkish immigrants (cf. North Africans in France) and which were reaffirmed in 1983 with the Act to Promote the Preparedness of Foreign Workers to Return.[80] Just as the immigration issue had come to be seen mainly as a problem of black immigrants in Britain, and as a problem of Arab immigrants in France, the 'foreigners problem' in Germany had come to be seen predominantly as a 'Turkish problem'.

The 1980s witnessed a growing recognition of immigrants as a permanent and structural feature of German society and an increasing concern for the integration of immigrant minorities, particularly those of the second and third generations who had been born or spent most of their lives in the Federal

Republic. A recent report issued by the Federal Minister of the Interior states that:

> approximately 60 percent of aliens staying in the Federal Republic of Germany have been living here for ten years or more ... More than two-thirds of foreign children and juveniles were born in the Federal Republic of Germany ... The Federal Government assumes that most of them will stay for a considerable period of time or that some of them will even stay for ever ... For these persons there is no convincing alternative to integration.[81]

A new Foreigners Act was passed in January 1991; its primary objective is stated as being the improvement of conditions for the integration of immigrants, and it includes for the first time 'a right to reside' for foreigners who have held a residence permit for eight years or more. However, this is dependent on the applicants' ability to prove that they can finance their living costs.[82]

There is little reference to the notion of 'multiculturalism' in official circles. Indeed, the emphasis is placed very firmly on improving immigrant minorities' social and economic status rather than on cultural matters. Nevertheless, the broadly assimilationist attitudes prevalent at the beginning of the 1980s are echoed in this Act, which states that:

> Integration as a process of adaptation to German conditions ... requires some participation of the aliens who have to accustom themselves above all to the values, norms and ways of living prevailing here ... Respect for our culture ... the acquisition of some knowledge of the German language, abandonment of excessive national-religious behaviours and integration into school and professional life ... are the prerequisites which have to be fulfilled.

Notwithstanding these attitudes, immigrants have generally enjoyed considerable cultural autonomy in Germany, not by virtue of a policy commitment to multiculturalism, but – as in France during the 1970s – as a result of policies which stressed the maintenance of a return-orientation among immigrant groups. However, the degree to which policy emphasized segregation/return or integration of immigrants varied from one region or city to another, because – unlike in France and more as in Britain – central state control over integration policies is limited relative to control assumed by the regional (*Länder*) and local authorities, especially over housing and education.

The Netherlands

The Netherlands is the only West European country apart from Sweden in which central government has attempted to translate an explicit endorsement of multicultural values into a coherent policy framework. Such an approach reflects the country's pluralist traditions: discussion has even turned at times to the possibility of encouraging the formation of a Muslim 'pillar' to match those of the Christian Churches and established secular or humanist bodies. The government has thus accepted some responsibility for helping minorities preserve, develop and express their cultural identity, on the basis of a notion that a strong group identity would help them overcome their social and economic disadvantage.[83]

This so-called 'minorities policy' did not appear until the 1980s, however. Indeed, during the first two decades of immigration, the prevailing view was similar to that of Germany, that the Netherlands 'was not and should not be an immigration country'.[84] Migration to the Netherlands was composed of both 'guest'-worker or recruited worker migration and post-colonial immigration, but the idea of worker 'rotation' and thus of temporary stay which characterized 'guest'-worker policy initially dominated approaches to immigrants' reception and integration. Reception facilities were 'meagre in general'[85] and developed as short-term responses to immediate problems as they arose. What cultural policies were pursued – such as the Mother-tongue and Culture programme for children from Mediterranean countries introduced in 1974 – were geared to facilitating immigrants' reintegration in the country of origin.

Policy changed radically after the late 1970s, however. Forced to some extent by hijackings and occupations by groups of young Moluccans in the mid-1970s, the idea of temporary stay was declared outdated and unrealistic for Moluccans, and in 1979 the Scientific Council for Government Policy issued a report on 'ethnic minorities' which stated that the presence of immigrants should in principle be regarded as permanent.[86] The conclusions of this report led to the announcement of a new 'overall ethnic minorities policy' in 1980, the draft Minorities Bill in 1981, and the final Minorities Bill in 1983. The policy approach was two-pronged: first, a tolerant multicultural society should be promoted in which cultural and ethnic differences would be accepted and supported; and, second, policy should be geared to overcoming immigrant minorities' social and economic disadvantage.

Policy was to be guided by the principle that immigrants are part of Dutch society. As such, they have constitutional rights in Dutch society, and are at the same time free to maintain and develop their own culture and identity. Unlike in France, their minority status was given explicit recognition, facilitating group-specific measures in both the cultural and social and the economic fields. The minorities themselves were to play an active part in servicing their own particular needs as minorities, particularly as regards culture. Meanwhile, the state would concentrate on promoting equal opportunities by improving the accessibility of facilities and institutions and fighting discriminatory behaviour. In this respect, Dutch policy came to resemble British policy, although the Dutch state has been more willing to identify specific target groups for the new policy.

However, worried by the continuing and in some cases worsening social and economic marginalization of many immigrant groups, the government began shifting the balance of its minorities policy at the end of the 1980s to give the 'anti-deprivation' element more weight. As argued in the Scientific Council's second report on 'immigrant policy', issued in 1990:

Apart from facilities to combat deprivation, the government's present policy also provides cultural facilities. This combination has ... placed excessive emphasis on the creation and maintenance of facilities designed to promote a multi-cultural society. One result is that too little has been achieved in reducing inequalities in the fields of education and employment. In the Council's view, the institutionalization of ethnic pluralism need not be regarded as an independent objective of government policy. A multi-ethnic society should be regarded as a social datum, and hence as a starting point for policies leaving room for cultural diversity in various fields ... Immigrants who so wish should be able to maintain and develop their own cultural identity ... however, this forms part of the responsibility of the individual groups themselves. The government's task is confined to helping eliminate the barriers experienced by ethnic groups as a result of their non-indigenous origins.[87]

Italy

Like Europe's traditional receiving states, Italy has adopted the dual policy of restricting immigration while at the same time promoting the integration of those who have already settled within its borders. Italian immigration policy has developed only recently, however, as a response to the new escalation in immigrant inflows and in an effort to bring its immigration control and treatment of immigrants more in line with that of other EC member states. Italy's first major policy response to immigration was Law no. 943, passed in December 1986. This was followed in February 1990 by Law no. 39, commonly referred to as the 'Martelli Law'. Perhaps the most significant integration measures to arise out of these laws were the amnesties providing for large-scale regularization of 'irregular' or undocumented immigrants, comparable with the regularization carried out by the French authorities in 1981/2. According to one estimate, roughly 80% of North African immigrants were in Italy on an irregular basis before 1986.[88] Law 943 came into effect in January 1987 with an amnesty initially intended to last for a period of three months, but extended by successive amendments up to September 1988. Law 39 introduced the second amnesty, which provided for the registration of undocumented immigrants who were present in Italy on 31 December 1989 and who came forward to register before 29 June 1990.

It was hoped that these regularizations would not only benefit the state by introducing a greater degree of control over the immigration phenomenon, but would also benefit the immigrants themselves by virtue of the general social and economic rights associated with legal residency status. However, neither amnesty proved particularly successful: only about 10% of irregular immigrants came forward under the first one,[89] and it is estimated that up to 50% of immigrants currently in Italy are present and/or working on an irregular basis.[90] A number of reasons are put forward for the very low regularization rate, perhaps the most important being that most immigrants saw more disadvantages than advantages in registering.[91]

A comprehensive framework of integration policies which could substantially affect the living and working conditions of immigrants is only at an early stage of development in Italy. Law 39 is concerned primarily with immigration control; thus, apart from the 1981 law ratifying the 1975 ILO Migrant Workers Convention[92] (ratified in the context of Italian emigration), Law 943 still stands as the primary piece of Italian legislation dealing with integration. While appearing relatively far-reaching in its intention to guarantee 'all non-Community workers ... and ... their families equality of treatment and full equality of rights to the use of social and health services ... to the maintenance of cultural identity, to schooling and to the availability of housing',[93] this legislation has not been backed up by an effective enforcement machinery. In practice, it places considerable responsibility with local authorities and on the voluntary sector, but does not provide clear guidelines on what policies should be implemented. According to a recent survey, the 'variegated world of voluntary associations performs a vital task in helping immigrants with social, bureaucratic and work-related problems'. However:

> analysis of local policies ... shows the fragmentary and incoherent nature of most interventions ... [which] range from a total abandoning of responsibility and buck-passing to (rarely) full integration ... What is needed is a coherent policy which promotes immigrants in both job-related and cultural fields and which seeks to construct a forum for the dignified exchange of views.[94]

In connection with a National Conference on Immigration held in Rome in 1990,[95] the Bocconi University was commissioned to carry out an analysis of the immigration and integration policies of France, Germany, the Netherlands and Great Britain so as to provide information on the main types and forms of immigration policies that could potentially be applied in Italy. The conclusions presented at the conference included 'the necessity of ... an integration which neither produces ghettos nor is complete assimilation ... of structures which ... would monitor the various aspects of integration ... [and] a promotion of greater understanding and respect between ethnic groups.'[96] It remains to be seen what direction Italy's integration policies will take under the country's new right-wing government.

Immigrant settlement and integration: social and economic rights and opportunities

Despite the variations in approaches to integration, there is a common element linking the discourse in every country: a concern with communities which are both economically disadvantaged and which display a distinct ethnicity based on a culture, race, religion, language and/or national identity with roots elsewhere. It is not the immigrant status of these groups which seems to matter so much as their cultural, racial or religious 'difference' from the receiving society, reinforced by social and economic marginalization.

Thus it is on communities of immigrant origin which are at once visible and disadvantaged that integration policies have focused. As expressed in a report for the European Commission on immigration policies and the social integration of migrants, 'integration is inescapable as a policy if we are setting out to defuse the tensions inherent in the immigration of generally poor, inadequately equipped and ethnically different people'.[97]

Since the early to mid-1980s, there has been a growing recognition, at least in principle, that efforts are needed to strengthen and improve immigrant minorities' social and economic rights and opportunities. This is reflected in the European Commission's report on integration quoted above, which stresses the need for greater security of stay for immigrants and their offspring, and the need for action in the areas of employment and business, education and housing. The basic position of the majority of postwar immigrant minority groups in the European receiving states is broadly similar. If integration is understood as a process which prevents or counteracts the social, economic and political marginalization of minority groups, whatever the policies pursued, states have generally failed to achieve the secure integration of all immigrant groups.

This is particularly so in respect of communities that have been the primary focus of concern: those of non-European origin. Every state has expressed greater anxiety over certain immigrant groups than others. Indeed, it is generally possible to speak of a hierarchy of preference for immigrants of different origins. In France, Italians have been preferred over Portuguese, Portuguese over Tunisians, Tunisians over Algerians. In Germany, as noted above, it is the Turks who have traditionally been seen as presenting the most serious integration problems. To some extent this is reflected in a social and economic status hierarchy, the most marginalized groups often being those that are perceived as culturally or ethnically most 'different'. Thus it is difficult to compare the position of Italian immigrants in France or Germany with that of Algerians or Turks, or the position of Irish immigrants in Britain with that of Bangladeshis.

Of course, the status of different immigrant groups vis-à-vis the dominant society is determined by a range of factors including not only discrimination, but the timing of immigration, the sectors of housing and employment into which groups originally entered, and the levels of unemployment in the areas of high immigrant concentration. This is illustrated by the well-documented process of geographical concentration of immigrant groups in the inner-city areas of Britain's largest conurbations,[98] a process which is in many respects common to the main cities of all the postwar receiving countries. To what extent this concentration has been as a result of 'exclusion, attraction or retention'[99] is debatable, and would anyway have varied from group to group. In the case of Britain, the process may be very generally – if somewhat crudely – explained in terms of immigrants' original location in the housing and labour markets. The majority of immigrants initially filled unskilled or manual jobs in industries that were located in the cities. However, British society was at that time undergoing a major process of economic and social decentralization. Economic and technological developments were already under way which were favouring shifts in the industrial sector to cheaper out-of-city locations, from heavy to light industry, and from a reliance on cheap unskilled labour to a demand for skilled workers. This process was accompanied by a growth in real income among the white population and a significant population movement out of the inner cities to more desirable housing in the suburbs or smaller towns. Unable to compete equally in the housing markets (owing to discrimination and low income), and initially excluded from local authority housing, immigrants were generally forced into the cheapest and most marginal privately rented* or owner-occupied accommodation† in the declining inner cities. Because these types of accommodation tended to be concentrated in certain areas, and because immigrants tended to create and maintain distinct communities, the outcome was a significant spatial segregation.[100] The disadvantaged position of immigrants in the labour market has therefore to be explained not only in terms of discrimination, but also in terms of a combination of sectoral and spatial segregation: from the very beginning, immigrants became concentrated in sectors of the economy and in geographical areas that have been marked by a progressive decline in demand for labour and, eventually, by high levels of unemployment.

In France the process was somewhat different, explained as much by the state's direct involvement in immigrant housing after the destruction of the *bidonvilles* as by processes of discrimination in the general housing market and by inner-city decay. Three 'solutions' to the immigrant housing problem were adopted in the 1960s: normal social housing rented from one of the

---

*West Indian immigrants particularly, followed later by movement into council housing. Immigrants were initially excluded from local authority housing because eligibility depended on a certain period of residence in the area, and housing was generally allocated to those who had been waiting the longest.
†Particularly Asian immigrants.

regional social housing organizations ('*Habitat à Loyer Modéré*' or HLM), *cités de transit* and *foyers-hôtels*. The *cités de transit* were government-financed, purpose-built, low-standard housing designed specifically for immigrant families moved out of the *bidonvilles*. They were intended to provide temporary housing for those groups that were not deemed 'ready' to move into normal social housing since they were considered too culturally or socially different to share housing markets with the French population as a whole. The *cités* were therefore filled primarily by North African immigrants who would receive education during their stay 'in preparation' for a move to HLM housing. The move into social housing was very difficult for many families because of the restrictions the HLM put on numbers of immigrants and family size accepted, so for many the *cités* turned out to be not provisional staging-posts, but areas of permanent settlement and *de facto* segregation.[101]

A similar segregation was applied to single North African men, many of whom were housed in barrack-like conditions in the *foyers-hôtels* – hostels for single workers.[102] Movement of North African immigrants into social housing and privately rented or owned property has generally been accompanied by a process of concentration similar to that which developed in Britain. According to Paul White, this has not been so apparent in the case of European immigrant groups.[103]

The concentration of immigrant groups in Germany associated with the move out of employer accommodation has largely come about through a combination of 'exclusion' (discrimination and low income) and 'attraction' (development and maintenance of community networks). Alarmed by what it saw as a progressive 'ghettoization' among immigrant groups, the Federal government introduced foreign residence quotas for urban regions in 1975, whereby local authorities could declare themselves overburdened and stop any further settlement of immigrants if the foreign population rose above 12%. In fact the authorities could not effectively control immigrants' settlement patterns and the measure was discontinued in 1977. Similar dispersal policies tried on occasion in Britain also met with failure.[104] They were nevertheless significant, since they reflected a concern common to all receiving states over the social implications of immigrant concentration.[105] The worry was as much about the capacity problems of social infrastructures in areas of high immigrant population as about the longer-term implications for the integration of immigrants. Such policies represented an attempt to solve these problems through a direct manipulation of residence rather than through the elimination of disadvantage and discrimination.[106]

Dispersal policies have come into use again more recently in Germany as a result of efforts to cope with large numbers of asylum-seekers. In this context, concerns have focused more on the problem of sharing the asylum burden among different *Länder* and local authorities than on an interest in promoting the social and economic integration of asylum-seekers.* Indeed, in many respects this policy may be seen as working counter to integration, since large numbers of asylum-seekers have found themselves in areas with no other established immigrant communities (particularly in eastern Germany), and where they are forced to live in segregated housing, if only for protection against attacks from hostile majority or 'indigenous' communities.

More sophisticated approaches to the integration of immigrant minorities have, however, been developed over the past decade. Although too varied to summarize here, these have tended to be based on one of two general approaches: (i) policies aimed at equipping immigrants to compete better with the majority population (particularly education and training policies); and (ii) policies aimed at opening up the major institutions of society to greater immigrant participation (particularly in the areas of housing and employment). In both cases, there has been a constant tension between the institution of policies which directly target minorities (and therefore risk resentment from sections of the majority population) and those of more general application (which may benefit the majority population more than minorities). Whatever the approach adopted, in all areas of policy concerned with the social and economic integration of minorities the challenges and problems have become greater with the onset of economic recession, the rise in overall unemployment levels and the increasing financial squeeze on the welfare state.

The most prominent measures aimed at improving immigrant minorities' access to institutions are those taken in the field of employment, where policies have been introduced to overcome structural discrimination in the labour market. In a 1990 report on immigrant policy, for example, the Netherlands Scientific Council for Government Policy argued for the introduction of a non-punishable obligation on the part of employers to: (i) implement employment equity in consultation with employees' representatives; (ii) prepare a plan setting out the goals that the employer intends to

---

*Note that the unequal 'burden' imposed on different local authorities has also caused tension in other countries, including Belgium, Sweden and the UK, with the result that authorities have at times refused to take responsibility for particular individuals or groups.

achieve in respect of equity; and the introduction of a punishable obligation for employers to file an annual report concerning the extent to which members of 'visible' and other minorities are represented in the various positions of employment.[107] This policy corresponds broadly with that of 'positive action' as applied in the United Kingdom. It should not be confused with a policy of positive discrimination, which has not been pursued by any West European government.

As regards policies to tackle direct and indirect discrimination against immigrant minorities, only the United Kingdom has a comprehensive legal enforcement machinery of long standing. Moreover, recent moves to amend legislation in other countries have tended to be limited to the consideration of laws to combat overt racist behaviour.[108] The Council of Europe's Committee of Experts on Community Relations recommended in its final report in 1991 that member states strengthen their anti-discrimination laws and promote the use of the legal remedies available to minority members, a recommendation which was backed up by the Declaration and Plan of Action on combating racism, xenophobia, anti-Semitism and intolerance adopted at the Council of Europe summit in Vienna in October 1993.[109] This is a view shared by the European Commission and European Parliament.[110] However, there are no signs as yet that this will lead to a European instrument to combat discrimination against ethnic minorities.

An issue which has attracted particular attention is that of the integration of the so-called 'second' and 'third' generations, since it has become increasingly apparent that the marginal position of immigrants in housing, employment and public life has tended to be perpetuated in the case of their children and their children's offspring. Indeed, unemployment levels among descendants of immigrants are frequently higher than among the immigrants themselves. For example, in 1985, 'foreign' youths in West Germany were two to three times more likely to be registered as unemployed than their German peers. Furthermore, of those who were working, nearly 90% were employed as manual labourers, and only 20% of those as skilled workers.[111]

Anxious to prevent the formation of a permanent 'minority underclass', governments have developed policies aimed at improving opportunities for the younger age-groups through education and training. However, in all the postwar receiving countries, ethnic minority children continue to be over-represented in the slowest tracks of the education system and under-represented at the higher levels of secondary and tertiary education (although the extent of underachievement varies considerably from group to group[112]).

In all countries, certain groups have been targeted for special language classes (particularly the lowest age-groups[113]), since language has been seen as one of the most important factors contributing to their problems at school.[114] However, the significance of the language factor must decline as more and more children are born into an environment in which the host-country language is dominant. This points to the importance of connecting education with broader integration programmes, for it is becoming increasingly apparent that the entire basis of minority disadvantage must be tackled if significant progress is to be made in any one area.

Other efforts to improve employment opportunities for ethnic minority labour-market entrants have included programmes of vocational training (e.g. Youth Opportunities and Youth Training Programmes in Britain). However, these have failed to make any significant impact because training cannot guarantee jobs, particularly in areas of high unemployment. Furthermore, the ethnic minorities are frequently over-represented in programmes that offer little or no opportunity for skilled or more qualified occupations.[115] Aware that disadvantage among minority groups as a whole is often connected with economic stagnation in areas with high immigrant populations, governments have also instituted programmes of urban renewal and rejuvenation. These have generally not led to a substantial improvement in the position of immigrant groups. Indeed, a common pattern is the displacement of immigrant groups from areas that have undergone redevelopment[116] – a trend often associated with a process of 'gentrification', particularly in the inner cities.

Immigrant minorities: a 'class apart'?

Despite the *de facto* marginalization of many immigrants and immigrant groups in the social and economic spheres of society in Western Europe, most immigrants and descendants of immigrants in Europe now enjoy a relatively secure legal status that allows for permanent settlement and *de jure* equal treatment in areas such as housing, employment, education and welfare benefits. Thus most enjoy, at least formally, full economic and social rights, and – as indicated in the previous section – much of the effort made by governments and other authorities to secure the integration of immigrant groups is devoted to promoting and protecting immigrants' and minorities' access to and enjoyment of these rights.

However, while socio-economic status is undoubtedly a central factor explaining the position of many immigrant minorities in Western Europe, it is not the only one to be considered. It should be noted that immigrant minorities' socio-economic or class status does, in fact, vary considerably: many individuals and certain immigrant groups have been very successful as entrepreneurs or have competed successfully in the education and labour markets, and yet continue to experience problems in their relations with the majority population (or sections of it). And even those policies aimed at improving immigrants' social and economic mobility have run up against a number of problems behind which lie important questions relating to immigrants' juridical or perceived status as foreign. This becomes clear once one ventures into the realms of culture, political rights and citizenship. As noted by G.S. Cross in the context of France, foreign labour became a 'radically distinctive class in France. Not merely were immigrants predominantly propertyless and unskilled, but they were non-citizens.'[117]

Therefore, even if the majority of immigrant minorities were to enjoy full substantive socio-economic equality, the extent of their membership of the wider society in which they live might still be questioned. An important factor militating against the full integration of immigrant minority groups is the legal definition and/or wider perceptions of immigrants and their offspring as 'outsiders' in many countries. This is a particular problem for the 'second-generation' immigrants born and brought up in Western Europe. As observed by Czarina Wilpert in a study of Turkish immigrant groups in Berlin, 'there exists, for all second-generation Turks, a tension between their lack of a legitimate future and membership of German society (institutional marginality) and the *de facto* experience of a legitimate claim to belongingness through a life lived [in the Federal Republic] ... [This] conflict is enhanced by the ascriptive experiences of discrimination, denigration and youths' concomitant identification with their family and culture of origin.'[118]

One key to this tension can be found in the concepts of citizenship that apply in Western Europe today. Both in formal terms (membership of a state) and in substantive meaning (possession of a number of rights and duties in that state),[119] it is citizenship that may ultimately define who are 'insiders' and who are 'outsiders' in the modern West European state. As Tomas Hammar observes, the majority of postwar immigrants and immigrant minorities in Western Europe could be considered to be both insiders and outsiders, members and non-members of the societies in which they live, and therefore can be seen as forming a 'class apart' within these societies. Hammar thus identifies three categories of person in Western Europe according to citizenship status: foreigners (those with no rights associated with citizenship, e.g.

short-stay visitors), citizens and 'denizens'. He estimates that over half of all non-nationals resident in Western Europe (excluding the UK) fall into the third category. As he observes:

> Many foreign citizens have ... gained a secure residence status [in Western Europe]. Even if they are not citizens of the country, they can for example only be deported in extreme emergency situations. They may have lived such a long period in the host country ... [or] their family ties may be so strong ... that they in fact constitute a new category of foreign citizens whose residence status is fully guaranteed or almost so. Those who belong to this category have also in several countries been entitled to equal treatment in all spheres of life, with full access to the labour market, business, education, social welfare, even to employment in branches of the public service, etc. A new status group has emerged, and members of this group are not regular and plain foreign citizens any more, but also not naturalized citizens of the receiving country.[120]

Because members of this group usually enjoy full social and economic rights (at least formally), their status is substantively different from that of citizens, principally through their exclusion from participation in most areas of the formal political process. Thus, for example, although foreign nationals are generally allowed to express themselves politically in Western Europe (to form associations, to take part in union activities, to demonstrate and strike, and to join political parties), they are excluded from participation in national elections in all West European countries apart from the UK, and it is only in recent years that a number of states have introduced the right to vote for certain categories of foreign nationals in municipal or regional elections.[121] As a result, a substantial proportion of immigrants and immigrant minorities are not represented politically and have no formal political voice. This not only raises questions as to the health of representative democracy in Western Europe, but may also be seen to constitute a significant challenge to the substantive integration of many immigrant minority groups. Because the promotion of immigrants' interests through formal political channels has to take place on the basis of an often weak and distorting filter-through process (or outside such channels altogether), the potential for immigrants to have any meaningful say in the policies developed to promote their integration is likely to be limited. Moreover, with no formal political voice, there exists little incentive or, indeed, little potential for such groups to develop any significant sense of political citizenship.[122]

This implies a danger of alienation and disaffection, and a persistent orientation to the country of origin among many immigrants, an orientation which may be not only political but also social and cultural in nature, and which is likely in turn to work against the processes of social and economic integration which the host governments are so keen to promote. Czarina Wilpert observed in Berlin, for example, the persistence of a return-orientation (or 'myth of return') not only among first-generation migrants, but also among their children, a situation which she ascribed in part to their imposed status as 'outsiders' or 'denizens'.[123]

In this context, however, generalization is problematic. Just as approaches to the social and economic integration of immigrants differ from country to country and group to group, so do policies affecting the substantive and juridical citizenship status of immigrant minority communities. Policy in the United Kingdom is the most obvious exception: the majority of immigrants who arrived in the UK during the postwar period did so as British subjects with full citizenship (and thus full political) rights; naturalization and dual citizenship are comparatively easy to attain; most offspring of immigrants born in the country are accorded British citizenship; and all Commonwealth citizens migrating today gain the right to vote in national elections after one year's residence in the UK. In France, the situation differs in that most immigrants did not enter with citizenship rights. Nevertheless, naturalization has been relatively easy for settled immigrants, and all offspring of immigrants born in France were, until recently, automatically granted French citizenship. However, foreign nationals cannot vote in either local or national elections in France. In Germany, on the other hand, not only most first-generation immigrants but also the majority of second- and third-generation offspring of immigrants born in Germany remain unnaturalized, and thus remain foreigners in the juridical sense. Long-settled foreign nationals can vote in some *Länder*, but not in others.

Such variation can be partly explained in terms of differing concepts of citizenship, which in turn derive from the historical development of nation-states in Western Europe, a process specific to each country in question. Thus the relative openness of both Britain and France to the acceptance of foreigners as nationals or citizens in the juridical sense can be traced back in part to the fact that centralization and bureaucratic statehood as they developed in these countries assisted the processes of creating the modern

French and British 'nations'. As a consequence, residence, allegiance to the state and submission to its jurisdiction became the hallmarks of citizenship, and thus territorial concepts – place of birth (according to the principle of *jus soli*) and place of residence – came largely to determine nationality in these countries.[124] Such concepts lent themselves to a perception of the populations of these states' empires as attached juridically to the centre as subjects or citizens. Meanwhile, the Netherlands' relatively liberal stance on foreigners' voting rights can be explained in terms of the country's pluralist history and political structures.

In Germany, by contrast, the centralized nation-state developed much later, and in such a way that encouraged the formulation of citizenship as derived from *jus sanguinis* rather than *jus soli*. As Ra'anan describes, 'it is not where an individual resides and which state has jurisdiction over him that determines his nationality, but rather who he is – his cultural, religious and historic identity, i.e. his ethnicity, a heritage received from his ancestors and carried with him, in mind and body, irrespective of his current place of domicile'.[125] In the case of Germany, this meant membership of the German *Volk*. Thus, recently, large numbers of so-called 'ethnic Germans' or *'Aussiedler'* have been able to migrate to Germany with automatic access to citizenship, whereas at the same time the majority of foreign immigrants and those born of foreign immigrant parentage in Germany remain 'foreigners' and thus non-citizens.

The official language used to denote immigrant minority communities in these countries is indicative of these differing models. As noted earlier, in Germany immigrants and descendants of immigrants continue to be referred to as 'foreigners' or 'aliens',[126] while in Britain and the Netherlands such groups are generally referred to as 'minorities'. In France, the term 'minorities' runs counter to the French insistence on a unitary state, and thus it is more common to refer to 'immigrants' and 'populations of foreign origin'. It is interesting to note that both 'minorities' and 'immigrants' denote groups with a specific status within the politico-legal structure of the nation-state, while the term 'foreigners' clearly places immigrant communities outside the structure of state membership.

In substantive terms, however, the significance of this variation should probably not be over-emphasized. The problems that France has experienced since the 1950s in accepting immigrants of different cultures, and the United Kingdom's difficulties in coming to terms with the new multiracial nature of its society, demonstrate the limits to the territorial or 'civic' basis of membership and citizenship of these states. Indeed, in Britain, the experience of black and Asian immigration during the postwar period resulted quite directly in the decline in the importance of territorial principles as the foundation of British citizenship. The distinction made between 'patrial' and 'non-patrial' citizens introduced in the 1970s – criticized so much at the time because it was seen to discriminate against potential migrants from the so-called 'New Commonwealth' countries (non-white) – demonstrated a growing emphasis on the principle of *jus sanguinis* in the operation of British citizenship laws, and thus a retreat from policies which had allowed the entry, settlement and exercize of citizenship rights to substantial numbers of non-white and non-Christian immigrants. Similarly, the French nationality law was revised in July 1993 such that children born in France of foreign parents would no longer automatically become French nationals at the age of 18.* Meanwhile, there is growing domestic pressure on the German government to liberalize its nationality laws to facilitate immigrant minorities' integration and allow for dual citizenship. The citizenship question is still a very thorny issue in most countries, particularly in the context of political rights, naturalization and dual citizenship. This indicates not only that traditional concepts of citizenship or membership have become more difficult to apply, but also that no clear alternative structure has yet been found to take their place.

It has been suggested that the colonial experience of France, Britain and the Netherlands implies a greater acceptance of foreign immigration. As argued in a recent Council of Europe report, 'countries with a colonial past ... have more historical familiarity with people from overseas' and thus 'have been more open than others to the possibility of permanent immigration.'[127] However, the colonial experience almost certainly did more to reinforce ideas of racial or cultural superiority than to foster tolerance. The French insistence on cultural assimilation in the past and, more recently, the controversy over the wearing of headscarves in French schools; the Salman

---

*The revised law was published in the French Official Journal on 23 July 1993. As of 1 January 1994, children born in France of foreign parents must declare their intention to become French nationals between the age of 16 and 21. In addition, foreign parents of children born in France are no longer able to apply for French citizenship for their children under the age of 18; children born in France of parents themselves born in former French colonies or overseas territories before becoming independent (e.g. Algerians born in Algeria before 1962) no longer become French at birth as of 1 January 1994 – one of the parents must have resided at least 5 years in France for such a child to be declared French at birth; and foreigners who marry French nationals now have to wait one year before being able to apply for French citizenship.

Rushdie affair in Britain; the resurgence in extreme anti-immigrant sentiment as a mainstream political force in France; and the increase in racial
violence in the UK: all are testimony to significant levels of intolerance on
French and British soil.

All 'nation-states' in Western Europe were built in the absence of large
racially, culturally, or religiously distinct immigrant communities, and thus
in all states, ideas of 'belongingness' became tied to those of cultural,
linguistic, ethnic and/or religious identity – an identity which defined the
community not only in terms of itself, but also in terms of its relations with
outsiders. Those who have least easily conformed to this identity have often
been those who have remained the most marginalized. Despite efforts to speed
immigrant and ethnic minorities' integration in terms of improving their
social, economic and (to a lesser extent) political rights and opportunities, it
is not at all clear that West European society is reconciled to the cultural and
ethnic diversity which the past few decades of immigration have brought
about. The variations and shifts in governments' approaches to the cultural
dimension of immigrant status in themselves indicate the difficulties that
European receiving states have had in coming to terms with the presence of
culturally, ethnically or religiously distinct immigrant minority communities.
As Philip Ogden argues in reference to France, the 'ultimate failure' of the
'series of twists and turns in government policy' is 'best illustrated by the
extraordinary hold which immigration has established on ... political
consciousness in the early 1990s.'[128]

At a time of considerable economic and political uncertainty, when the
traditional frontiers of the state are being eroded by a range of transnational
and global economic, political and social forces (including migration), there
is a potential for societies in Western Europe to turn increasingly to negative
symbols of identity (i.e. to base their identity on opposition to the identities
of others). Nothing demonstrates this more clearly than the upsurge in
extreme anti-immigrant opinion in Western Europe and the increase in
incidents of racial violence and harassment in recent years.

Extreme anti-immigrant opinion and racial violence and harassment
As noted by Robin Oakley in his 1991 report on racial violence and
harassment for the Council of Europe, racism is not a new phenomenon in
European history: anti-Semitism, for example, has been present in Europe for
over a millennium. Yet postwar immigration has introduced 'a new chapter'
in the history of racism in Europe. Whether it has emerged as a question of

true 'racial' difference, as in Britain, or, more commonly, as a question of cultural difference, Europe's 'new racism', according to Oakley:

> confronts many of the Mediterranean and Third World immigrants who form its new 'internal colonies' with a form of xenophobia which ... articulates a deep-rooted though previously latent Eurocentrism which appeals to the superiority and inherent proprietorship of certain life-styles and 'civilized' values. This strong and assertive form of xenophobia has displaced earlier intra-European rivalries, and has become manifest in the ideologies of right-wing movements across Europe, some of which have achieved considerable electoral success.[129]

The recent increase in strength of extreme right-wing anti-immigrant political movements has attracted considerable attention over recent years, as the most organized expression and manifestation of racism in contemporary Europe. Less attention has been paid, however, to the significance of the linked (but not necessarily causally related) increase in racial violence and harassment, and thus – with the partial exception of the United Kingdom – official recognition of this issue has been slow to develop.[130]

Both forms of racist expression have tended to be treated in isolation in official circles, as a failing in a particular minority of the population. While the causes of extreme racism of this kind are complex and can only be examined in terms of individual national and local circumstances, the ugliest expressions of racism tend to be found among 'persons who feel threatened and who do not have access to other forms of personal and institutional power'.[131] There is indeed a strong link between, on the one hand, overt racism and racial violence and, on the other, poverty, insecurity and competition for jobs and housing; and thus it is not entirely surprising that extreme anti-immigrant attitudes and incidents of racial violence and harassment should increase during periods of economic recession and high unemployment, whether at the local, regional, national or European level.

Nevertheless, these forms of racist expression and behaviour cannot be properly understood in isolation from the broader and deeper tendencies towards racial or cultural exclusion and domination in contemporary European societies. As argued by Liz Fekete, it is not enough to see the growth of right-wing organizations 'as confined to the extremities of society ... like a gangrenous limb that needs amputation'. It can only be properly examined 'within the framework of the body politic as a whole, [involving] the health of the whole organism, so to speak.'[132] It is, indeed, because the most overt forms of racist behaviour have wider resonance in terms of community relations as a whole – or are seen to have such resonance by members of the victim communities – that their impact is so significant. Racial violence and harassment do not only affect the individuals directly involved, for it is not the violent acts themselves which have so much impact on the wider community but the racist message which they convey; indeed, everyday 'low-level' forms of harassment may carry as much force as more isolated incidents of extreme violence. As Oakley notes, 'Such harassment is an effective means of maintaining racial boundaries at the local level ... [and] of keeping victim communities subordinated.' Moreover, 'few individuals need to be actively involved in the use of force to establish or maintain the pattern of inter-group relations; provided others condone or at least do not oppose the action, the racial order at the collective or group level will still have been successfully imposed'.[133]

It is because of what isolated or localized forms of racism and inter-group tension say about relations in society as a whole that the Council of Europe report on community relations lays great stress on the need for integration policies and other forms of political action which start from the basis that integration is a process involving society as a whole: 'It is no longer appropriate to think of the migrant population and the host population as separate, possibly even antagonistic groups; rather, we should think of society as a single whole in all its ethnic and cultural diversity.'[134]

It should not be forgotten that European societies also have a powerful anti-racist impulse which has deep roots in European liberal traditions, as illustrated by the strength of such movements as the Anti-Nazi League in the United Kingdom and *SOS Racisme* in France. This impulse is in constant tension with nationalistic, xenophobic and exclusionist tendencies, and it is for this reason that political leaders have a central role to play in influencing community relations by virtue of the messages they convey through their policies and public statements. The immigration issue has always been a subject easily manipulated for political advantage. Whether explicitly or implicitly, politicians have tended to find more immediate advantage in playing on people's fears and insecurities by drawing on xenophobic and exclusionist tendencies in society. While this may have proved an effective way of winning votes, its more significant effect is likely to have been in souring community relations and increasing inter-group tensions at the local and national levels.

Immigrant minority integration and the promotion of good community relations is a complex and difficult process for all European countries, particularly at a time of increasing economic and social insecurity. The substantive obstacles are considerable and the challenges enormously varied. There are no 'quick fixes' available to governments and no single mix of policies which would be appropriate to all countries and all localities in all situations. But if there is one goal which could be seen as applicable to Europe as a whole, it is that of reconciling populations to the ethnic and cultural diversity which the past few decades of immigration have brought about, for only when the multicultural and multiethnic nature of European societies takes as strong a hold as exclusionist identities have done until now will members of immigrant and ethnic communities be able to feel that they are accepted as an integral part of society. As argued by the Council of Europe's Committee of Experts on Community Relations, 'open, welcoming and tolerant attitudes are the only sound basis for good community relations.'[135]

The messages currently being conveyed by West European leaders are at best confused in this regard. Governments have expressed a positive commitment, at both the national level and in the European Union or Council of Europe, to securing the successful integration of immigrant minority populations, yet they have shown a tendency to react more to negative than to positive attitudes relating to immigrants among the public; and, as argued in the concluding chapter, they have done little to ensure that immigrant minorities feel or are seen to be an integral part of the 'European project'.

Chapter 7

Europe's Receiving States in the 1990s: Towards a Common Migration Policy?

As demonstrated in earlier chapters, international migration emerged as an important component of the process of economic expansion and liberalization which took place in Western Europe after the Second World War. Whether as migrant-receivers (Northwestern Europe) or as migrant-senders (Southern Europe), all states became linked into an expanding migration 'system' which soon extended beyond the region, incorporating former colonies and other states to the south and to the east. Despite the general clamp-down on foreign labour recruitment which followed the oil crisis in 1973, immigration continued, dominated by family reunion and – after the mid-1980s – undocumented 'economic' immigration and asylum inflows, not only into the longer-standing 'receiving' states, but also into what had traditionally been the 'sending' states of Southern Europe.

This migration system is now, as Zolberg notes, one in which all the 'various migratory streams are interconnected' and in which 'the policies of the various states pertaining to them are ... interactive.'[1] Yet whereas comparable developments in spheres such as trade and finance led to the emergence of international regulatory regimes, no strong international regime developed around migration as a policy area. Immigration policy remained principally the concern of individual states. In the context of 'economic' migration, this could be explained by the fact that, with an abundant supply of foreign labour, foreign workers could be recruited without receiving states having to cooperate with one another. However, equally important was the fact that control over the admission of aliens has traditionally been viewed as inherent in the concept of state sovereignty – reflecting the political, as well as economic, importance of the phenomenon. As a consequence, there has been considerable resistance to surrendering elements of this control to an international regulatory system or regime.

What international cooperation has emerged has tended to come about reactively as a result of either indirect or negative, as opposed to positive, interdependence. Thus, for example, provisions for the free movement of workers within the European Community which arose from the 1957 Treaty of Rome came about largely because a viable common market could not function without the circulation of all four economic factors: goods, services, capital *and* labour. Similarly, the subsequent extension of geographical mobility of workers to free movement of *persons* within the Community as set out in Article 8a of the Single European Act (SEA) was enacted less for its own sake than for the sake of creating an internal market comprising 'an area without internal frontiers in which the free movement of goods, persons, services and capital is ensured'. As regards immigration policy, recent moves to achieve closer cooperation have largely been forced both by efforts to suppress internal border controls, and by growing anxiety about increasing levels of 'unwanted' immigration which would seem to necessitate joint responses.

Nevertheless, irrespective of the basis for cooperation, pressure for closer coordination and integration of migration policy among the member states of the European Union (EU) has been mounting since the mid-1980s. Some progress has been made alongside the more general acceleration of West European political and economic integration. However, it is still very unclear what degree of policy harmonization[2] is likely to be achieved or what the overall nature and pattern of cooperation will be in the future, particularly as international cooperation in this area increasingly involves states outside the Union.

This chapter looks at the current direction of migration policy in Western Europe through the lens of the harmonization process. It begins by examining the development of policy coordination and integration to date, and then considers divergent trends in specific issue areas and current patterns of multilateral cooperation, both within Western Europe and throughout Europe as a whole. Although all the elements would seem to be in place for an extensive harmonization in this area, a closer analysis of a number of issues in question reveals that the road to common policies is unlikely to be a smooth one. Indeed, the numerous obstacles to harmonization which can be identified raise questions about the likelihood of a cohesive Union migration policy developing in the years to come.

Cooperation during the 1970s and 1980s: institutional developments
During the 1970s and 1980s, immigration came to be viewed by Europe's receiving states as more and more of a problem. As detailed in previous chapters, attention turned progressively towards issues such as family immigration, return migration, illegal and clandestine immigration, integration and – somewhat later – rising levels of spontaneous arrivals of asylum-seekers. The emphasis was on control. To what extent could family immigration be limited or regulated? How could foreign workers be persuaded to return home? How could those destined to stay be integrated? How could illegal immigration be prevented? What could be done about rising numbers of spontaneous asylum applications? Increasingly, these questions came to be seen as problems shared among all Europe's major receiving states.

The patterns of cooperation which emerged in Western Europe before the mid-1980s revealed a growing recognition of the commonality of such problems, but also reflected the highly restrictive climate which developed after the postwar recruitment period and the reluctance of states to relinquish their sovereign control over immigration. Until the early 1970s, formal cooperation among the member states of the European Community was limited to issues connected with the internal movement and residence of European Community workers, the self-employed, suppliers and recipients of services, and their family members, as provided for in the Treaty of Rome and subsequent secondary Community legislation and decisions of the European Court of Justice. There was virtually no discussion of matters associated with the movement of third-country nationals (i.e. nationals of states which were not members of the European Community), despite high levels of labour migration to Northwestern Europe during the 1960s and early 1970s. Migration which did not involve citizens of the member states was considered strictly the concern of individual countries.

During the early 1970s, however, this situation began to change. As discussed in Chapter 4, the period following the 1973 oil crisis marked an overall convergence in receiving states' immigration policies following the rather disparate approaches of the preceding two decades, and included a growing recognition of the importance of immigration as a factor of social policy in Western Europe. 1974 saw the adoption of a European Community Action Programme in Favour of Migrant Workers and their Families, followed in 1976 by a Resolution of the Council of Ministers advocating a Community approach to nationals of third countries and consultation on migration policies.

Nevertheless, overall commitment to international cooperation on immigration and the position of third-country migrants was still very weak; this was reflected in the fact that the Council of Ministers made no moves towards developing a legal instrument on the basis of the 1976 Resolution.[3] The Council of Europe went further by opening for signature the 1977 European Convention on the Legal Status of Migrant Workers, but at the time this was ratified by only five states, of which three were migrant-senders rather than migrant-receivers.[4] Limited Community competence in the area of certain groups of third-country immigrants was established by the Cooperation Agreements between the European Community and Algeria, Morocco and Tunisia in 1978, the Association Agreement between the European Community and Turkey in 1980, and the Cooperation Agreement between the European Community and Yugoslavia in 1983 (suspended in 1991). Yet this competence was generally limited to non-discrimination clauses and did not extend to control over labour recruitment or immigration as such.[5]

Although there was still little emerging in the way of formal policy integration or harmonization, dialogue between ministers and officials from different countries did intensify during the early 1980s within intergovernmental fora such as the Council of Europe's European Committee on Migration (CDMG) and its Ad Hoc Committee of Experts on the Legal Aspects of Territorial Asylum, Refugees and Stateless Persons (CAHAR), and the UNHCR's Executive Committee. The first signs of a further expansion of European-wide dialogue and cooperation in the mid-1980s were reflected in the establishment of the Intergovernmental Consultations on Asylum, Refugee and Migration Policies in Europe, North America and Australia in November 1985, following calls for new consultative arrangements at a meeting of 35 states convened by the UNHCR earlier that year. The intensification of intergovernmental dialogue in the area almost certainly encouraged informal policy alignment in certain areas – such as the adoption of carrier sanctions legislation by a number of states during the second half of the 1980s – and contributed to the recognition of a number of migration and asylum issues as common problems for the states involved.

For the member states of the European Community, the increase in momentum of the broader process of European economic integration in the mid-1980s proved more decisive for driving cooperative efforts in the area. A turning-point came in the mid-1980s with (i) the signing of the Schengen Agreement on the gradual abolition of controls at their common frontiers by Germany, France and the Benelux countries, which undertook to create a frontier-free space for the movement of goods, services and persons, and thus to harmonize a wide range of policies including controls on immigration from third countries; and (ii) the signing of the Single European Act (SEA) by all the Community member states in 1986, which, when ratified in 1987, introduced a new article[6] into the EEC Treaty of Rome stipulating that an internal market be established by the end of December 1992. The Schengen Agreement was to be implemented ahead and in anticipation of free movement within the European Community as a whole.[7]

Not only did these developments represent a changing environment for the movement of persons within the Schengen grouping and the European Community, but they also introduced a new necessity for closer cooperation among member states on matters connected with migration into the two groupings from outside, since the suppression of internal borders meant that the external borders of each member state were effectively to become the external borders for the Schengen group and/or the Community as a whole. This was expressed in a Communication on immigration issued by the European Commission in 1991, which stated that:

> The inauguration within the European Community of the free move-
> ment of persons on 31 December 1992 and the suppression of internal
> frontiers ... could entail a risk that the absence of checks at internal
> borders will render any control of immigration impossible ... This has
> led the Member States to recognize the need for a common approach
> by the Twelve and to discuss ways in which they can cooperate. The
> interdependence of various national situations, taken together with the
> permeability of borders, requires joint action, if only on the grounds
> of efficiency.[8]

Yet, given the paucity of prior formal cooperation among member states, the development of 'a common approach' could not proceed automatically. There was first a need to reach closer consensus and consistency among member states through a harmonization of what was still – despite general convergence – a very disparate assortment of migration policies operating in the different states. Moreover, not only were member states still anxious to guard their national sovereignty in such matters, but it was already clear then, as now, that many of the interests and concerns of the member states did not entirely overlap. The member states resisted pressure from the Commission to acknowledge Community competence in the area and therefore opted to continue with the intergovernmental and largely *ad hoc* approach of preceding years.

Even with the emphasis on problems linked directly to controls at the internal and external borders, the process of cooperation and policy harmonization was set to be slow and complex. This was reflected in the structure of different institutional bodies which emerged after the signing of the SEA and which were concerned directly or indirectly with the harmonization process. Matters connected directly with migration were to be dealt with primarily by a group of ministers and senior civil servants responsible for immigration, the so-called Ad Hoc Group on Immigration, established in 1986. This body grew out of the Trevi Group, set up in 1975, which brought together officials responsible for law enforcement – European Justice and Interior Ministers and senior civil servants – and which itself extended its area of interest in the 1980s to include the examination of questions connected with undocumented immigration and asylum inflows. The Ad Hoc Group was charged with looking into matters such as stronger checks at external frontiers, internal checks, coordination of visa policies, cooperation to avoid the abuse of passports, and common policies to 'eliminate abuse of the right of asylum'. After 1988, the Ad Hoc Group worked in tandem with a third body, following the decision of the European Council at Rhodes in December 1988 to set up a Group of Coordinators consisting of senior officials of the member states and representatives of the European Commission which was to be responsible for supervising activities associated with the implementation of free movement.

The recommendations of the Group of Coordinators led to the so-called 'Palma Document', issued by the Council of Ministers in 1989, which listed problems to be solved if the free movement of persons in the Community was to be achieved. The list reflected the continuing emphasis on problems linked directly to border controls, leaving aside for future discussion the development of a common immigration policy and common agreements on the status of third-country nationals. The two most important instruments to arise from the recommendations of the Palma Document were the so-called 'Dublin Convention' (Convention Determining the State Responsible for Examining Applications for Asylum), signed in June 1990,[9] and the draft Convention on the Crossing of External Borders,[10] both of which are considered essential mechanisms to compensate for the loss of control over internal borders.[11]

The emphasis on measures connected directly with the suppression of internal border controls is similarly reflected in the Schengen Implementing

Convention, signed in 1990, which, in respect of provisions affecting the movement of persons, mirrored the instruments formulated at EC level (including state responsibility for asylum applications, and the crossing of external frontiers). This reflects *inter alia* the high degree of inter-group influence and consultation that has characterized the intergovernmental process. However, this level of consultation has not been matched by dialogue with national parliaments, the European Parliament or non-governmental bodies, and, as a result, the Ad Hoc, Schengen and Trevi Groups came under severe criticism for the secrecy with which negotiations were carried out.[12]

Cooperation during the early 1990s

That the Palma Document was felt necessary reflected the complexity of the negotiations over the movement of persons, and a certain anxiety over the (disputed) need to meet the deadline of 31 December 1992. This deadline (which was, in fact, missed) would have been difficult to meet at the best of times, but was made even more so by the events which took place in Central and Eastern Europe in 1989. The euphoria at the collapse of the Eastern bloc soon gave way to a growing sense of anxiety which focused increasingly on migration. Worries began to be voiced over the apparent threat of 'mass' east–west migration, worries which only added to what was already a growing sense of anxiety over rising numbers of asylum-seekers and illegal immigrants from the 'South'.

These concerns had two somewhat contradictory impacts on cooperation in migration policy in the European Community. By heightening sensitivity to unwanted immigration, they had the effect of increasing the tension between member states' interest in achieving the Single Market and their interest in maintaining national competence over immigration matters. This development threatened, at best, a much reduced chance of migration policy being transferred to Community competence, and, at worst, a fragmentation of the intergovernmental negotiating process.[13] The potential for fragmentation was heightened further by the more general crisis of confidence in the processes of EC integration which began to emerge after 1990, and which became particularly manifest after the signing of the Treaty on European Union (TEU).

However, this centrifugal force was counterbalanced, first, by continuing progress within the Schengen grouping, as signalled by the signing of the Implementing Convention (on the basis of which the Schengen states could pursue closer integration without being hampered by the reservations of more hesitant states); and, second, by a consensus that only on the basis of joint action could Europe's new migration problems be adequately tackled. As expressed in a Work Programme on migration and asylum policy adopted by the Council of Ministers at Maastricht in December 1991:

> The pressure of immigration on most Member States has increased significantly in recent years. The conviction that, confronted with these developments, a strictly national policy could not provide an adequate response has been consistently gaining ground ... [and on] that basis, it would appear advisable to define a common answer to the question of how this immigration pressure can be accommodated ... [The] aim is to make the problems manageable for the entire Community. This will require ... an extended form of cooperation among Member States.[14]

Developments during 1990 and 1991 demonstrated both a new sense of urgency in the negotiations and a shift in emphasis as the agenda widened to take account of broader concerns connected with the build-up of external migration pressures and increasing inflows of asylum-seekers and undocumented immigrants. Further cooperation in the area of migration policy (beyond that necessary for the completion of the internal market) was no longer seen simply as a desirable long-term objective (cf. the Palma Document), but as a necessity if member states were to maintain control over migratory flows. This was reflected in the conclusions of the Luxembourg European Council in June 1991 which, on the basis of a proposal from the German delegation, included an undertaking on the part of member states to 'commit themselves under the Treaty on Political Union to harmonizing, both formally and substantively, their policies on asylum, immigration and aliens'. The European Commission noted in its most recent Communication on immigration and asylum that whereas '[h]itherto the efforts of the Community and its Member States had been primarily directed towards new forms of cooperation ... that would be needed to manage the frontier-free area', the Luxembourg European Council's decision reflected 'a recognition that the geopolitical and socio-economic background against which immigration and asylum issues had to be viewed was changing rapidly and called for a different level of cooperation than before, moving beyond procedure into substance'.[15]

The European Council therefore invited the ministers responsible for immigration to submit proposals on the harmonization of policy in these areas, and this in turn led to the adoption of the Ad Hoc Group's Work Programme on migration and asylum policy at Maastricht the following December.[16] Under migration policy it set out five main categories requiring further work:

(1) the harmonization of admission policies;
(2) a common approach to the problem of illegal immigration;
(3) policy on the migration of labour;
(4) the situation of third-country nationals; and
(5) migration policy 'in the broad meaning of the term' (including action to tackle migration pressures).

The Work Programme was to be carried out, if possible, before the entry into force of the TEU, and therefore did not make reference to the question of institutional competence, as this was to be decided upon at the Maastricht European Council.[17] Two months prior to the Maastricht Council, the European Commission had issued two Communications to the Council and European Parliament, one dealing with the right of asylum and one with immigration;[18] the report on immigration touched *inter alia* on the question of institutional competence in these areas. These Communications reflected a concern on the part of the Commission to have some involvement in the deliberations at Maastricht and represented its first official input into the intergovernmental discussions of these issues.[19] In its Communication on immigration, the Commission argued that:

The European dimension is one of the areas in which dialogue must be continued. The Community's activity is still hampered by the fact that areas of competence are too narrow, thus denying it the opportunity to take comprehensive, consistent action. However, it has proved to be essential for fostering the necessary climate of trust between Member States, in order to achieve common objectives, especially the creation of a frontier-free area as provided by the Single Act. The implementation of this objective justifies the Community's action. The Commission has no wish to shirk this obligation.[20]

The TEU, as agreed at Maastricht and now in force, may be seen as a compromise between a Community and an intergovernmental approach to migration and asylum matters.[21] Yet the intergovernmental approach clearly dominates, with visas being the only area transferred to full Community competence under Article 100c of the Treaty (the 'first pillar' of the TEU, i.e. Community matters).[22] Almost all other areas of migration and asylum policy are listed as matters of 'common interest' under Title VI (provisions on cooperation in the fields of justice and home affairs) – the so-called 'third pillar' – and thus fall within the framework of intergovernmental cooperation. The areas of common interest listed under Title VI, Article K.1 (1) to (6) include asylum policy, the crossing of external borders,[23] and immigration policy (conditions of entry and residence, movement of third-country nationals, and the treatment of unauthorized immigration).

Article K.3 of the Treaty lays down a procedure for the adoption of legal instruments in these fields, and, importantly, includes the right of the Commission to initiate proposals,[24] a possibility of granting jurisdiction to the European Court of Justice, and an obligation for the Presidency to consult the European Parliament on these matters. Thus, as noted by the Commission in its Explanatory Memorandum accompanying its recent proposal for a decision establishing the Convention on the Crossing of the External Frontiers of the Member States[25] (based on its right of initiative under Article K.3), 'the Member States can ... no longer conclude conventions between one another in the areas listed in Article K.1 in the traditional manner prescribed by public international law'.[26] Moreover, Article K.9 introduces the possibility for matters listed under Article K.1 to be transferred to Article 100c, and thus to Community competence. However, such transfers can be brought about only through unanimous agreement by the Council of Ministers, and so the likelihood of any significant shift in overall competence in the area of migration and asylum remains doubtful. The 'Declaration on Asylum' attached to the Final Act of the Treaty specifies asylum policy as a priority matter in this regard, inviting member states to consider the transfer of asylum policy to Article 100c by the end of 1993. Accordingly, in November 1993, the Commission issued a report to the Council on the possibility of applying Article K.9 to asylum policy. Although the report stressed the advantages of transferring asylum policy to Article 100c, including 'gains in terms of transparency, the full involvement of the European Parliament and potentially speedier decision-making', the Commission's concern not to move too far out of step with the member states is reflected in its conclusion that 'the time is not yet right to propose the application of Article K.9 so soon after the entry into force of the Treaty on European Union'.[27]

Thus the principal effect of the TEU in these areas has been to strengthen and institutionalize the intergovernmental negotiating framework relating to migration and asylum policy. This is clearly disappointing for the Commission, the European Parliament and sectors of the non-governmental lobby which favour the greater transparency and firmer judicial and democratic control that is associated with the Community framework. Yet in its most recent Communication on these issues, the Commission argues that the new institutional framework introduced by the TEU does at least represent an advance on the previous *ad hoc* structures of cooperation:

> The Treaty on European Union provides ... a new political commit-
> ment; a clear set of rules, procedures and possible instruments; an
> opportunity for all the institutions and Member States of the Union to
> involve themselves in new areas of major public and political concern;
> and rationalised and better coordinated structures for preparing
> political-level decisions. Since there is also a potentially significant
> agenda for these new structures to address, the Union owes it to itself
> and to its citizens to put the possibilities offered by the Treaty to early
> and effective use.[28]

It is also important to note that the TEU introduces a Treaty commitment to cooperate on a permanent basis in the areas of immigration and asylum;[29] the SEA, by contrast, merely brought about an indirect pressure to cooperate, and only in areas necessary for the completion of the single market. Yet despite this new commitment, and despite the new 'rationalized' and 'coordinated' structures,[30] there are already signs that continuing reliance on the intergovernmental framework may be hampering the full harmonization of migration policy among the Union member states. The lack of progress may be partly attributed to problems which have arisen in connection with the processes set in motion by the SEA, namely the introduction of provisions deemed necessary for the suppression of internal controls on the movement of persons. The draft External Borders Convention has still not been signed owing to a disagreement between the UK and Spain over the status of Gibraltar; and the so-called European Information System (EIS) – a database designed to contain information on persons and objects for the purposes of border checks, visas, residence permits, etc. – has yet to be fully developed. Indeed, once developed, the implementation of the EIS will depend on the prior adoption of a regulating convention which has still to be formulated.[31]

Similarly, the entry into force of the Schengen Implementing Convention has been continually postponed, owing principally to technical and legal problems associated with the setting up of the Schengen Information System (SIS).[32]

Moreover, member states have still to agree on what 'an area without internal frontiers' actually entails; the UK, Irish and Danish governments take the position that limited documentation checks on persons entering from other member states are compatible with Article 8a of the SEA (now Article 7a of the TEU). Indeed, one might go so far as to question the commitment of all the member states to suppressing internal border controls. Delays in the implementation of the Schengen Agreement have also been blamed on the French government's anxieties concerning the efficacy of compensatory measures, including the SIS; and the European Parliament has repeatedly expressed concern over an apparent strengthening, rather than weakening, of internal border controls throughout the Community over recent years.[33] As noted by Giuseppe Callovi, member states are trying to reach a compromise between 'requirements for security' and 'a "reasonable" degree of free movement of people within the EEC territory'.[34] This is reflected in recent moves to step up surveillance at certain internal borders – such as between the Netherlands, Germany, Belgium and Denmark – in the effort to detect undocumented immigrants and asylum-seekers.[35]

Perhaps more important, however, is the extra burden which has been imposed on the harmonization process by the widened agenda. Indeed, given the still very divergent positions held by different states on a number of key policy issues, the widened agenda initially threatened to bring the cooperative process to a grinding halt. As a result, the emphasis shifted away from efforts to achieve full harmonization on the basis of legally binding treaties, towards a more flexible approach aimed at what might be better termed policy 'alignment', on the basis of agreements with political, but little or no legal, force.

Thus, for example, at the London meeting of the Ad Hoc Group in November/December 1992, ministers agreed on a number of 'Resolutions', 'Conclusions' and 'Recommendations' on different areas of migration and asylum policy, but left 'to be examined' the possibility of giving any practical effect to certain principles agreed upon in the form of a binding convention. The possibility of taking the Resolutions adopted in 1992 'as a basis for formulating joint action or a convention' was still listed only as a question for 'examination' in the second inter-ministerial Work Programme on asylum and immigration drawn up by the Justice and Home Affairs Council in

November 1993.[36] As observed by the European Commission in its November 1993 report on asylum policy, 'The effectiveness of this approach will only be fully tested when it is seen how far Member States are in practice willing to go to bring their national legislation into line with these resolutions and recommendations.'[37] The Commission goes on to argue that 'the type of approach adopted to date may not prove to be the most appropriate for introducing the sort of harmonization envisaged by the Maastricht European Council and needed in an area without internal frontiers'.[38] In its most recent Communication on immigration and asylum policies, the Commission notes that:

> The development of common rules and practices ... is still at a preliminary stage. Immigration Ministers have adopted a number of resolutions, which are not of a legally binding nature and their interpretation is left to each Member State. There has been no attempt yet to create a mechanism to monitor the implementation of those resolutions. The present stage of the process could therefore best be described as approximation rather than harmonisation of immigration and asylum policies.[39]

Divergence in the 1990s

As one would expect, particular rules, standards and procedures relating to immigration vary considerably from one state to another. Thus, for example, the nature of specific authorities responsible for taking decisions on questions such as the issuing of visas and residence permits, or the development of integration programmes, differs according to their degree of independence from central government. Integration policy has been considerably more centralized in France than in the United Kingdom or Germany, for example. Similarly, mechanisms for taking decisions on individual cases vary according to the role played by national courts or other administrative bodies. In the area of asylum policy, for instance, appeals against negative decisions in the United Kingdom are taken to an independent adjudicator or Immigration Appeals Tribunal, whereas in the Netherlands appeals are submitted to the Minister of Justice.

In many areas, harmonization of the details of national immigration procedures might not appear to be of pressing importance. For example, the Ad Hoc Group's 1991 Work Programme argues in reference to asylum policy that if 'too much emphasis were put on uniform procedures in the Twelve, the harmonization process could become bogged down quite simply through the complexity of the issue', reflecting as it does 'matters which concern fundamental aspects of a state's organization'.[40] However, specific procedures are of central importance where they reflect or lead to substantive differences in the functioning and outcome of the policies in place. As discussed below, it is precisely in the area of asylum policy that differences in the procedures followed by different states have proved most significant in this respect.

In a number of policy areas, it is not only the particular procedures that vary, but also the more fundamental bases and aims of policy, and it is in this respect that the harmonization – or even a less ambitious 'alignment' – of policies is likely to prove most problematic. Actual or potential problems of this kind can be identified in most of the policy areas referred to in Article K.1 of the TEU, including immigration control, visa policies, the admission and reception of asylum-seekers, the rights of third-country nationals, and policies on worker immigration.

Control measures

There is consensus among all states in Western Europe that unregulated immigration should be restricted as much as possible on the basis of direct control measures. The most obvious measures are 'external' controls, i.e. those which prevent initial entry into the state in question. These include restrictive visa policies, documentation checks at the main points of entry, and border or coastal patrols. These methods are further strengthened by the now increasingly important forms of what may be termed 'externalized' controls, including the imposition of penalties for carriers found to be transporting foreigners without the requisite documentation,[41] and the creation of 'buffer zones' by means of readmission agreements with third countries of emigration or transit (discussed below).

Immigration controls, however, do not operate only at the borders of a state. Because state borders are so difficult to police, and because a substantial proportion of unregulated immigration takes place initially through legal entry channels (e.g. immigrants who enter on short-term visas and subsequently overstay), most countries also rely on 'internal' controls, such as the requirement to carry identity cards or other proof of legality, 'stop-and-search' documentation checks, and employer sanctions (i.e. the fining of companies found to be employing unauthorized workers). The 1993 Priority Work Programme in the field of Justice and Home Affairs calls for a study on the improvement of member states' methods of checking up on undocumented third-country nationals, with the aim of harmonizing the conditions for combating undocumented immigration and employment.[42]

Yet despite an overall agreement among member states that undocumented immigration should be restricted, both forms of control – external and internal – raise a number of important questions as regards their application. For example, the states of Southern Europe now faced with controlling undocumented flows from the African continent – particularly Italy and Spain – were predominantly 'senders' rather than 'receivers' of migrants until the 1980s.[43] A sudden growth in immigration during the second half of the 1980s, coupled with the prospect of the Single Market (and the implementation of the Schengen Agreement), forced these states to rush to introduce new immigration controls in line with those operating elsewhere in Western Europe. However – considering the speed with which such controls have had to be developed, the fact that these states had no previous tradition of regulating immigration, and the extent of migration pressures currently experienced in the Mediterranean region – the capacity of these states to control immigration to the degree possible elsewhere in the Union must be questioned. Moreover, the labour markets of Southern Europe have further important implications for the control of undocumented immigration owing to the close linkages which exist between the 'informal' economy and undocumented immigration and employment. According to one estimate, the informal sector comprised 20% of GDP in Italy as compared with 4% in France in 1990.[44] Where there is a strong informal economy, one must question the capacity – and perhaps the will – to enforce strict internal control measures such as employer sanctions.

Nevertheless, none of these states have explicitly challenged the basic methods or objectives of immigration control. In particular, none have expressed strong reservations in connection with a stepping-up of internal surveillance. This is important, as the strengthening of internal control measures is seen as unavoidable if the suppression of border controls within the European Union and European Economic Area is not to result in a further loss of control over migration flows into and within the West European region. The shift towards strengthened internal controls called for by the establishment of the Single Market (and/or Schengen economic space) is, in fact, accepted by almost all EU governments, since the majority of states have for some time used internal controls as a means not only to regulate the residence and movements of immigrants, but also to keep a check on a range of activities of their own nationals.

However, because of its particular geography and political traditions,[45] the United Kingdom has relied almost exclusively on border controls to regulate immigration. As a consequence, the population – both indigenous and foreign – is subject to relatively little explicit institutionalized scrutiny once within the country. There is no obligation to carry identification, no established system of identity cards,[46] and, indeed, no enforced personal registration system. With no tradition of explicit internal surveillance, the prospect of such measures being introduced in Britain is viewed with considerable suspicion among the general public (particularly by members of ethnic minorities), and with a high degree of scepticism among the immigration authorities.[47]

These and other linked reservations have already led to a conflict between the UK government and the European Commission, with the former, as noted above, interpreting Article 8a of the SEA (Article 7a of the TEU) in a way that allows for continued – albeit relaxed – checks on entries from other member states,[48] and the latter holding that all such controls should be removed and replaced with internal checks to whatever extent is deemed necessary.[49] The resulting impasse has contributed to the delay in completing the Single Market, and hence to the European Parliament's recent complaint filed before the European Court of Justice against the Commission for the latter's failure to ensure the full implementation of free movement by the deadline of 31 December 1992.[50]

Implicit in this debate is the UK government's lack of confidence in the ability of other member states to prevent undocumented immigration, which hints at a potential for wider tension within the European Union in the future. Indeed, as noted above, it is not only the UK government which has been demonstrating a certain anxiety over the suppression of internal border controls. The recent stepping-up of surveillance at the borders between the Netherlands, Germany, Belgium and Denmark indicates a certain mutual lack of trust in measures to control movement across the external borders of the Union area and to control the movement of third-country nationals between member states.[51]

Thus tension can be expected if any one of the Twelve suspects undue laxity on the part of another as regards the policing of external borders. It is interesting to note, for example, that in early 1994 Germany was putting pressure on Denmark to carry out more effective checks on entries from outside the Union so as to reduce the numbers of Kosovo Albanians entering Germany from Denmark. In April 1994, the Netherlands decided to set up observation posts at the borders with Germany and Belgium and introduce checks on trains coming in from abroad to identify 'admissable' and 'inadmissable' asylum-seekers. This caused a dispute with the Belgian Interior Ministry. In August 1993, a new law on identity checks came into force in France which, in anticipation of the implementation of the Schengen Agreement, introduced new provisions for an extensive system of identity checking within new 20km 'border zones'. As noted above, French lack of confidence in measures to compensate for the suppression of border controls within the Schengen area has contributed to delays in the implementation of the Schengen Agreement.[52]

Such concerns also carry the implication that any unique or exceptional immigration measures taken by one state can no longer be isolated from the interests of other member states. As noted by the Ad Hoc Group on Immigration:

> The volume of third-country nationals is at present still completely determined by national admission policies ... If the Twelve wished to grant further rights to third-country nationals it would be necessary to have at least a probable estimate of the size of the group. In other words, Member States will have to have such confidence in each other's policies that the consequences of a gradual extension of rights may be readily evaluated and that an effective integration policy is not constantly undermined by the addition of further groups of third-country nationals.[53]

For example, in recent years Italy, Spain and Portugal have opted for large-scale legalization or 'amnesty' programmes to deal with the problem of substantial and growing undocumented immigrant populations.[54] Although such action has been deemed necessary for these states to gain better control over immigrant populations and over the immigration process, if it were repeated after the suppression of border controls within the Union and/or Schengen grouping, it could spark off protests from other member states. This problem has been noted by the European Commission, which stated in its 1991 Communication on Immigration that:

> It seems essential that Member States show greater determination [to control illegal immigration] ... Schemes to give legal resident status to illegal residents, as carried out in certain Member States, make this responsibility weigh even heavier inasmuch as this tends to make

illegal residence a long-term route to legal immigration. Irrespective of the humanitarian motives behind such steps, it comprises a fundamental problem.[55]

This issue does not only concern states' policies on the admission of third-country nationals. Germany's exceptional admission of 'ethnic Germans'[56] from Eastern and Central Europe, Greece's admission of ethnic Greeks from the former Soviet Union, and Portugal's confirmation of citizenship rights to Macau residents all signify the continuing importance of varying citizenship policies in place in different countries – policies which may at times give rise to inflows of, or extension of citizenship rights to, substantial numbers of immigrants in such a way that might conflict with the wider restrictive interests of the Union. The issue also points to what has always been an important overlap between states' immigration policies and wider domestic and foreign policy interests and traditions.

Visa policy
Differing foreign policy concerns within the European Union – despite the provisions of the second pillar of the TEU – also raise questions relating to the formulation of a common visa policy among the Twelve. The new draft External Borders Convention includes an article stipulating that member states undertake to harmonize their visa policies progressively,[57] and includes provisions for the formulation and operation of a uniform visa. The TEU goes further by stipulating that: 'The Council, acting by unanimity [and by qualified majority after 1 January 1996] on a proposal from the Commission and after consulting the European Parliament, shall determine the third countries whose nationals must be in possession of a visa when crossing the external borders of the Member States.'[58] Accordingly, a list of 130 'visa-national' countries was submitted to the Council of Ministers by the European Commission in November 1993,[59] representing a first step towards a common visa policy among the Twelve. The proposal specifies that:

divergences between the regulations and practices of Member States should be authorised for a limited period as a transitional measure ... [yet] it should be stipulated that this transitional regime shall expire on 30 June 1996 and that prior to that date the Council shall decide with respect to each third country whether its nationals are to be subject to a visa requirement or are to be exempted from that requirement.[60]

The proposed transitional period reflects the fact that up to 1 January 1996, placing a country on the visa list will require a unanimous decision by the member states, but after that date it will require only a qualified majority vote. The strict stipulations set by the Commission reflect the fact that a common visa policy is listed not merely as a matter of 'common interest' within the third pillar of the TEU, but as a binding Article within the 'first pillar' and thus of the Treaty establishing the European Communities.

At first sight the adoption of a common policy may not seem particularly problematic, since all countries share an interest in containing and controlling immigration from existing or potential 'migrant-sending' countries. Moreover, an informal core list of countries for which visas are required for entry into all European Community states has existed for a number of years. However, the introduction of a visa requirement for nationals of another state is frequently designed as – or is perceived to be – a politically significant act, and thus each country's visa policy has tended to reflect a particular pattern of foreign relations. In the case of the UK, for example, the 1981 British Nationality Act, the 1988 Immigration Act, and the introduction of visa restrictions on the admission of nationals of certain former colonies in the 1980s signalled *inter alia* the UK's progressive dissociation from the countries of its former empire. On the other hand, the fact that many former colonies still enjoy what could be argued to be privileged status as regards UK visa requirements reflects the continuing importance attached to the Commonwealth – an attitude not shared by other member states of the European Union.

A fully harmonized Union visa policy thus begs the question of foreign policy integration within the Union, the future of which is still highly uncertain. It is likely that during the transitional period member states will, as now, maintain variable policies in respect of the countries listed by the Commission. Yet, because of the binding nature of Article 100c, tension can be expected to increase once the transitional period expires. In the Explanatory Memorandum accompanying its recent proposal, the Commission notes that, ideally, it:

> would have wished at this stage to place every third country either on the negative list or on a 'positive list' of countries whose nationals are to be exempted from visa requirements. Manifestly, this is what is contemplated by Article 100c. However, this proved impossible in view of the very large number of third countries for which the

practices of Member States diverge and the sensitive nature of the decision to be taken with respect to many of those countries. Accordingly, the Commission accepts that Member States may decide whether or not to impose visa requirements on nationals of third countries not listed in the Annex, subject to the two conditions set out in the preamble, namely: that it does not give rise to any controls contrary to Article 7A EC (formerly Article 8A EEC); and that it is only applicable for a strictly limited period of time, whereupon each third country must be governed either by the positive or the negative list. This situation can only be compatible with the Treaty if these two conditions are met.[61]

Because the list proposed by the Commission is based on the Schengen 'visa list', the Schengen states are unlikely to raise serious objections to the proposal as it stands. The inclusion of former French colonies, for example, is not problematic for France, as France already requires visas for nationals of all these countries. However, reservations are already evident on the part of the non-Schengen states, and particularly on the part of the UK in respect of a number of Commonwealth member states which are included in the list but are so far exempt from a UK visa requirement. It was for this reason, for example, that the British delegation to the Socialist Group of the European Parliament abstained from the adoption in April 1994 of a report on the Commission's proposal drawn up by the Parliament's Committee on Civil Liberties and Internal Affairs.[62] Although it is too early to predict exactly what the prospects for a Union visa policy will be, it is possible that states will periodically or continually depart from the agreed policy or that the 'common' visa policy will be more limited in application than envisaged by Article 100c so as to sidestep national sensibilities.

Asylum policy

There is an overlap between the future visa policy and future asylum policy of the Union to the extent that it is increasingly common for states to impose visa requirements on nationals of particular states generating refugees. Britain, for example, introduced visa requirements for all nationals of Sri Lanka and Turkey in the 1980s following a rise in the number of asylum applications from people originating from these countries. Indeed, the TEU states that 'in the event of an emergency situation in a third country posing a threat of a sudden inflow of nationals from that country into the Community, the Council may ... *introduce'* – rather than remove – 'a visa requirement for nationals from the country in question' (emphasis added).[63] Such practice, in conjunction with the use of carrier sanctions,[64] effectively reduces the chances of certain groups of potential asylum-seekers reaching states in which they might wish to lodge an asylum application.

As in the case of visa policy generally, varying foreign and domestic policy considerations frequently impinge on the decision as to whether or not to impose visa requirements in such cases, and these considerations are by no means uniform across the member states of the Union. They may have little to do with the appraisal of the particular human rights situation in the country of origin, since visa requirements concern the restriction of access to asylum procedures, as opposed to the actual application of asylum policies. Thus, for example, a state may choose to impose a visa requirement on nationals of a particular country simply because of the number of applications for asylum received from that country. It is worth noting, for example, that most, but not all, Union member states now require visas for nationals of Bosnia-Herzegovina.[65]

When it comes to the application of asylum policy to individual cases, much depends on the receiving state's own particular view of conditions in the country from which asylum-seekers have come. Indeed, since the granting of refugee status – like the issuing of visa restrictions – can be perceived as a political statement by either the sending or receiving state, or by both, foreign policy concerns may affect the application of asylum policy just as much as the formulation of visa policy.

The Ad Hoc Group's 1991 Work Programme on immigration and asylum takes note of the fact that, despite common ground within the member states of the Union based on their accession to the 1951 Geneva Convention and 1967 New York Protocol, considerable room exists for divergent appraisals of conditions in countries which are giving rise to asylum-seekers. Indeed, not only do different states adopt different positions in respect of country of origin conditions, but different authorities within states frequently disagree with one another on this question. Thus, for example, the UK's Home Office is not always in step with the Foreign Office; and in Germany there has been little or no consensus among the different *Land* Administrative Courts and the Federal Administrative Court over the safety of returning Albanians to Kosovo and Kurds to Turkey. In the autumn of 1993, the decision of a Belgian court – contrary to the view of the Belgian government – to consider as admissible the asylum applications of a Basque couple from Spain sparked a row which resulted in Spain blocking any decisions on asylum policy at the November Justice and Home Affairs Council in November 1993. In January 1994, a Special Adjudicator in the UK ruled that Sweden was 'not a safe country' for the return of Kosovo Albanians, given Sweden's particularly tough stance towards this group.[66]

Such divergent assessments may arise not only from varying interests as regards relations with the sending state and the numbers of asylum-seekers arriving from a particular country, but also, as the Ad Hoc Group notes, from differing interpretations of the provisions of the United Nations refugee instruments, including differing interpretations of what constitutes 'persecution' in the country of origin. The Work Programme emphasizes the need for greater harmonization of substantive asylum law so that 'the chances of being granted refugee status or admission will be the same everywhere'. A Centre for Information, Discussion and Exchange on Asylum (CIREA) has been set up within the Council of Ministers. This is intended *inter alia* to keep countries better informed of one another's policies and to promote more informed and more consensual appraisal of the situations in countries of origin. Moreover, the Council's 1993 Priority Work Programme in areas related to asylum and immigration includes the harmonized application of the definition of a refugee as a matter for priority action. However, no significant progress has yet been made in this area.[67]

Indeed, despite the Ad Hoc Group's reference to the importance of harmonizing substantive asylum law, almost all intergovernmental efforts have so far focused on measures to restrict asylum-seekers' access to asylum procedures and to accelerate these procedures so as to reduce the 'load' on national asylum systems. This emphasis is reflected in the 1992 Resolutions on 'manifestly unfounded applications for asylum' and 'host third countries', and the 1992 Conclusion on the concept of countries 'in which there is generally no risk of persecution' (the 'safe country' principle).[68] The provisions of these agreements are now being progressively incorporated into member states' national legislation. However, their future uniform interpretation and application remain an open question. For example, the European Commission notes in its most recent Communication on immigration and asylum policy that the Resolution on manifestly unfounded applications leaves it up to Member States whether to introduce a separate procedure for such cases or simply to speed up the regular procedure. The Commission argues that 'ensuring legal certainty in this matter for both asylum applicants and the Member States may warrant the subject matter of those resolutions also being dealt with more comprehensively by way of a Convention'.[69]

As noted earlier, the question of judicial and administrative procedure is particulary important in the context of asylum policy. In its 1991 Communication on the right of asylum, the European Commission called for studies to begin on the role, structure and operation of possible common judicial machinery, with the aim of reducing disparities between Member States in the interpretation of the law on asylum and harmonizing administrative practices. However, in its most recent Communication on these issues, the Commission notes that no such studies have been started.[70] Indeed, as yet there has been no progress as regards agreement on the basic principles underlying asylum procedures in the different member states. Thus no general framework has been formulated which defines basic criteria for 'fairness and efficiency' in the application of asylum policy, including, for example, 'pre-screening procedures' (aimed at excluding certain categories of asylum applications) and applicants' appeal rights, which at present vary considerably from one state to another. In the absence of agreed basic procedural standards, the chances of being granted refugee status or admission will not be the same throughout the Union. In May 1994, for example, the UNHCR expressed the opinion that Greece could not be considered a 'safe country' for asylum-seekers as asylum procedures there did not guarantee effective protection.[71] This is an extremely important issue, given the imminent entry into force of the Dublin Convention and, indeed, its current 'informal' application in the form of the 'third host country principle'.

Nevertheless, given the universally restrictive stance on the admission of asylum-seekers which has developed in Western Europe over recent years, an overall policy alignment in the area of admission can be expected during the 1990s, despite some variation in positions adopted towards specific groups or countries of origin, and some remaining variation in specific admission policies and procedures.[72] Recent experience indicates that the chances of asylum-seekers being granted admission or refugee status in the European Union will be universally lower, rather than higher, than in the past, as is indicated by the Resolutions on manifestly unfounded applications for asylum and safe third countries, and by the amendment of Germany's asylum law effected in 1993.

Whether an alignment of admission policies will lead to an extensive harmonization or alignment of protection and reception policies and procedures, however, is more questionable. Of particular importance in the context of protection is the category of asylum-seekers who are not found to fit the (narrow) UN definition of refugees,[73] but who nevertheless are considered to be in need of some kind of protection, as standards of protection in respect of this category are not codified in international law. This is an increasingly important group not only because of the progressively restrictive interpretation of the UN refugee definition by the state authorities, but also because of the increase in numbers of war refugees arriving in Western Europe, particularly from the former Yugoslavia. Indeed, the majority of asylum-seekers in Western Europe now fall into this group. Since the mid-1970s, the Council of Europe has been pressing for a regional instrument to establish a codified system of protection for this category, but its efforts have not been successful.[74] Consequently, although the majority of so-called 'de facto' refugees have been accorded some form of temporary refuge, they continue to be considered on a discretionary basis by individual states. As a result, the legal and procedural bases upon which protection is offered and rights attached to 'de facto' or temporary protective status are highly variable. In the absence of an appropriate regional legal instrument, they are likely to remain so. At the Copenhagen Justice and Home Affairs Council in June 1993, ministers adopted a Resolution on the protection to be offered to particularly vulnerable groups from the former Yugoslavia. However, as noted by the Commission, this Resolution 'does not attempt ... to harmonize the kind of temporary protection which national laws and legislation provide'.

Similarly, variations in reception conditions affect those who have not been granted full refugee status according to the UN refugee protection instruments more than those who have, as the 1951 UN Convention on the Status of Refugees sets out detailed provisions defining the rights and duties of those that it covers. A study on reception policies carried out for the United Nations High Commissioner for Refugees in 1993 found that:

> In comparing the social conditions of the [different] categories of persons in need of international protection our main finding is that there is least variation in the social conditions of refugees; the reception schemes for asylum seekers vary considerably; and the social conditions of persons granted temporary protection are of an equal or higher standard than those of asylum seekers.[75]

The 1993 Priority Work Programme in the field of Justice and Home Affairs calls for an alignment of conditions for the reception of asylum-seekers in the member states, particularly of their rights and obligations.[76] But according to the report on reception policies produced for the UNHCR, the harmonization of all aspects of reception policies is not feasible, given differences in national social welfare systems, public education and health systems, the general reception and integration policies for foreign migrants in specific states, and even the extent to which there is a public or corporate housing sector. The report also notes the potential importance of an unequal distribution of refugees and asylum-seekers between different states, as an increasing number of persons in need of protection may lead to changes in reception schemes.[77]

In view of the progressive convergence in policies governing the admission of asylum-seekers in Western Europe, concerns connected with the unequal distribution of asylum-seekers and refugees within Western Europe might be expected to prove less of a problem in the future. Indeed, one of the express reasons for aligning admission policies is to prevent the burden of asylum shifting 'towards those countries where the arrangements are relatively more favourable'.[78] However, even though there is already a high degree of policy convergence in this respect, certain states continue to receive significantly higher numbers of asylum applications than others, and/or disproportionate numbers of applications from specific countries of origin. In particular, Germany remains the principal destination for asylum-seekers in Western Europe, despite the fall in numbers following the introduction of its new, more restrictive, asylum law.

The sudden exoduses from Albania in 1990 and 1991, and refugee flows out of the former Yugoslavia since 1992, indicate that a number of factors may result in one state being faced with considerably larger asylum inflows than others: not only the nature of asylum policies in force in particular countries, but also the geographical position of potential receiving countries, and migration-related or other links between sending and receiving regions. Thus, with more attention being paid to regional cooperation in the area of asylum and refugee policy generally, the issue of burden-sharing has risen up the political agenda over recent years. For the German government, the move towards harmonization of asylum policies has been viewed overall as a positive step, since it has provided a justification for the introduction of restrictive measures while simultaneously opening up a possible route to greater burden-sharing with other members of the Union. However, in other states which have hitherto experienced much lower numbers of asylum applications, the idea of burden-sharing has not been greeted positively, implying as it does either a greater financial burden, or the acceptance of greater numbers of asylum-seekers and refugees.

Perhaps owing to the sensitivity of the issue, no mention of the principle of burden-sharing was made in the Ad Hoc Group's 1991 Work Programme, the European Commission's 1991 Communications on immigration and the right of asylum,[79] the draft External Borders Convention, or the Treaty on Political Union. The Dublin Convention[80] deals with the question of state responsibility for processing asylum claims, but its aim is to reduce the potential for 'refugees in orbit' rather than to tackle the wider question of burden-sharing. Indeed, by stipulating that asylum claims should be processed by the country of first arrival, the Dublin Convention acts implicitly against the principle of burden-sharing, as does the Resolution on 'third host countries'.[81]

Yet burden-sharing has emerged as the issue of greatest potential disagreement between member states in respect of asylum questions. At the September 1992 meeting of European Community foreign ministers, for example, Klaus Kinkel, referring to his country's disproportionate asylum burden, complained that Germany couldn't 'do everything alone'. At the Fifth Council of Europe Conference of Ministers Responsible for Migration Affairs in November 1993, Germany, Austria, Denmark, Norway, Switzerland and Sweden presented a draft Resolution pressing for more equal burden-sharing in the provision of protection for refugees from Bosnia. The draft Resolution refers to the fact that these six countries have granted protection to about 90% of the almost one million persons who have fled the former Yugoslavia. However, the Resolution was not adopted owing to opposition expressed by other participating states, notably the UK, France and the Netherlands.[82] In the EU intergovernmental context, the first explicit mention of burden-sharing appears in the 1993 Priority Work Programme as a result of German demands that the issue be considered. Reflecting other member states' reservations in the area, however, the Work Programme does not endorse the idea, calling only for a detailed examination of the question.[83] The most recent Commission Communication on migration and asylum policy argues for the introduction of a mechanism for 'some matching of national absorption capacities' in cases of sudden mass influxes, but qualifies this suggestion by stating that '[s]uch a matching system would not necessarily have to amount to a formal arrangement for burden sharing'.

The Commission, however, does endorse a proposal from the European Parliament for the establishment of a 'European Fund for Refugees'[84] which might be used for emergency situations facing member states. As the Commission points out, such a fund (or, indeed, more general burden-sharing measures) could prove particularly important for a number of Central and East European states which, as a result of tighter policies in Western Europe and the application of the 'third host country' principle, are facing ever-increasing numbers of asylum applications with which they are ill-equipped to cope.[85] Yet there is little prospect of a consensus emerging on the issue of burden-sharing among the EU member states, even in respect of assistance to Central and East European countries.[86]

Free movement of third-country nationals
While the social and political organization and traditions of different states have some bearing on variations in asylum policies, they are likely to have more far-reaching implications for the varying status and rights of immigrant minority populations in the European Union. The TEU lists 'conditions of entry and movement' and 'conditions of residence' by third-country nationals as 'matters of common interest' under Article K.1. However, the only issue to have been given any significant consideration by the Ad Hoc Group on Immigration or the Justice and Home Affairs Council is that of conditions of entry. Although the Ad Hoc Group's 1991 Work Programme on immigration and asylum listed the 'situation of third-country nationals' as an area requiring further work, the only item mentioned under this heading related to rights to free movement, not touching on the wider question of immigrant minorities' integration – i.e. the issue of their social, economic, cultural and political rights and status.

It is important to note the distinction between 'free circulation' and 'free movement' provisions or rights in this context. 'Free circulation' provisions for third-country nationals can be understood as those that allow for short visits to other member states, whereas 'free movement' rights encompass the wider range of rights associated with 'the free movement of persons' under Article 8a of the SEA (Article 7a TEU), including the right of establishment and access to the labour market.[87] The Schengen Agreement provides for a right of free *circulation* for legally resident third-country nationals for visits of less than three months to member states other than that in which they are normally resident. Similarly, the new draft External Borders Convention proposed by the European Commission includes a provision for residence permits to have the equivalent value of a visa for the same purpose, and the Commission intends to come forward with a proposal which would allow legally resident third-country nationals to visit another member state without a visa. However, neither the Schengen Agreement nor the draft External Borders Convention touches on the question of free *movement*.

The Ad Hoc Group's 1991 Work Programme on immigration and asylum went further by suggesting the possibility of extending free movement rights to certain foreign nationals who have been resident for some time in one of the member states, and called for the examination of 'the possibility of granting third-country nationals who are long-term residents in a member state certain rights or possibilities, for example concerning access to the labour market'.[88] This was echoed both in the European Commission's 1991 Communication on immigration – which suggests that 'consideration could be given to ... granting access to employment in another member state ... to certain categories of non-European Community nationals already allowed to reside permanently in one of the member states'[89] – and in a request made in May 1992 by the Social Partners represented in the Permanent Committee on Employment.[90] So far, however, no progress has been made in this area. The Commission has proposed in its most recent Communication on immigration that '[a] first step ... would be for Member States to accord priority to third-country nationals permanently and legally resident in another Member State, when job vacancies cannot be filled by EC nationals'.[91] However, at the June 1994 Justice and Home Affairs Council in Luxembourg, at which ministers adopted a Resolution on limitations of third-country nationals to the Member States for employment, the question of free movement for legally resident third-country nationals between the member states was not included in the discussions.

Moreover, such proposals beg the question of differences between member states in the status as regards rights and residence accorded to immigrants and their family members and descendants. No moves have as yet been made to create a jointly agreed permanent residence entitlement. Thus immigrants in those states in which permanent or secure residence is granted more liberally would almost certainly have an advantage over those in which residence is less secure. And in the absence of an agreed policy on free movement for third-country nationals, only immigrants – or the descendants of immigrants – possessing citizenship of the country in which they are resident (and therefore Union citizenship) will enjoy full rights in respect of free movement and settlement rights within the Union. Therefore, a far higher proportion of immigrants or members of immigrant minority groups resident in countries with relatively liberal citizenship laws will be accorded these rights than in countries where access to citizenship is more restricted. One can contrast, for example, the situation in the UK, where citizenship is comparatively easy to acquire on the basis of qualified *jus soli* and where the majority of immigrants who entered during the 1950s and 1960s did so as British subjects with full citizenship rights, with the position in Germany, where citizenship laws, based on the principle of *jus sanguinis*, are considerably more restrictive.

Thus the only categories of third-country nationals who so far can be said to benefit from a common approach among the Twelve in the area of free movement are nationals of the EFTA countries which have joined the European Economic Area (EEA), since, under the EEA Treaty, they benefit from the same free movement rights enjoyed by Union nationals; and providers of services from Central and East European countries linked to the Union by the new Europe Agreements (right of establishment).

The Council's 1993 Priority Work Programme in the fields of Justice and Home Affairs moves beyond the Ad Hoc Group's 1991 Work Programme by calling for the 'consideration and, if necessary, possible harmonization' of the position of third-country nationals established on a long-term basis in the member states. However, no indication is given of what is meant by 'position'. Proposals in this area usually stress the need for common approaches to the social, economic, political and legal position of immigrants. The Commission's most recent Communication on immigration issues notes the numerous calls by the European Parliament for the Commission to prepare and table framework directives relating to integration policies for third-country immigrants, as well as the use that could be made of the TEU, which provides for the possibility of joint action and common approaches to policy regarding nationals of third countries. In addition, the Commission notes that Article 2(3) of the Agreement on Social Policy provides for Community legislation in the area of employment conditions of third-country nationals who are legally resident in the territory of the Community, and that it thus provides a basis for proposals by the Commission in the area of the labour market and integration. A number of measures are suggested in the Communication with the aim of: (i) improving the legal situation of third-country nationals; (ii) creating the right economic and socio-cultural conditions for successful integration; (iii) promoting constructive dialogue and improving information on the position of third-country nationals; and (iv) combating racial discrimination and tackling the problem of racism and xenophobia.[92]

Yet, given the divergence in approaches to these issues followed by the different member states, and given that these questions touch on fundamental issues of citizenship and thus on varying concepts of national or state membership and identity,[93] common approaches will take a long time to develop, if they develop at all. Because conditions of nationality frequently determine immigrants' access to rights or benefits, it is important to note the 'Declaration on Nationality of a Member State' attached to the Final Act of the TEU, which confirms that the question of whether an individual possesses the nationality of a member state shall be settled solely by reference to laws of the member state concerned. Thus, it is not only free movement rights, but immigrant minorities' access to a wide range of rights and duties within member states and within the Union as a whole, that will continue to vary. Political rights, including voting rights, pose one of the most serious challenges in this respect, being the issue on which there is probably least agreement among member states.[94]

Worker immigration

Like immigration control and the status of third-country nationals, labour market policy has traditionally been seen as the sovereign concern of individual states. However, the Ad Hoc Group's 1991 Work Programme argued that 'full harmonization of admission policy linked to employment presupposes that this policy will cease to be defined exclusively at national level, as it will no longer be possible unilaterally to extend or tighten the national labour market when conditions for admission are determined at European level'.[95] Given that all member states have adopted relatively restrictive positions on labour immigration, concern over efforts to harmonize policy in this respect might seem somewhat unnecessary. However, 'economic' or worker immigration into Western Europe continues, whether authorized or not, and this may create problems for a full harmonization of policy in the area.

The persistence of worker immigration is due, in large part, to external migration pressures, such as rising unemployment in 'migrant-sending' countries to the east and to the south. However, it is also due to continuing demand for immigrant workers within Western Europe, despite high levels of unemployment and the current economic downturn. Demand can be identified at both the upper and the lower levels of Western Europe's labour markets, reflecting their progressive segmentation, which is in turn linked to difficulties in overcoming rigidities and effecting economic restructuring. At the upper end, the demand is for highly skilled technical, professional and managerial workers, and mobility within this sector is now a growing feature of movement within Western Europe and into the region from outside. This type of migration is, however, relatively easy to regulate, and is generally not seen as a problem for receiving countries – it tends rather to be seen as a problem for sending countries experiencing a net emigration of skilled workers, in the form of the so-called 'brain-drain'. Indeed, growing skill deficits among the advanced industrialized economies have brought about competition to attract such workers.

Thus it is the persistence of the immigration of workers to fill jobs at the lower end of the labour market spectrum that is seen as a primary problem in Western Europe, especially immigration which is unauthorized. Demand for workers persists in marginal and relatively unregulated sectors of the economy which depend on a cheap and exploitable workforce to remain competitive; this is particularly the case in labour-sensitive service industries (e.g. hotels and catering), certain labour-intensive industries (e.g. textiles and clothing), and agriculture. Unauthorized immigrant workers are particularly appealing in these sectors because they are generally cheaper than either legal immigrants or indigenous workers, and 'totally flexible' with regard to wage rates and working conditions. Although this demand is present to a greater or lesser degree in all member states, it is probably strongest in Southern Europe. This is a reflection of specific structural characteristics of these countries' labour markets, including a large agricultural sector and a strong 'informal' service sector.

As long as labour markets within the European Union continue to differ, so will the level and nature of worker immigration into each state; and as labour markets are more difficult to change than immigration policies, it is likely that their demands will have more of an influence over policies on the admission of foreign workers than admission policies will have over labour market policies, at least in the short term. Thus, for example, the European Commission argues that:

It will ... be necessary to monitor closely labour market developments in order to ensure that admission policies are capable of adapting to new demands. Such analyses should also be capable of distinguishing between short-term conjunctural developments and structural changes, as what is needed is a clear picture of the long-term development of labour supply and demand. If it were to be established that there was a long-term need for additional labour supply, the analysis should proceed by defining costs and benefits of allowing for migration in order to fill up these gaps.[96]

Of course, it is highly unlikely that we will witness a return to the recruitment policies of earlier decades, as not only would this be politically very difficult (if not impossible), but the nature of demand has changed. Overall, policies are likely to remain restrictive; however, where the absence of an admissions policy, or an over-restrictive admissions policy, results in important labour deficits or continuing or increasing undocumented immigration, states are likely to continue to respond independently by opening or maintaining 'windows' for specific categories of worker immigration – such as for seasonal agricultural workers – if only to gain better control over the process. Thus, for example, quotas for immigrant workers have been set in Spain, and have been under consideration in Italy; the Italian authorities have been examining rules which could be introduced to formalize the status of seasonal workers;[97] and bilateral agreements have been reached between Germany and certain Central and East European countries which allow limited numbers of workers to enter Germany for 'vocational and linguistic training' or for seasonal work (particularly in agriculture, hotels and catering, entertainment and construction), or under 'work contracts' (for foreign sub-contractors bringing in their own workforce). In practice this amounts to a limited 'guestworker' system.[98]

Thus, just as differing foreign policy interests are likely to hamper the development and eventual functioning of a common visa policy, and differing citizenship and immigrant integration policies will hamper the development of a common approach to the rights and status of immigrant minorities, so differing labour market interests are likely to hamper the development or application of harmonized policies on the admission of foreign workers. One can expect either that states will continually derogate from such policies, or that future agreements reached at Union level will be sufficiently vague as to allow states leeway to pursue different policies at the national level. According to a Resolution on limitations on the admission of third-country nationals to the member states for employment adopted at the June 1994 Justice and Home Affairs Council in Luxembourg, member states will endeavour to seek to ensure that by 1 January 1996 their national legislation is in conformity with the principles of the resolution, namely that admission of third-country nationals (other than EEA nationals and foreign workers covered by Community agreements with third countries) may be considered only as 'a very narrow exception'. The Resolution – aimed principally at regulating the entry of seasonal workers, trainees, frontier workers, qualified and 'indispensable' personnel and businessmen – seems to be aimed more at dissuading member states from liberalizing their national policies than at obliging them to render these policies universally more restrictive.[99] It should also be noted that no common position has yet emerged among member states on the question of regularizing the status of undocumented immigrant workers.

New partnerships and prospects for an integrated Union policy on migration

The reluctance to transfer competence in migration matters to the Community/Union, and the (at least temporary) retreat from the introduction of legally binding instruments connected with migration matters, have left room not only for the generalized heterogeneity in different areas of migration policy to persist within the Union, but also for varying patterns of cooperation and policy integration to emerge or persist among different member states in relation to the policy area as a whole – a process rendered even more complex by the increasing involvement of non-member states and other overlapping international groupings.

This is perhaps most evident when one considers the relationship between the Schengen grouping* and the European Union as a whole. The original motivation for the 1985 Schengen Agreement was the desire on the part of the signatory states to make greater progress than had been achieved in the context of the European Community. To a large extent, the Schengen initiative has been looked upon positively by the European Commission and other EC member states, as it has been seen as a 'laboratory' for developments planned to take place within the European Community/Union as a whole. However, Article 142 of the Implementing Convention hints that the Schengen grouping may turn out to be more than a simple stepping-stone towards the completion of the Union's internal market. This Article states that when conventions are concluded between the member states of the European Community, the contracting parties will agree on the conditions under which the provisions of Schengen are to be replaced or amended, and

*Note that the original signatory states have subsequently been joined by Italy (1990), Spain (1991), Portugal (1991) and Greece (1992). However, the long process of ratification and mutual approval upon which these states' full membership depends was still to be completed at the time of writing.

adds that the provisions of the Schengen Convention may provide for more extensive cooperation than that resulting from conventions concluded by the Twelve.

As long as the External Borders Convention remains unsigned and as long as disagreements persist among the Twelve over the issue of border controls, Schengen seems set to overtake efforts involving the Union as a whole, and may already be seen to represent in a concrete form a 'two-speed' Europe as regards cooperation in the areas of immigration control and the movement of persons.[100]

That Schengen may represent a break away from efforts to establish a unified Union approach to such matters is also indicated by the agreement reached between the Schengen states and Poland on the readmission of persons in an irregular position, an agreement which entered into force in May 1991; and by the fact that the Schengen states have started discussions on the possibility of inviting Austria, Finland and Sweden to join (although in principle this would seem to depend on these states first joining the European Union).

These developments are also significant in terms of what they say about the future shape of cooperation between Schengen and Union member states and non-member states in Europe in the context of migration and the movement of persons. They seem to reflect above all the influence of policy developments within the European Union (including Schengen) over the policies of non-member states in Europe, despite what appears to be considerable confusion and uncertainty on the matter among the member states themselves.

As regards the EFTA states, it is clear that these countries are set to become more fully integrated with the emerging regime governing policy on migration and the movement of persons in the European Union. This is an inevitable consequence of the erosion of the EFTA grouping and the establishment of the European Economic Area (involving the relaxation of common frontiers and the rights of free movement for nationals of the signatory third countries), and of the accession of these states to the European Union (according to the principle of *acquis communautaire*). It is worth noting, for example, that negotiations are already under way on the development of a parallel Convention to extend the regime set up by the Dublin Convention, of which the EEA/EFTA states will be the primary signatories. Given that the immigration problems faced by these states are in many respects the same as those faced by the present EU member states, cooperation with them is not likely to be significantly more problematic than it is among the Twelve. Nevertheless, simply by virtue of the increase in the number of countries involved in the various negotiations and agreements connected with migration policy, and the greater variation in the degrees of institutional integration (according to states' membership or otherwise of the Schengen grouping, the European Union, the European Economic Area, and EFTA), it is almost certain that the 'widening' of the policy regime to encompass other West European states will hinder even further its 'deepening' in terms of policy harmonization.

The increasing involvement of other West European states stems at least in part from the growing emphasis on joint action as member states became more aware of the potential migration problems on the European continent following the collapse of the Eastern bloc. In this respect, however, cooperation has not been confined to the principal West European economic groupings. Against the background of a general breakdown in old international frontiers and old institutional boundaries, and in the context of increasing anxiety surrounding all aspects of the migration issue, other institutions, other states and other state groupings have become involved. These include existing or potential migrant-'transit' or migrant-'sending' states in Central and Eastern Europe, which have been viewed by West European receiving states not only as sources of unwanted immigration, but also as important partners in migration control, i.e. as migration 'buffer states'. The hands of the Central and East European states are tied in this respect, for their economic and political relations with the EU member states depend on their cooperation in matters connected with migration.

The early 1990s have witnessed an explosion of multilateral activities in the migration field. According to one observer, there are now 15 multilateral fora dealing with migration issues in Europe, as compared with five in the mid-1980s.[101] Extending beyond the Schengen, EU, EEA and EFTA groupings, these include the activities of organizations with a well-established role in the field (such as the Council of Europe,[102] the International Organization for Migration, the United Nations High Commissioner for Refugees, and the OECD), others which have only recently started examining the issue (such as the Conference on Security and Cooperation in Europe) and new groupings which have developed to tackle specific aspects of the phenomenon (including the so-called 'Vienna Process'[103] and the 'Berlin/Budapest' grouping[104]).

Considerable institutional crowding has been caused by a failure to synchronize and streamline activities carried out within the various fora, which in turn derives from the complexity of the issues and – in the context of a widened policy agenda and broader state representation – from the failure of governments to think out and agree on a comprehensive plan of action at the pan-European level. At the same time, however, the way has been opened for a more fluid, and thus in many cases pragmatic structure of cooperation and integration in the area of migration policy – albeit a complex and confused one. Within this structure, different EU member states have been able to pursue different aims in their dealings with non-member states, according to their specific concerns – acting sometimes individually and sometimes alongside others.

Thus, for example, Germany and Denmark have been able to use the Council of Europe as a forum within which they could join forces with states outside the European Union to put pressure on other EU member states to share the burden of protecting refugees from Bosnia-Herzegovina (as noted above). And aided by consultation with Central and East European states in the context of the 'Berlin/Budapest' process, Germany has led the way in pursuing bilateral 'readmission agreements'[105] with various states in the region without waiting for a joint Union initiative on readmission.

It may be that the Schengen states will develop a more unified approach to readmission; it is notable that the 1991 Schengen–Poland readmission agreement is so far the only multilateral agreement of this type to have been reached,[106] and that France has been pushing for readmission agreements with Mediterranean migrant-sending countries within the framework of Schengen, rather than unilaterally. However, the fact that France is looking south while Germany looks east is again indicative of the differing concerns of member states in terms of the sources and control of immigration. Therefore, despite pressure for a more integrated approach to readmission (deriving in part from an interest in sharing the financial burden associated with these agreements), it is likely that bilateral readmission agreements and informal forms of bilateral cooperation will continue to predominate. It is worth noting that the Action Plan on Immigration and Asylum presented at the meeting of the Justice and Home Affairs Council in November 1993 goes no further than suggesting that 'principles be adopted which must appear in bilateral and multilateral readmission agreements' and that 'a link be established where appropriate between Europe association and co-operation agreements concluded by the Community and its Member States and the practices of third countries regarding readmission'.[107]

The present shape of migration policy in Europe thus appears to indicate the emergence of a complex mosaic of cooperative arrangements, not only in terms of relations between the Union member states and third countries, but also within the Union itself. Different spheres of cooperation seem to be developing, with the greatest integration being achieved in respect of policies connected directly with the completion of the internal market and the European Economic Area (suppression of internal border controls, the strengthening of external controls, and the free movement of citizens) – first within the Schengen grouping, second within the European Union, and third within the newly established EEA.

The integration of broader areas of immigration policy in the EU context seems set to take place more slowly and less comprehensively, halted by member states' differing interests in this sphere, and by their concern – and ability – to protect national sovereignty over such matters. Cooperation in this context is likely to remain within the intergovernmental framework until the harmonization of policies in particular areas (e.g. asylum admissions policy) is considered sufficiently advanced to create few problems if transferred to Union competence. For the present, many of the interests and concerns of the member states will not coincide, particularly if Union membership is appreciably widened. Thus, in most policy areas, a general alignment is more likely than any extensive harmonization, reflecting shared interests but not a high degree of positive interdependence. Cooperation with third countries is likely to remain flexible and thus variable, a pattern which will be reinforced by the existence of other overlapping, and to some extent competing, multilateral fora involving both member and non-member states.

Thus, even with the existing EU membership, it is unlikely that a fully cohesive Union migration policy will emerge, at least in the short to medium term. Indeed, given the complexity of the issues involved, it is not clear that a fully unified approach would be suited to all the challenges ahead, particularly in the context of cooperation with countries outside the boundaries of the European Union. However, in the areas where a degree of harmonization and policy integration are achieved, confusion, 'piecemeal' cooperation and tension will be avoided only if this integration is backed up with legally binding instruments which ensure uniform application and interpretation of common policies and judicial and procedural safeguards to protect both the EU citizens and the third-country nationals affected.

Chapter 8

Conclusion

Migration has always played an important part in the economic, political and social development of European society, and it is a process which has, on balance, proved enriching. For countries such as France, the United Kingdom and the Federal Republic of Germany, the immigration of foreign workers from the 1950s to the 1970s constituted a key element in the postwar economic boom, and the immigrants have contributed in many important and positive ways to the cultural and social life of the countries in which they settled. Indeed, one may reflect that if international migration could not prove a positive economic, social and political force, the Single European Act would have been unlikely to call for the free movement of persons within the European Community after January 1993. According to a recent study carried out in Germany, the inflow of 3.8 million people to Western Germany between 1988 and 1991 increased the gross national product by 3.5% and created one million additional jobs.[1] Thus, even if 'economic' migration into Western Europe is to escalate in the years to come, it is not at all clear that the effects will be overwhelmingly damaging for receiving states.

However, it is also evident that – coming now at a time of very high sensitivity to the issue in Western Europe – any substantial and unmanaged 'economic' immigration could have complex social and political ramifications which most receiving states would seek to avoid. In particular, a widespread perception among the public that control over immigration is largely lacking, or has been lost, could certainly contribute to a further strengthening of anti-immigrant sentiment in Western Europe which would be destabilizing for society as a whole. Moreover, in the light of what seems to be a growing potential for inter-ethnic conflict, civil war and generalized political instability in the former Eastern bloc and in countries to the south, it is clear that 'economic' or 'voluntary' migration is not the only issue for concern; large-scale refugee movements, are – particularly with the emergence of new refugee movements within and out of the Balkans – increasingly pin-pointed as the primary migration challenge facing Europe in the 1990s. Caused usually by traumatic political events, such movements are generally highly volatile and disruptive for every state affected, as well as tragic in terms of the human suffering involved.

Nevertheless, the potential for new 'mass movements' towards Western Europe should not be exaggerated. External 'economic' migration 'pressures' do not necessarily translate directly into actual migration, as economically motivated migration is sensitive to a variety of factors, including demand or 'pull' factors in receiving areas and immigration controls. As noted in a recent OECD report on migration trends, 'past experience shows that it is impossible to predict the scale and direction of future migratory flows'.[2] Similarly, recent refugee flows in the former Eastern bloc indicate that – with the partial exception of the former Yugoslavia – most refugee movements in this part of the world are likely to take place between contiguous states and thus are unlikely to give rise to large-scale migration towards Western Europe. Indeed, in the face of what are already extreme 'pressures' in areas bordering on Western Europe – rapid population growth, high and rising under- and unemployment, falling incomes and political instability to the south; growing inter-ethnic tension, civil war and economic and political uncertainty to the east – what is perhaps surprising is that so few, rather than so many, people are currently moving towards Western Europe.

This, of course, does not mean that intensifying external 'migration pressures' are not or should not be of concern to the states of Western Europe. But at the same time it should be stressed that the issues at stake extend far beyond the question of migration, for if the factors identified as 'migration pressures' intensify in neighbouring regions and other areas of the world, they are likely to have an increasingly destabilizing and, in some cases, catastrophic effect on political and economic conditions in those regions, which may in turn pose new problems or challenges for Western Europe unrelated to actual or potential levels of migration.

In view of the seriousness of the issues at stake, the new rhetoric on the need to 'address the root-causes of migration' should be greeted as a positive development. Policy-makers are talking more and more of the need to tackle 'unwanted' or disruptive migration through greater cooperation with governments of existing or potential sending states, and through policies which target pressures such as unemployment and population growth or, in the case of refugee movements, inter-ethnic tensions, arms proliferation and human rights abuses in areas of actual or potential refugee movement. The current refugee crisis caused by the conflict in the former Yugoslavia is already forcing politicians and policy-makers to link migration with issues which are qualitatively different from those that have traditionally shaped migration and refugee policy, including foreign policy questions touching on the protection of minority and human rights, the principle of self-determination, the sanctity of borders, and intervention.

To counter any undue optimism, however, two major reservations ought to be noted. First, in terms of concrete policy, most substantive measures currently on the table indicate a continuing, and even growing, reliance on old-style approaches to migration control, such as border controls and visa regimes. The economic and political uncertainty of the 1990s and the intractability of many of the problems associated with migration have frustrated the development of more comprehensive and long-term approaches to the issue. Attention is still focused almost exclusively on migration problems in the receiving states in Western Europe, and on short-term protective measures. Indeed, direct parallels could be drawn between statements and measures being introduced today and those of the interwar period, when West European governments talked of their countries' saturation with immigrants and refugees and their reluctance or inability to accept any more. The outcome of this response in the late 1930s, and thus the potential outcome of such a response today, needs little elaboration.

Second, the new concern with 'root-causes' appears to be founded in the same defensive thinking that is simultaneously encouraging greater emphasis on direct immigration restrictions and controls, and in this respect it does not reflect a significant departure from approaches of the past. There are, of course, certain important areas where there is obvious and immediate potential for constructive action (in particular, limiting arms exports, encouraging respect for human rights and supporting the development of democratic institutions in existing or potential regions of refugee generation). However, experience indicates that here progress is likely to be slow and uncertain. In other areas – such as measures to prevent or resolve conflicts and to improve social and economic conditions in the countries of emigration – the prospects for any substantial results seem faint, at least in the short term.

Moreover, an approach which places too much emphasis on migration could encourage fire-fighting responses which divert attention from many of the wider problems at issue. Developments in the former Yugoslavia have highlighted the problems that will almost certainly beset any efforts to prevent or resolve the kind of complex conflicts which are likely to dominate in the post-cold war era; and to talk realistically of improving social and economic conditions in potential or existing migrant-sending regions begs fundamental questions relating to the structure of the international economy and, in particular, the structural economic imbalances at the root of much of today's migration. Progress in such areas is likely to be achieved only in the longer term, and then only on the basis of clear and realistic objectives backed up by a level of political and economic commitment which has so far been largely lacking.

Given the uncertainty which surrounds the 'root-cause' approach, perhaps a first active step for governments would be to face up to the fact that Western Europe is a region of immigration, and that they therefore have a responsibility both to their own populations and to the 'sending' countries to implement positive measures aimed at introducing a degree of equity and order into the management of migration flows. Barriers against the entry of 'unwanted' migrants may certainly prove effective as a short-term protective measure, but if introduced in the absence of more positive steps to implement a system of managed (albeit limited) immigration, receiving states are in the end likely to weaken, rather than strengthen, their hold over the migration process. At the same time, governments have a responsibility – if only for reasons of self-interest – to try to prevent the pressures associated with the 'root-causes' of migration from translating into more intractable problems of conflict or economic collapse in countries to the east and to the south. The challenges are enormous, but if the countries of Western Europe shrink from them and retreat into what is the rather fragile shell of 'fortress Europe', they will only grow greater.

Notes

Preface

1 Myron Weiner, 'On International Migration and International Relations', in *Population and Development Review*, vol. 2, no. 3, 1985, pp. 441–55, at p. 441.

Chapter 1: Introduction

1 Eugene Kulischer, *Europe on the Move. War and Population Changes 1917–1947*, Columbia University Press, New York, 1943, p. 9.

2 Note also a recent increase in indenture-type labour, including an unknown, but certainly significant, number of foreign domestic servants held in virtual bondage in Britain and other industrialized countries in the West.

3 See, for example, definitions of different types of 'worker' migration as set out in the UN Convention on the Protection of the Rights of All Migrant Workers and Members of Their Families, 1990 (reproduced in the United Nations Press Release, Department of Public Information, *Resolutions and Decisions Adopted by the General Assembly During the First Part of Its Forty-Fifth Session: From 18 September to 21 December 1990*, pp. 471–96). The Convention includes definitions of frontier workers, seasonal workers, seafarers, offshore installation workers, project-tied workers, itinerant workers, specified employment workers, professional, technical and professional workers, and self-employed workers.

4 See John Salt, 'Contemporary Trends in International Migration Study', *International Migration*, vol. 25 (1987), no. 3, pp. 241–7. See also Charles W. Stahl, 'Overview: Economic Perspectives', in Reginald Appleyard, ed., *The Impact of International Migration on Developing Countries*, OECD, Paris, 1989, p. 362; and Claudio Stern in R. Appleyard, ed., *International Migration Today* (vol.1), UNESCO, 1988.

5 Jonas Widgren, 'International Migration: New Challenges to Europe', report prepared for the Third Conference of European Ministers Responsible for Migration (Council of Europe), Porto, Portugal, 13–15 May 1987. Reprinted in *Migration News* no. 2, International Catholic Migration Commission, Geneva, 1987. This figure includes legally employed foreign workers and their dependants, undocumented workers, and official and unofficial refugees.

6 Sharon Stanton Russell and Michael S. Teitelbaum, *International Migration and*

International Trade, World Bank Discussion Paper, no. 160; World Bank, Washington DC, 1992, p. 1.

7   Ibid., p. 29. Russell and Teitelbaum note that theirs represents the first, and possibly only, attempt to calculate the total global volume of remittance flows. They draw on IMF balance-of-payments data for 193 countries. A figure of $65.6 billion is quoted in the publication cited, but subsequent calculations by the same analysts suggested the figure of $60.9 billion as more accurate.

8   Louis Emmerij, 'The International Situation, Economic Development and Employment', paper presented at the OECD International Conference on Migration, Rome, March 1991, p. 9.

9   Russell and Teitelbaum, *International Migration and International Trade*, p. 9. All are conservative estimates.

10   Immigrant populations in Europe are difficult to quantify owing in part to the operation of different citizenship and nationality laws in different countries. Both figures should be taken as very provisional. The term 'foreigners' is used here in a very loose sense and includes EC nationals living in another Community state and immigrants in Britain who hold British citizenship.

11   Russell and Teitelbaum, *International Migration and International Trade*; *World Refugee Survey 1992*, US Committee for Refugees and American Council for Nationalities Service, Washington DC, 1992; OECD Continuous Reporting System on Migration (SOPEMI), *Trends in International Migration*, OECD, Paris, 1992; *Demographic Statistics 1992*, Eurostat, Luxembourg, 1991.

12   See also SOPEMI, *Trends in International Migration*, pp. 13–15.

Chapter 2: Western Europe and International Migration

1   The World Bank, *World Population Projections, 1989-90 Edition: Short- and Long-Term Estimates*, The Johns Hopkins University Press, Baltimore and London, pp. xiv–xvi.

2   Ibid.

3   OECD (Continuous Reporting System on Migration), *SOPEMI 1992. Trends in International Migration*, OECD, Paris, 1992, Tables 34 and 36; and Demetrious Papademetriou, 'International Migration in North America: Issues, Policies and Implications', paper prepared for the UNECE/UNFPA Informal Expert Group Meeting on International Migration, Geneva, July 1991, p. 36 (fn.).

4   *SOPEMI 1992. Trends in International Migration*, Tables 2, 3 and 4, pp. 132–3.

5   Ibid., Table 5, p. 133. This figure is based on data provided for Austria, Belgium, France, Germany, Luxembourg, Netherlands, Sweden, Switzerland, United Kingdom.

6   S. Stanton-Russell, K. Jacobsen and W.D. Stanley, *International Migration and Development in Sub-Saharan Africa, Volume I*, World Bank Discussion Papers, Africa Technical Department Series, no. 101, World Bank, Washington DC, 1990, p. 1.

7   Eurostat, *Demographic Statistics 1991*, Eurostat (Statistical Office of the European Communities), Official Publications Office of the European Communities, Luxembourg, 1991, p. 152 (Table H-1). The table provides an aggregate figure for immigrants from African countries, with a breakdown on those from Algeria, Morocco and Tunisia. Subtracting immigrants of North African origin from the total figure for

African immigrants leaves roughly 0.5 million. The statistics should be assumed inaccurate.

8   See, for example, Manolo Abella, 'International Migration in the Middle East: Patterns and Implications for Sending Countries', paper prepared for the UNECE/ UNFPA Informal Expert Group Meeting on International Migration, Geneva, July 1992, p. 7; See also J.S. Birks and C.A. Sinclair, *International Migration and Development in the Arab Region*, International Labour Office, Geneva, 1980, p. 77.

9   Abella, 'International Migration in the Middle East', p. 12.

10   Ibid., p. 16; and Asian Regional Programme on International Labour Migration, *Statistical Report 1990: International Labour Migration from Asian Labour-Sending Countries* (UNDP-ILO Asian Regional Programme on International Labour Migration), International Labour Organisation, Regional Office for Asia and the Pacific, Bangkok, Thailand, 1990. This figure is only a rough estimate. It includes those who left to work as seafarers (630,000) and female domestic workers, but excludes undocumented migration.

11   World Bank, *World Development Report 1991: The Challenge of Development*, Oxford University Press for World Bank, Washington DC, 1991, Table 1 (Basic Indicators), p. 204.

12   Abella, 'International Migration in the Middle East', Table 9, p. 37; Lin Lean Lim, 'International Labour Migration in Asia: Patterns, Implications and Policies', paper prepared for the UNECE/UNFPA Informal Expert Group Meeting on International Migration, Geneva, July, 1992, Table 6, p. 64.

13   UNDP/ILO Asian Regional Programme on International Labour Migration, *Statistical Report 1990: International Labour Migration from Asian Labour-Sending Countries*, International Labour Organisation (World Employment Programme), Regional Office for Asia and the Pacific, Bangkok, Thailand, 1990.

14   World Bank, *World Development Report 1991*, Table 26 (Population Growth and Projections), p. 255.

15   See, for example, John Bauer, 'Demographic Change and Asian Labour Markets in the 1990s', in *Population and Development Review*, vol. 16, no. 4, pp. 615–45.

16   Lim, 'International Labour Migration in Asia', pp. 25–6.

17   Mr Kayutaba Shigemi, Deputy Director, General Affairs Division of the Immigration Bureau, Ministry of Justice, Tokyo, Japan. Quote taken from a statement to the International Labour Office: 'Recent Changes in Immigration Control Act and Recent Developments in the Immigration of Foreign Workers to Japan' (ILO, Asia Regional Office, Bangkok).

18   Ibid., pp. 5–6.

19   See OECD, *SOPEMI 1993 (Annual Report). Trends in International Migration*, OECD, Paris, 1994, pp. 57–62.

20   Ibid., pp. 58 and 61.

21   See, for example, E.G. Ravenstein, 'The Laws of Migration', *Journal of the Royal Statistical Society*, no. 52, London, 1889; Arthur W. Lewis, 'Economic Development with Unlimited Supplies of Labour', The Manchester School of Economic and Social Studies, vol. 22, Manchester, 1954; and Michael Todaro, 'A Model of Labor Migration and Urban Unemployment in Less Developed Countries', *American Economic Review*, vol. 59, March 1969.

22   See, for example, John Salt, 'A Comparative Overview of International Trends and Types, 1950–1980', *International Migration Review*, vol. 23, no. 3, 1989.

23 A. Golini, G. Gerano and F. Heins, 'South–North Migration with Special Reference to Europe', *International Migration*, June 1991, p. 253.

24 Myron Weiner, 'On International Migration and International Relations', in *Population and Development Review*, vol. 2, no. 3 (1985), pp. 441–55, at p. 489.

25 Papademetriou, 'International Migration in North America', p. 5.

26 Weiner, 'On International Migration and International Relations', p. 489.

27 I.J. Seccombe, 'International Migration in the Middle East: Historical Trends, Contemporary Patterns and Consequences', in R. Appleyard, ed., *International Migration Today*, vol. 1, UNESCO, 1988, p. 199; and W.A. Shadid, E.J.A.M. Spaan and J.D. Speckman, 'Labour Migration and the Policy of the Gulf States', in F. Eelens, T. Schampers and J.D. Speckmann, eds, *Labour Migration to the Middle East: From Sri Lanka to the Gulf*, Kegan Paul International, London and New York, 1992, p. 72.

28 See, for example, David North, 'Why Democratic Governments Cannot Cope with Illegal Immigration', paper presented at the International Conference on Migration, Rome, March 1991, OECD (OCDE/GD(91)22), Paris, 1991.

29 For example, the USA in 1987/8, France in 1982, Italy in 1987/8 and 1989/90, Spain in 1985 and 1991, and Portugal in 1992/1993.

30 Georges Tapinos, 'The Macroeconomic Impact of Immigration: Review of the Literature Published Since the Mid-1970s', in OECD, *SOPEMI 1993*, pp. 172–3.

31 See Chapter 6.

32 US Department of Labor, Bureau of International Labor Affairs: Immigration Policy and Research Report 2, *Employer Sanctions and U.S. Labor Markets: First Report* (prepared by the Division of Immigration Policy and Research as part of the Department of Labor's submission to 'The President's First Report on the Implementation and Impact of Employer Sanctions'), Washington DC, July 1991, p. 7.

33 See Papademetriou, 'International Migration in North America'.

34 See, for example, 'Life, Liberty and Try Pursuing a Bit of Tolerance Too', *The Economist*, 5–11 September 1992.

35 See, for example, L. Dinnerstein and D.M. Reimers, *Ethnic Americans: A History of Immigration*, 3rd Edition, Harper and Row, New York, 1988.

36 UNHCR, Regional Office for the European Communities, Brussels, 1991.

37 See, for example, Gil Loescher, *Refugee Movements and International Security*, Adelphi Paper 268, Brassey's for the International Institute for Strategic Studies, London, 1992, p. 10.

38 See, for example, G. Coles, 'Changing Perspectives of Refugee Law and Policy', in V. Gowlland and K. Samson, eds, *Problems and Prospects of Refugee Law*, The Graduate Institute of International Studies, Geneva, 1992, pp. 34–5.

39 UNHCR, Regional Office for the European Communities, Brussels, 1991.

40 See US Committee for Refugees, *World Refugee Survey 1992*, American Council for Nationalities Service, Washington DC, 1992.

41 Ibid.

42 UNHCR, Regional Office for the European Communites, Brussels, 1991.

43 US Committee for Refugees, *World Refugee Survey 1993*.

44 The Statute of the United Nations High Commissioner for Refugees (1950); the 1951 United Nations Convention Relating to the Status of Refugees (*United Nations Treaty Series*, vol. 189, no. 2545, p. 137), and its 1967 Protocol (UNTS, vol. 606). Texts of the UNHCR Statute and the 1951 UN Convention are reproduced in Guy Goodwin-Gill, *The Refugee in International Law*, Oxford University Press, 1983.

The 1967 Protocol removed the temporal limitation included in the 1951 Convention which limits application to refugees who acquired their status as a result of events occurring before 1 January 1951. Over one hundred states have acceded to the 1951 Convention and 1967 Protocol.

45 See Louise Holborn, *The International Refugee Organisation: A Specialised Agency of the United Nations, Its History and Work, 1946–52*, Oxford University Press, London, 1956.

46 Gil Loescher and John A. Scanlan, *Calculated Kindness: Refugees and America's Half-Open Door, 1945 to the Present*, Free Press and Collier Macmillan, New York and London, 1986.

47 James C. Hathaway, 'Reconceiving Refugee Law as Human Rights Protection', in V. Gowland and K. Samson (eds.), *Problems and Prospects of Refugee Law*, Graduate Institute of International Studies, Geneva, 1992, pp. 9–30, at p. 11.

48 See Elizabeth Ferris, *The Central American Refugees*, Praeger, New York, 1987.

49 The 1969 OAU Convention Governing the Specific Aspects of Refugee Problems in Africa, OAU Document CM/267/Rev.1. Reproduced in Goodwin-Gill, *The Refugee in International Law*.

50 See A. Zolberg, A. Suhrke and S. Aguayo, *Escape from Violence: Conflict and the Refugee Crisis in the Developing World*, Oxford University Press, New York and Oxford, 1989.

51 Jonas Widgren, 'The Management of Mass Migration in a European Context', paper delivered at the Royal Institute of International Affairs, London, 12 March 1991; and J. Widgren, 'Movements of Refugees and Asylum-Seekers: Recent Trends in a Comparative Perspective', paper presented at the International Conference on Migration (OECD), Rome, 1991.

52 Sadruddin Aga Khan, Hassan Bin Talal, et al., *Refugees: The Dynamics of Displacement; A Report for the Independent Commission on International Humanitarian Issues*, Zed Books Ltd, London and New Jersey, 1986, p. 38.

53 Although in the case of the Federal Republic of Germany, which had particularly liberal asylum procedures and policies, this pattern was becoming less clear-cut by the mid- to late 1980s.

54 In connection, for example, with efforts to introduce a new Asylum Bill in the United Kingdom in 1991 and 1992. See House of Commons debates (i) 13 November 1991 (567-617 CD3/2-3/52); (ii) 2 November 1992, issue no. 1598, vol. 213 (21–120)

55 See Sarah Collinson, *Beyond Borders: West European Migration Policy Towards the 21st Century*, Royal Institute of International Affairs/Wyndham Place Trust, London, 1993, Chapter 4.

56 Ibid.

57 J.-P. Hocké, 'Beyond Humanitarianism', in Gil Loescher and Laila Monahan (eds.), *Refugees and International Relations*, Oxford University Press, 1989.

58 S. Ogata, 'Refugees: a Comprehensive European Strategy', statement made at the Peace Palace, The Hague, 24 November 1992.

Chapter 3: From Babylon to Berlin

1 Eugene Kulischer, *Europe on the Move. War and Population Changes 1917–1947*, Columbia University Press, New York, 1943, p. 8.

2 Ibid., p. 96.

3 The King of Babylonia who ordered the deportation of much of the Jewish population

of Southern Judaea after 586 BC. See Sven Tagil, 'From Nebuchadnezzar to Hitler', in Göran Rystad, ed., *The Uprooted: Forced Migration as an International Problem in the Postwar Era*, Lund University Press, Lund, 1990. See also Kulischer, *Jewish Migrations: Past Experiences and Post-War Prospects*, American Jewish Committee, New York, 1943, p. 14.

4   For a full discussion of the emergence of sovereign power in Europe, see F.H. Hinsley, *Sovereignty*, 2nd Edition, Cambridge University Press, 1986.

5   See, for example, Adam Smith, *An Inquiry into the Nature and Causes of the Wealth of Nations*, Whitestone, Dublin, 1776.

6   Alan Dowty, *Closed Borders*, Yale University Press, New Haven and London, 1987, p. 29.

7   Jews, Moriscos, Protestants from France and the Low Countries, German Catholics. Aristide Zolberg, 'Contemporary Transnational Migrations in Historical Perspective: Patterns and Dilemmas', in Mary M. Kritz, ed., *US Immigration and Refugee Policy. Global and Domestic Issues, USA and Canada*, Lexington Books, Lexington MA, 1983, p. 21.

8   Kulischer, *Europe on the Move*, p. 17.

9   Roughly 100,000. Ibid., p. 18.

10   Ibid., p.18.

11   Dowty, *Closed Borders*, p. 33.

12   Estimates for the number of Huguenots who left France at this time vary (ranging between 150,000 and 900,000). See Tagil, 'From Nebuchadnezzar to Hitler', p. 68 and fn. 23. Tagil notes that the difficulty in estimating a figure for this group is compounded by the fact that the Huguenots were accompanied by other French migrants trying to escape famine and social disorder. See also Aristide R. Zolberg, Astri Suhrke and Sergio Aguayo, *Escape from Violence. Conflict and the Refugee Crisis in the Developing World*, Oxford University Press, New York and Oxford, 1989, p. 6.

13   Zolberg, et al., *Escape from Violence*, p. 8.

14   Tagil, 'From Nebuchadnezzar to Hitler', p. 69.

15   Aristide R. Zolberg, 'Patterns in International Migration Policy: a Diachronic Comparison' in C. Fried, ed., *Minorities: Community and Identity*, Life Sciences Research Report Series no. 27, Springer-Verlag, Berlin, 1983, pp. 232–3. Many Europeans left for the New World under some form of bondage. See, for example, H.J.M. Johnston, *British Emigration Policy 1815–1830: Shovelling out Paupers*, Clarendon Press, Oxford, 1972, pp. 6–7. Johnston notes that between 1717 and 1775 as many as 225,000 Ulstermen arrived in America, most as indentured servants. Many of those who left for the New World were religious dissenters escaping a combination of persecution and economic hardship, including high numbers of Huguenots. See also Zolberg, et al., *Escape from Violence*, p. 8.

16   Kingsley Davis, 'The Migrations of Human Populations', *Scientific American*, no. 231, September 1974, p. 96.

17   See Philip D. Curtin, *The Atlantic Slave Trade: A Census*, University of Wisconsin Press, Madison, 1969, pp. 12–13 and 275–82. Curtin notes that estimates of slave imports into the Americas range between 3.5 and 25 million. He criticizes many estimates as being based on 'insubstantial guesswork'. Curtin's estimate for slave imports into the Americas and Europe is close to 9.6 million for the period 1451–1870; of these, he estimates that about 7.8 million were taken to the New World.

18   Davis, 'The Migrations of Human Populations', p. 97.

19 Quoted by Dowty, *Closed Borders*, p. 43. The French Revolution itself gave rise to a flow of some 129,000 refugees (Zolberg et al., *Escape from Violence*, p. 9), approximately 8,000 of whom arrived in the United Kingdom over the three years after 1789. It is interesting to note that this influx resulted in Britain's first Alien Bill, which was designed to control the entry of French migrants by way of sanctions imposed on transporters not providing customs officers with details of any foreigners transported, etc. This influx took place during a period of deteriorating relations between Britain and France. Within three years, France had introduced similar controls over aliens within its territory. See Richard Plender, *International Migration Law*, Sijthoff, Leiden, 1972, p. 44. In 1797 France adopted a Passports Law, which can be seen as the starting-point for modern aliens registration. See Grahl-Madsen, *The Status of Refugees in International Law*, vol. 1, Sijthoff, Leiden, 1966, p. 11. In 1798 the USA approved its first Bill providing for the control of immigration.

20 For a succinct analysis of the thinking of theorists such as Locke and Smith in the context of free movement of people and the right to emigrate, see F.G. Whelan, 'Citizenship and the Right to Leave', in *American Political Science Review*, no. 75, September 1981.

21 Frank H. Knight, *Risk, Uncertainty and Profit*, Houghton Mifflin, Boston, 1921, p. 77. Quoted in J.R. Stansfield, *The Economic Thought of Karl Polanyi: Lives and Livelihood*, Macmillan, London, 1986, p. 128.

22 Karl Polanyi, *Origins of Our Time: The Great Transformation*, Victor Gollancz, London, 1945, p. 75.

23 Thomas Robert Malthus, *An Essay on the Principle of Population*, edited by Patricia James, Cambridge University Press for the Royal Economic Society, Cambridge and New York, 1989.

24 Smith, *The Wealth of Nations*.

25 Zolberg, 'Contemporary Transnational Migrations in Historical Perspective', pp. 21–2.

26 Dowty, *Closed Borders*, p. 45.

27 The Passenger Act of 1803, introduced largely in reaction to increased voluntary emigration from the Scottish Highlands. The Highlands and areas of Northern Ireland had a history of emigration to the New World dating back at least as far as the mid-18th century. Between 1717 and 1775, roughly 225,000 Ulstermen arrived in America. See H.J.M. Johnston, *Shovelling out Paupers*, Clarendon Press, Oxford, 1972, pp. 1 and 6–7.

28 Ibid.

29 See Plender, *International Migration Law*, p. 46.

30 By 1886, there were over 250,000 Italian workers in France. See Frank Thistlethwaite, 'Migration from Europe Overseas in the Nineteenth and Twentieth Centuries', *Rapports*, vol. 5, 1960, p. 42. Thistlethwaite notes the significance of France as a country of immigration, particularly after the United States began restricting entry of aliens towards the end of the nineteenth century.

31 Thistlethwaite, 'Migration from Europe Overseas', p. 41. See also Brinley Thomas, *Migration and Economic Growth. A Study of Great Britain and the Atlantic Economy*, Cambridge University Press, 1954. Thomas examined how nineteenth-century migration was related to rhythms of economic growth in Britain and the United States, and found changes in Britain to be more decisive in determining levels of emigration.

32 Thistlethwaite, 'Migration from Europe Overseas', p. 47.

33   Davis, 'The Migrations of Human Populations', p. 98. Other destinations included South America, Southern Africa, Central Asia and Australia. About 30% of those who left eventually returned. See M. Piore, *Birds of Passage*, Cambridge University Press, 1979, p. 150.

34   Poire, *Birds of Passage*, p. 98.

35   Davis, 'The Migrations of Human Populations', p. 99.

36   Johnston, *British Emigration Policy*, p. 165. Kingsley Davis estimated in 1974 that had it not been for emigration up to that date, the population of Ireland would be nearly 12 million instead of 3 million. See Davis, 'The Migrations of Human Populations', p. 99.

37   See Piore, *Birds of Passage*.

38   Thistlethwaite, 'Migration from Europe Overseas', p. 48.

39   Ibid., p. 50, quoting W.D. Forsyth, *The Myth of the Open Spaces: Australian, British and World Trends of Population and Migration*, Melbourne University Press, Melbourne, 1942, pp. 16–17.

40   Tomas Hammar, ed., *European Immigration Policy*, Cambridge University Press, 1985, p. 240.

41   Zolberg, 'Patterns in International Migration Policy', p. 237. Note that Ireland was still part of the United Kingdom.

42   Ernest Gellner, *Muslim Society*, Cambridge University Press, 1981, p. 96.

43   Michael Marrus, *The Unwanted; European Refugees in the Twentieth Century*, Oxford University Press, New York and Oxford, 1985. See also Zolberg, et al., *Escape from Violence*, pp. 10–11.

44   Hannah Arendt, *The Origins of Totalitarianism*, Harvard University Press, Harvard, 1973, p. 269.

45   Marrus, *The Unwanted*, p. 23.

46   Of a total US immigration figure of 27.5 million for same period; see E. Kulischer, *Europe on the Move*, p. 24.

47   Between 1875 and 1914. See Plender, *International Migration Law*, p. 55.

48   See Zolberg, 'Patterns in International Migration Policy'.

49   Mr Justice Gray in *Nishimura Ekiu vs. USA*, quoted in Plender, *International Migration Law*, p. 51.

50   Ibid., p. 55.

51   The Dillingham Report, which also recommended introduction of provisions for deportation of certain aliens. Ibid., pp. 55–6.

52   Including Australia's 1901 Immigration Registration Act, marking the beginnings of the 'White Australia Policy' which prevailed until the 1970s. Ibid., p. 48.

53   Marrus, *The Unwanted*, p. 25.

54   Ibid., p. 37, and Plender, *International Migration Law*, pp. 56–7 and fn. 114. Marrus notes that in practice the new law had limited effect, but that it was significant in that it represented a shift away from the attitude that refugees should have an automatic right to enter Britain.

55   Zolberg et al., *Escape from Violence*, p. 13.

56   Marrus, *The Unwanted*, p. 45.

57   Convention of Adrianople, November 1913. In fact most of those affected by the agreement had already moved.

58   See S.J. Shaw and E.K. Shaw, *History of the Ottoman Empire and Modern Turkey*, vol. 2, Cambridge University Press, 1977, pp. 347–8.

59   Quoted in Marrus, *The Unwanted*, p. 105.

60   Already before Lausanne, Greece had to absorb about 1 million refugees from the Turkish War of Independence, and after 1920 was faced with settling refugees numbering up to one quarter of the total Greek population of the time. See Marrus, pp. 102–3. Armenians were among those groups who fled to Greece, but the majority were Greeks from Thrace and Western Anatolia.

61   Arendt, *The Origins of Totalitarianism*, p. 277.

62   Estimate made by Sir John Hope Simpson, *The Refugee Problem: Report of a Survey*, Oxford University Press for the RIIA, London, 1939, pp. 80–87. Zolberg et al. note that many estimates of the time (e.g. 3 million) were inflated owing to the inclusion of displaced Poles and Germans returning home. They suggest a figure of around one million refugees outside the boundaries of the old empire. See Zolberg, et al., *Escape from Violence*, p. 17.

63   League of Nations Doc. C.277.M.203.1921.III (1921). The provision of the so-called 'Nansen Passports' (named after the High Commissioner) was agreed to in 1922.

64   Zolberg, 'Contemporary Transnational Migrations'.

65   According to one migration expert, 20–25 million Europeans fell within a nationally alien jurisdiction after the peace settlements. See Marrus, *The Unwanted*, p. 70.

66   The League Council was called upon to extend the identity certificate programme to Armenians in September; the other categories listed fell into December 1926 resolution, named explicitly as groups requiring assistance in 1928. League of Nations OJ 967 (1924) and 155 (1927).

67   Zolberg et al., *Escape from Violence*, p. 18. See also Marrus, *The Unwanted*, p. 51; and Kulischer, *Europe on the Move*, pp. 248–9.

68   The Dillingham Report. Quoted in Plender, *International Migration Law*.

69   See Dowty, *Closed Borders*, p. 90.

70   Ibid., pp. 90–91. Note that France took over as one of the most important countries of immigration as America began restricting inflows. Between 1919 and 1928 about 1.5 million foreigners entered France (many of whom were refugees). See Marrus, *The Unwanted*, p. 114.

71   Hope Simpson, *The Refugee Problem*, pp. 515–16. See also Marrus, *The Unwanted*, p. 138. Of these at least 100,000 had emigrated overseas, including at least 45,000 who left for Palestine (Marrus, p. 132).

72   The right-wing regimes of these countries were becoming increasingly hostile to their Jewish populations which numbered about 3 million in Poland, 445,000 in Hungary and 757,000 in Romania. See Marrus, *The Unwanted*, p. 142. Sir John Hope Simpson estimated the total population of Jews east of Germany, excluding the USSR, to be about 5 million in 1938. See Hope Simpson, *The Refugee Problem*, pp. 515–16.

73   See Marrus, *The Unwanted*, pp. 170–72.

74   See Sir John Hope Simpson, *Refugees: A Review of the Situation Since 1938*, Oxford University Press for the RIIA, London, 1939, pp. 1–30.

75   Tagil, 'From Nebuchadnezzar to Hitler', p. 9.

76   Nicolai Tolstoy, *Stalin's Secret War*, Cape, London, 1982, p. 112. See also Marrus, *The Unwanted*, p. 197.

77   Marrus, *The Unwanted*, p. 199.

78   Tolstoy, *Stalin's Secret War*, pp. 201 and 222–3. See also Marrus, *The Unwanted*, p. 197.

79   Marrus, *The Unwanted*, pp. 200–2.

80   Kulischer, *Europe on the Move*, p. 305.

81   Michael Marrus, 'The Uprooted: an Historical Perspective', in Rystad, ed., *The Uprooted*, pp. 47–57.

82   See Louise Holborn, *The International Refugee Organisation*, Oxford University Press, London, 1956.

83   The 1951 United Nations Convention Relating to the Status of Refugees, United Nations Treaty Series, vol. 189, no. 2545, p. 137. See also its 1967 Protocol, UNTS, vol. 606. The 1967 Protocol removed the temporal limitation. Texts of the UNHCR Statute and 1951 Convention reproduced in Guy Goodwin-Gill, The Refugee in International Law, Oxford University Press, 1983, pp. 241–6 and pp. 270–74.

84   Despite growing numbers of refugees in other parts of the world over the following years, it was not until 1967 that the temporal limitation was removed by a protocol; the optional geographical limitation was left intact. Over one hundred states have acceded to the 1951 Convention and 1967 Protocol.

85   Note that the first major refugee movements to be experienced in the Third World took place at this time: the partition of India in August 1947 displaced 14 million people, and the formation of Israel resulted in the immediate displacement of at least 700,000 Arabs and subsequent movement of over 750,000 Jews who had been living in Arab countries. See Aristide Zolberg, 'The Refugee Crisis in the Developing World: A Close Look at Africa', in Rystad, ed., *The Uprooted*, pp. 87–8. See also Zolberg et al., *Escape from Violence*, p. 23.

86   Quoted by Dowty, *Closed Borders*, p. 97.

87   Ibid., pp. 100–1.

88   Dowty, *Closed Borders*, p. 116.

89   Jean-Pierre Hocké, 'Beyond Humanitarianism', in Gil Loescher and Laila Monahan, eds., *Refugees and International Relations*, Clarendon Press, Oxford, 1989.

90   See Gil Loescher and John Scanlan, eds., *Calculated Kindness: Refugees and America's Half-Open Door, 1945 to the Present*, Free Press and Collier Macmillan, New York and London, 1986.

Chapter 4: Immigration Policy in Postwar Europe

1   Note that colonial ties had already given rise to small numbers of migrants moving from Algeria to France, from the Caribbean to Britain and from Indonesia to the Netherlands during the 1930s. See Alan Dowty, *Closed Borders*, Yale University Press, New Haven and London, 1987, pp. 56–7.

2   No case-study is taken from the new immigration states of Southern Europe (Italy, Spain, Portugal, Greece), since these countries, traditionally sending states, have only begun introducing coherent immigration policies over the past few years. During the 1980s, however, these states emerged as important countries of immigration (although, it should be noted, Portugal remains a country of net emigration). As noted in Chapter 7, the overall convergence in immigration policies which has taken place in Western Europe since the mid-1980s includes the countries of Southern Europe.

3   'Le problème de la population représente ... le problème numéro un de toute la politique économique française', in 'Documents relatifs à la Première Session du Conseil du Plan (16–19 mars 1946)', Commissariat Général du Plan de Modernisation et d'Equipment, Paris, 1946. Quoted in Georges Tapinos, *L'immigration étrangère en France, 1946–1973*, Institut National d'Etudes Démographiques no. 71, Presses Universitaires de France, Paris, 1975, p. 16.

4   See Tapinos, *L'immigration étrangère*, p. 129, and Catherine Wihtol de Wenden,

Les immigrés et la politique, Presses de la Fondation Nationale des Sciences Politiques, Paris, 1988, p. 93.

5   2 November 1945. Note also the Ministerial Order of 19 October 1945 establishing the 'Code de la Nationalité Française', including arrangements to facilitate naturalizations.

6   'Au printemps de 1946, un vaste programme d'immigration semblait sur le point de prendre place dans une audacieuse politique de relèvement national, où les exigences démographiques se seraient conciliées heureusement avec les nécessités économiques', in Xavier Lannes, *L'immigration en France depuis 1945*, Nijhoff, Dordrecht, 1953, p. 18, see Wihtol de Wenden, *Les immigrés et la politique*, p. 95.

7   See Dowty, *Closed Borders*, p. 98.

8   Ibid., p. 122.

9   Wihtol de Wenden, *Les immigrés et la politique*, p. 95.

10   Tapinos, *L'immigration étrangère*, p. 28. Accord dated 11 March 1947.

11   See Zig Layton-Henry, 'British Immigration Policy and Politics', in Michael C. LeMay, ed., *The Gatekeepers. Comparative Immigration Policy*, Praeger, New York, 1989, pp. 59–94.

12   Over 100,000 'volunteered' under this scheme, most notably Lithuanians, Ukrainians, Latvians and Yugoslavs. See J. Tannahill, *European Voluntary Workers in Britain*, Manchester University Press, Manchester, 1958.

13   Stephen Adler, *International Migration and Dependence*, Saxon House, Farnborough, Hants, 1977, p. 60.

14   G. Tapinos and Yann Moulier, 'France', in Daniel Kubat, ed., *The Politics of Migration Policies: The First World in the 1970s*, Center for Migration Studies, New York, 1979, pp. 127–43.

15   Wihtol de Wenden, *Les immigrés et la politique*, p. 92.

16   'La constitution de colonies inassimilables sur le territoire national', in ibid., p. 92, quoting Pierre Bideberry, 'Bilan de vingt années d'immigration, 1946–1966', in *Revue Française des affaires sociales*, no. 2, April–June 1967, p. 7.

17   22 February 1946, 24 November 1946, etc. See Wihtol de Wenden, *Les immigrés et la politique*, p. 96.

18   Tapinos, *L'Immigration étrangère*, p. 28.

19   Ibid., p. 33.

20   Wihtol de Wenden, *Les immigrés et la politique*, p. 100.

21   Layton-Henry, 'British Immigration Policy', pp. 61–2.

22   Ibid., p. 62. See Ministry of Labour, 'Report of the Working Party on Employment in the UK of Surplus Colonial Labour', Ministry of Labour Papers 26/226/7503, Public Records Office, 1948.

23   Quoted by Layton-Henry, 'British Immigration Policy', p. 64. See Royal Commission on Population, Cmnd. 7695, HMSO, London, 1949, pp. 226–7.

24   These arrivals were not, in fact, strictly the first immigration flows from the British colonies. By the mid-eighteenth century, several black communities had been established in Britain as a result of the slave trade (e.g. 20,000 immigrants in London in 1764, most of whom were ex-slaves and escapees). During the First World War, 15,000 troops were recruited in the Caribbean, and many other West Indians joined the merchant marine. Many of these settled in existing black communities in Britain or began new settlements in ports such as Cardiff and Liverpool. These ports were the scenes of racial violence in 1919. During the Second World War, over 7,000 West Indians volunteered for the Royal Air Force, factory work (through the Over-

seas Volunteer Scheme) and the merchant marine. Many settled, and many of those who returned to the West Indies subsequently remigrated to the United Kingdom. According to Stuart Hall, the return migration to the West Indies played an important part in triggering new migration to the United Kingdom beginning in 1948. See Stuart Hall, 'Migration from the English-speaking Caribbean to the United Kingdom, 1950–80', in Charles W. Stahl, ed., *International Migration Today. Vol. 2: Emerging Issues*, UNESCO, Paris, 1988.

25 Note also emigration of British population to the 'Old' Commonwealth at this time. In the late 1940s and 1950s, emigration from Europe overseas accounted for a net loss of 3 million people for the whole of Europe. See Stephen Castles, Heather Booth and Tina Wallace, *Here for Good: Western Europe's New Ethnic Minorities*, Pluto, London, 1984, p. 1.

26 It is worth noting that as a result of past British colonial policies, many Commonwealth immigrants had a good knowledge of the English language, which served as a facilitating factor both in the migration process itself, and in the ease with which immigrants could fill gaps in the labour market.

27 Hall, 'Migration from the English-speaking Caribbean', p. 269.

28 Staff shortages in London Transport persisted well into the 1960s and 1970s. See Paul E. Garbutt, *London Transport and the Politicians*, Ian Allen, London, 1985.

29 Tom Rees, 'The United Kingdom', in Kubat, *The Politics of Migration Policies*, p. 77.

30 Tapinos, *L'Immigration étrangère*, p. 22. Note the lesson that this experience could teach policy-makers today, given the current emphasis on strict control policies which leave little room for the recognition of a demand for immigrant labour, and thus are ill-equipped to manage flows that are taking place irrespective of policies designed to prevent them. This is a theme raised in Chapter 8.

31 'L'établissement définitif et l'insertion des étrangers dans la société française', in Tapinos, *L'Immigration étrangère*, p. 20.

32 Agreements concluded with Greece and Spain 1960, Turkey 1960, Morocco 1963, Portugal 1964, Tunisia 1965, Yugoslavia 1968, further agreements with Turkey 1971 and 1972. See 'Survey of the Policy and Law Regarding Aliens in the Federal Republic of Germany', Federal Minister of the Interior (V II 1-937 020/15), Bonn, 1991, Annex 1. See also Richard Plender, *International Migration Law*, revised second edition, Nijhoff, Dordrecht, 1988, pp. 566–77 and refs. Note the Association Agreement concluded between the EC and Turkey in 1963 involving an agreement to step-by-step measures towards freedom of movement between Turkey and the EC to be completed by 1 December 1986. This regulation did not enter into force in 1986.

33 28 April 1965.

34 Marilyn Hoskin and Roy C. Fitzgerald, 'German Immigration Policy and Politics', in LeMay, ed., *The Gatekeepers*, p. 95.

35 Unemployment within the immigrant population increased from 0.2% in 1966 to 1.5% in 1967. See Castles et al., *Here for Good*, p. 145. Between June 1966 and January 1968, numbers of foreign workers in Germany declined by about 31% (nearly one million non-EC immigrants remained). The economic upturn which followed the recession was accompanied by a renewal in immigration streams. By 1974 the number of foreigners legally resident in the Federal Republic had passed the four million mark. See Hoskin and Fitzgerald, 'German Immigration Policy and Politics', p. 151; and OECD, *Continuing Reporting System on Migration (SOPEMI)*, Paris, 1981, p. 33.

36 Note the formal abolition of barriers to free movement of workers within the

European Economic Community in 1968 in accordance with Article 3c of the 1957 Treaty of Rome. Since Italy and Germany were both members of the EEC, the Rome Treaty rendered the labour agreement between the two countries obsolete. After 1968 all Italians could enter Germany freely to take up employment. This development did not lead to a large-scale influx of Italian workers, since emigration pressures in Italy had by this time declined to the point where many migrants were returning.

37 By 1969 the proportion of immigrants present in France who had regularized their status after entry had reached 80%. Tapinos and Moulier, 'France', p. 131.

38 Including large numbers of French settlers returning from Algeria, labelled as the '*pieds-noirs*'. This influx had the effect of encouraging subsequent Algerian and other immigration flows as the need for extra housing increased demand for labour in the construction industry.

39 'Il s'agit d'une immigration largement non controlée, caractérisée par la grande variété des pays d'origine et des cadres légaux (ou illégaux) par lesquels ils sont entrés inorganisés, insécurisés, privés de droits politiques, faiblement intégrés dans les organisations ouvrières et peu politisés', in Wihtol de Wenden, *Les immigrés et la politique*, p. 126.

40 Defining Algeria's relationship with France following independence.

41 April 1964. The so-called 'Nekhache-Grandval' agreement, which included a protocol allowing for numbers of Algerians entering France to be fixed according to the labour-market situations in both countries. See Adler, *International Migration and Dependence*.

42 Ibid.

43 'L'immigration clandestine elle-même n'est pas inutile, car si l'on s'en tenait à l'application stricte des règlements et accords internationaux, nous manquerions peut-être de main-d'oeuvre', in Jean-Marcel Jeanneney, 28 March 1966. See Wihtol de Wenden, *Les immigrés et la politique*, p. 161 and fn.

44 Including the UK, the Federal Republic, France, Belgium, the Netherlands, Luxembourg, Austria, Switzerland, Denmark, Norway and Sweden.

45 Castles et al., *Here for Good*, p. 88. Percentages are quoted for 1970. Percentages as a proportion of the working population would have been higher in every country.

46 OECD, *SOPEMI*, Paris, 1975 and 1976.

47 Roughly 500,000 New Commonwealth citizens settled in Britain between 1955 and 1962. See Layton-Henry, 'British Immigration Policy', p. 69.

48 Category 'A' issued to those with a specific job to come to; Category 'B' issued by the British High Commissions overseas to those with skills or qualifications of which there was a shortage in the United Kingdom; Category 'C' issued to anyone on a first-come-first-served basis. Note that entry of foreign nationals from outside the Commonwealth was still controlled by the Alien Acts of 1914 and 1919 and the rules drawn up under these acts (except, subsequently, EC nationals wishing to enter to take up employment, offer services, etc.).

49 *Sunday Telegraph*, 18 October 1964. Quoted in Patrick Cosgrave, *The Lives of Enoch Powell*, Bodley Head, London, 1989, p. 235.

50 Note the uproar caused by his speech delivered in Birmingham on 20 April 1968.

51 Cosgrave, *The Lives of Enoch Powell*, p. 244.

52 1965 Race Relations Act, followed by a second Race Relations Act in 1976.

53 See Vaughan Bevan, *The Development of British Immigration Law*, Croom Helm, London, 1986, pp. 195–9.

54 Note that this subsequently affected the immigration of Asians from Uganda.

55 Her Majesty's Stationery Office, London 1971. Reproduced in Peter Wallington
    and Robert Lee, eds., *Blackstone's Statutes on Public Law*, Blackstone, London,
    1988, p. 79.
56 Wihtol de Wenden, *Les immigrés et la politique*, p. 160.
57 The second specifying 31 October 1973.
58 See Belkacem Hifi, *L'immigration algérienne en France: origines et perspectives de
    non-retour*, L'Harmattan/CIEM, Paris, 1985.
59 23 November 1973. This was followed a year later with a restriction on granting of
    work permits for first employment to aliens residing in the Federal Republic of
    Germany (13 November 1974).
60 Federal Minister of the Interior, 'Survey of the Policy and Law Regarding Aliens in
    the Federal Republic of Germany', Bonn, January 1991, p. 49.
61 Note, for example, the European Convention on Human Rights, which calls for
    respect of family life; the Universal Declaration of Human Rights, which states that
    'the family is the natural and fundamental group unit of society and is entitled to
    protection by society and state' (Art. 16); the International Covenant on Civil and
    Political Rights; and the Final Act of the Helsinki Conference on Security and
    Cooperation in Europe, which sets standards for family reunification.
62 For example, France maintained a ban on family immigration from July 1974 to July
    1975, and during the late 1970s family immigrants were allowed to enter only on the
    condition that they would not demand access to the labour market; similarly, the
    Federal Republic issued dependants and family members residence permits without
    work permits until 1979.
63 *Immigration Observations on the Report of the Select Committee on Race Relations
    and Immigration*, Secretary of State for the Home Department, HMSO, London, July
    1978, Cmnd. 7287, paragraphs 15 and 16.
64 Federal Minister of the Interior, 'Survey of the Policy and Law', p. 47.
65 OECD, *SOPEMI*, Paris, 1986.
66 Ibid., p. 9.
67 Ibid., p. 28.
68 See Chapter 6 for a discussion of fertility rates among immigrant groups.
69 'L'Europe ... doit s'efforcer de définir en commun des objectives et d'organiser avec
    les pays un modèle exemplaire de coopération où l'immigration trouve son exacte
    place', quoted in Wihtol de Wenden, *Les immigrés et la politique*, p. 195.
70 ILO, 'Convention Concerning Migration in Abusive Conditions and the Promotion of
    Equality of Opportunity and Treatment of Migrant Workers', ILO Convention no.
    143, Cmnd. 6674, Geneva, 24 June 1975. See Plender, *International Migration Law*,
    Chapter 5.
71 Plender, *International Migration Law*, p. 256. Note that at the time of writing, the
    European Convention on the Legal Status of Migrant Workers had only been ratified
    by Sweden, Portugal, Spain, Turkey, the Netherlands, France and Norway. It had
    been signed by Germany, Greece, Italy, Luxembourg and Belgium. It entered into
    force on 1 May 1983. See Council of Europe, *Activities of the Council of Europe in
    the Migration Field* (CDMG (93) 10 E), Council of Europe, Strasbourg, 1993, p. 15.
72 Wihtol de Wenden, *Les immigrés et la politique*, p. 224.
73 Gilles Verbunt, 'France', in Tomas Hammar, ed., *European Immigration Policy. A
    Comparative Study*, Stockholm University Centre for Research in International
    Migration and Ethnicity, Cambridge University Press, 1985, p. 142.

74 Federal Minister of the Interior, 'Survey of the Policy and Law Regarding Aliens', pp. 6–7.

75 Ibid.

76 Wihtol de Wenden, *Les immigrés et la politique*, p. 124.

77 Layton-Henry, 'British Immigration Policy'. See Bevan, *The Development of British Immigration Law*, Chapter 5, pp. 191–223. Note also the Immigration Act 1988, which introduced a wide range of further provisions designed to restrict immigration.

78 This date was repeatedly postponed until the first parliamentary term of 1982. See Wihtol de Wenden, *Les immigrés et la politique*, p. 281.

79 Ibid, p. 290; and Claude-Valentin Marie, 'L'immigration clandestine in France', in *Travail et Emploi*, no. 17, July–September 1983, pp. 27–39.

80 *Immigration: Observations on the Report of the Select Committee on Race Relations and Immigration*, paragraphs 6 and 24.

81 Note that in France entry of visitors staying for a period of less than three months became subject to stringent conditions in addition to visa requirements, including guarantees of intention to return (proof of sufficient funds to cover period of stay, completion of an arrival card, an attestation of reception signed by the person to be visited, etc.). See Ministère des Affaires Sociales et de la Solidarité Nationale, *1981–1986. Une nouvelle politique de l'immigration*, La Documentation Française, Paris, 1987.

82 See Federal Minister of the Interior, 'Survey of the Policy and Law Regarding Aliens', pp. 51–2. Note the UK 1987 Carrier Liability Act, which allows for air and sea carriers to be penalized in the same way. Reproduced in Wallington and Lee, *Statutes on Public Law*, p. 275.

83 See Presidenza del Consiglio dei Ministri, *Norme Urgenti in Materia di Asilo Politico, Ingresso e Soggiorno dei Cittadini Extracomunitari e di Regolarizzazione de Cittadini Extracomunitari ed Apolidi Già Presenti Nel Territorio Dello Stato*, Law of 28 February 1990, no. 39, converting Decree no. 416 of December 1989, Collana de Testi e Documenti, Dipartimento per L'Informazione e L'Editoria (Istituto Poligrafico e Zecca Dello Stato), Rome, 1990, including English translation, pp. 27–47.

84 Centro Studi Investimenti Sociali (CENSIS), *Immigrati e Società Italiana*, Editalia-Edizioni d'Italia, Rome, 1991, p. 329; CENSIS, *Atti Della Conferenza Nazionale dell' Immigrazione*, Editalia-Edizioni d'Italia, Rome, 1991, p. 484.

85 Council of Europe, *Conclusions and Resolution adopted at the Fourth Conference of European Ministers responsible for Migration Affairs* (MMG-4 (91) 9 final), Council of Europe, Strasbourg, 1991.

86 European Council, 'Declaration on Principles Governing External Aspects of Migration Policy', in the Conclusions of the Presidency (SN 456/1/92 REV 1), Edinburgh, December 1992.

87 Commission of the European Communities, *Policies on Immigration and the Social Integration of Migrants in the European Community*, Experts' report drawn up on behalf of the Commission of the European Communities, Brussels, September 1990 (SEC(90) 1813 final), p. 32.

88 Federal Minister of the Interior, Survey of the Policy and Law Regarding Aliens in the Federal Republic of Germany (Translation), Bonn, January 1991 (V II 1-937 020/ 15), p. 8.

89 Ibid.

90 See, for example, Institute of Race Relations, Race and Class, *Europe: Variations on a Theme of Racism*, Russell Press, Nottingham, 1991. See also European Parliament (Rapporteur: Mr Glyn Ford), *Report of the Committee of Enquiry into Racism and Xenophobia*, Brussels, European Parliament Sessions Document, Brussels, 1989.

91 Commission of the European Communities, *Policies on Immigration*, pp. 37 and 32.

92 Myron Weiner, 'Security, Stability and International Migration', in *International Security*, vol. 17, no. 3 (1993).

Chapter 5: The Sending Countries

1   D. Papademetriou, 'International Migration in a Changing World', in R. Appleyard, ed., *International Migration Today. Vol. 1: Trends and Prospects*, UNESCO, Paris, 1988.

2   International Labour Office, *Some Growing Employment Problems in Europe*, Report II, Second European Regional Conference, Geneva, 1974, pp. 98–9. Quoted in Philip L. Martin, *The Unfinished Story: Turkish Labour Migration to Western Europe*, Geneva, ILO, 1991, p. 17.

3   Stephen Adler, *Swallow's Children – Emigration and Development in Algeria*, Geneva, ILO, 1980.

4   See John Salt, 'Contemporary Trends in International Migration Study', *International Migration*, vol. 25, 1987, no. 3, pp. 241–7. See also Charles W. Stahl, 'Overview: Economic Perspectives', in R. Appleyard, ed., *The Impact of International Migration on Developing Countries*, OECD, Paris, 1989, p. 362; and Claudio Stern in Appleyard, *International Migration Today*, vol. 1.

5   Papademetriou, 'International Migration in a Changing World'.

6   Ibid.

7   See, for example, E.M. Petras, 'The Global Labour Market in the Modern World Economy', in M.M. Kritz, C.B. Keely and S.M. Tomasi, eds., *Global Trends in Migration: Theory and Research on International Population Movements*, Center for Migration Studies, New York, 1983.

8   Stephen Adler, *A Turkish Conundrum: Emigration, Politics and Development*, ILO World Employment Programme research working paper, Geneva, 1981, p. 82; quoted in Rinus Penninx, 'A Critical Review of Theory and Practice: The Case of Turkey', in *International Migration Review*, vol. 16, 1982, no. 4, pp. 781–818.

9   Note also Turkey's 1963 Association Agreement with the European Communities.

10 'Le Gouvernement français et le Gouvernement turc, désireux d'organiser dans l'intérêt commun le recrutement de travailleurs turcs, sont convenus de ce qui suit: *Art. 1er.* – Le Gouvernement français fait connaître périodiquement au Gouvernement turc ceux de ses besoins en main-d'oeuvre qui conviendraient aux travailleurs turcs....Ces informations préciseront, en particulier, les conditions d'âge, de spécialisations, d'aptitude professionnelle et de santé. Le Gouvernement turc fournit au Gouvernement français des indications aussi précises que possible sur le nombre, l'âge et la qualification des travailleurs turcs désirant travailler en France', Convention de Main-d'Oeuvre Entre La France et La Turquie, 8 April 1965. *Journal Officiel de la République Française*, 15 June 1965, p. 4940.

11 Martin, *The Unfinished Story*, p. 3; (source: Ali Gitmez, 'Turkish Experience of Work Emigration: Economic development or individual well-being', *Yapi Kred: Economic Review*, vol. 3, no. 4, pp. 3–27).

12   Office des Travailleurs Tunisiens à l'Etranger, de l'Emploi et de la Formation Professionelle.
13   I.J. Seccombe and R.I. Lawless, 'State Intervention and the International Labour Market: A Review of Labour Emigration Policies in the Arab World', in Appleyard, ed., *The Impact of International Migration.*
14   Stephen Adler, *International Migration and Dependence*, Saxon House, Farborough, Hants, 1977, p. 161.
15   Ibid., p. 69.
16   A progressive move away from free circulation as articulated in the Evian Accords: (i) the Nekhache-Grandval Accord of 1964, which held that arrivals of Algerians in France should be fixed according to the needs of the French (and Algerian) labour market (an annual contingent of 12,000) and which imposed new restrictions on the entry of Algerian tourists; (ii) the 1968 Agreement concerning the Movement, Employment and Residence of Algerian Nationals and their Families in France, which set a new annual contingent of 35,000, to be renegotiated after 3 years; (iii) the negotatiation of a new annual contingent in 1971 - reduced to 25,000, and publication of a procès-verbal stating the intention to bring the regulation of Algerian immigrants more in line with that of other nationalities (e.g. Spaniards and Portuguese as processed through ONI).
17   In 1968, migrants' remittances were roughly equal in value to tax revenues from oil exports, whereas by 1973 the value of remittances represented only a fraction of the value of oil revenues. See Lawless and Seccombe, 'North African Labour Migration: The Search for Alternatives', *Immigrants and Minorities*, vol. 3, no. 2, July 1984, pp. 151–66.
18   Adopted after a referendum in 1976, the Charte Nationale defined the fundamental principles of the organization of Algerian society. Quoted in Seccombe and Lawless, 'State Intervention and the International Labour Market', p. 81.
19   Adler, *International Migration and Dependence*, p. 77.
20   1976 ILO World Employment Conference, paragraph 42. See Martin, *The Unfinished Story*, pp. 98–9; and W.R. Böhning, *Studies in International Migration*, International Labour Office, London, 1984, p. 9.
21   Barbara Schmitter Heisler, 'Sending Countries and the Politics of Emigration and Destination', in *International Migration Review* (Special Issue: 'Civil Rights and the Socio-political Participation of Migrants'), vol. 19, 1985, no. 3, pp. 469–84.
22   Seccombe and Lawless, 'State Intervention and the International Labour Market', pp. 69–89.
23   See Martin, *The Unfinished Story*, p. 52.
24   And members of the Village Development Cooperatives. This policy was designed to encourage return migration (as it was felt that members of cooperatives would maintain closer ties with their village or region of origin and would have a greater incentive to return). Despite the stated policy aims, the Turkish authorities exercised very little control over worker emigration. Of the 800,000 emigrants processed by the TES, roughly one-third were classed as skilled, and the majority were employed prior to departure. Ibid., p. 52.
25   Allan Findlay and Anne Findlay, *The Geographical Interpretation of International Migration: a Case Study of the Maghreb*, Centre for Middle Eastern and Islamic Studies, Durham, 1982.
26   Moroccan migration policy was largely laissez-faire. See Seccombe and Lawless, 'State Intervention and the International Labour Market'.

27   Emigration out of Morocco was strongly localized. According to Findlay and Findlay, the 'acute localization of Moroccan emigration in certain parts of the country underlines the regional as opposed to national significance of emigration ... [and reflects] the existence of fundamental spatial disequilibrium'. Findlay and Findlay, *The Geographical Interpretation of the International Migration*, p. 39. The geographical concentration of emigrant sources in Morocco also illustrates the importance of 'networks' in determining migration flows.

28   Penninx, 'A Critical Review of Theory and Practice', p. 793. See also Abadan-Unat et al., *Migration and Development: A Study of the Effects of International Labour Migration on Bogazliyan District*, Ajams-Turk Press, Ankara, 1976.

29   Martin, *The Unfinished Story*, p. 52. Source: Kutlay Ebiri, 'Impact of Labor Migration on the Turkish Economy', in Rosemarie Rogers, ed., *Guests who Come to Stay: the Effects of Labor Migration on Sending and Receiving Countries*, Westview Press, Boulder, Colorado, 1985, pp. 207–30. A similar story is reflected in Stuart Hall's discussion of Caribbean emigration to the UK. Hall cites a number of studies which indicate that 'compared with the population as a whole, the [UK] intake contained a high proportion of skilled workers' – a situation described in some areas as 'a serious "loss of skilled and productive elements in the labour force"'. Hall notes that the percentage of working-age persons in Jamaica declined from 47% in 1943 to 40% in 1960. Stuart Hall, 'Migration from the English-speaking Caribbean to the United Kingdom, 1950–80', in C.W. Stahl, ed., *International Migration Today*, vol. 2 (UNESCO), 1988, pp. 271–3.

30   Bundesanstalt für Arbeit (FRG), *Repräsentativ-Untersuchung 1972, Beschäftigung ausländischer Arbeitnehmer* ('Representative Survey 1972, Employment of Foreign Workers'), Nurnberg, 1973. See Penninx, 'A Critical Review of Theory and Practice', p. 795.

31   The country with probably the most comprehensive return policy was Yugoslavia. According to Zvonimir Baletic, Yugoslav policy was 'designed to keep the migration temporary ... [this was] explicitly defined'. The Yugoslav government sought 'to promote the collective interest of Yugoslav workers in foreign countries ... by organizing their social and cultural life, by attempting to preserve their attachment to their home country and by encouraging them to return home ... the country's economic and social development policy takes into account their return and reintegration into economic and social life'. Zvonimir Baletic, 'International Migration in Modern Economic Development: with special reference to Yugoslavia', *International Migration Review*, vol. 16, 1982, no. 4, pp. 736–56.

32   Findlay and Findlay, *The Geographical Interpretation of International Migration*, p. 19.

33   See Catherine Wihtol de Wenden, 'L'échange de Lettres Franco-Algérien du 18 Septembre 1980 et Son Evolution en 1981 et 1982' in *Les Algériens en France*, CNRS, Paris, 1985, pp. 119–35. The 'aid to return' programmes were dubbed 'useless, ineffective and illusionary' by the Mitterrand administration in 1981. See Lawless and Seccombe, 'North African Labour Migration', p. 154; and G. Simon, 'Industrialisation, Emigration et Réinsertion de la Main-d'Oeuvre Qualifiée au Maghreb – le cas de la Tunisie et de l'Algérie', *Hommes et Migrations*, no. 902, 1976, pp. 4–14.

34   Suzanne Paine, *Exporting Workers: the Turkish Case*, Cambridge University Press, Cambridge, 1974, p. 129.

35   Adler, *A Turkish Conundrum*, p. 43. Quoted in Penninx, 'A Critical Review of

Theory and Practice', p. 795.

36 See Martin, *The Unfinished Story*. The Turkish government also supported the Turkish Workers' Companies set up by migrants in Germany.

37 By the early 1980s, most governments of the receiving countries were looking to cooperate more with the sending countries. This was reflected in a greater emphasis on training returning migrants. Note that, at least initially, the interests of receiving and sending countries in encouraging returns did not necessarily coincide, since both were most interested in the most skilled and enterprising migrants.

38 Heinz Werner and Ingeborg König, *Ausländerbeschäftigung: Wiederkehroption für ausländische Jugendliche*, Ausländisches Amt., Bonn, 1988. See Martin, *The Unfinished Story*. The further return incentives introduced by the FRG in 1983/4 encouraged more returns, but again the impact was minimal.

39 See *International Migration*, vol. 24, no. 1, March 1986, which includes a number of papers on return migration (policies, causes, impacts, etc.). See also F.P. Cerase, 'Migration and Social Change: Expectations and Reality. A Case Study of Return Migration from the United States to Southern Italy', *International Migration Review*, vol. 8, no. 2, pp. 245–62. Cerase talks of the return of 'failure', 'conservatism', 'retirement' and the (less frequent) 'return of innovation' in return migration flows. The motivation for return migration is usually not for reinsertion into the industrial sector of the country of origin. See also Böhning, *Studies in International Migration*, p. 178.

40 Many of the agreements reached between sending and receiving countries after 1973 dealt exclusively with questions relating to migrants' living and working conditions and social and economic rights. Note also the mounting concern among sending countries worldwide regarding the treatment of migrant workers. The nine co-sponsors of the first draft text of the UN Convention on the Protection of the Rights of All Migrant Workers and the Members of Their Families (adopted in 1990) were all sending countries, including Algeria, Turkey, Yugoslavia and Morocco. See *International Migration Review*, vol. 25, 1991, no. 4 (special edition on the UN Convention).

41 Adler, *International Migration and Dependence*, pp. 107–8.

42 M. Miller and P. Martin, *Administering Foreign-Workers Programs*, Lexington Books, Lexington MA, 1982. Quoted in Schmitter Heisler, 'Sending Countries and the Politics of Emigration', p. 477.

43 Ben Bella replaced the French Federation with the Amicale largely because the former had sided with the opposition GPRA. Ben Bella was anxious about the possibility of antigovernment action based within the emigrant community (which originated predominantly from the Kabylia region in Algeria). The Amicale was staffed by pro-Ben Bella appointees.

44 See Ali Gitmez and Czarina Wilpert, 'A Micro-Society or an Ethnic Community? Social Organisation and Ethnicity Amongst Turkish Migrants in Berlin', in John Rex, Daniele Joly and Czarina Wilpert, eds., *Immigrant Associations in Europe*, Gower, Aldershot, 1987, pp. 86–125.

45 Penninx, 'A Critical Review of Theory and Practice', p. 797.

46 Author's calculation. *Sources: IMF International Financial Statistics*, and *IMF Balance of Payments Yearbooks 1990*.

47 Ibid.

48 World Bank, *Trends in Developing Economies 1991*.

49 Author's calculation. *Sources*: Ibid.; World Bank, *World Development Report 1991:*

The Challenge of Development, Oxford University Press for the World Bank, Oxford, 1991.

50 Penninx, 'A Critical Review of Theory and Practice', p. 809.

51 See, for example, W.R. Böhning, 'Some Thoughts on Emigration from the Mediterranean Basin', *International Labour Review*, vol. 3, no.3, March 1975, pp. 251–77, reproduced in W.R. Böhning, *Studies in International Labour Migration*, Macmillan, London, 1984, pp. 165–90; Heiko Korner, 'The Experience in the Main Geographical OECD Areas: European Sending Countries', in *The Future of Migration*, OECD, Paris, 1987, pp. 64–85. For a very clear résumé of the main arguments, see C.W. Stahl, 'Overview: Economic Perspectives', in Appleyard, ed., *The Impact of International Migration*; for an authoritative assessment of the impacts in North Africa and the Middle East, see Ismail Serageldin, J.A. Socknat, S. Birks, Bob Li, and Clive A. Sinclair, *Manpower and International Labour Migration in the Middle East and North Africa*, Oxford University Press for the World Bank, Oxford, 1983; for an important contribution to the debate based on evidence from Asia, see Charles W. Stahl, *International Labor Migration: A Study of the ASEAN Countries*, Centre for Migration Studies, New York, 1986. For a detailed study of the effects of emigration on a particular region (Turkey), see Abadan-Unat et al., *Migration and Development*. This research project was part of a larger project called REMPLOD: Reintegration of Emigrant Manpower and Promotion of Local Opportunities for Development (studies carried out in Morocco, Tunisia and Turkey, financed by the Dutch Ministry for Development Cooperation).

52 Serageldin et al., *Manpower and International Labour Migration*, p. 107.

53 E.g. 11% on one-year US$ accounts in 1988.

54 Martin, *The Unfinished Story*, p. 33.

55 See, for example, Hassan Boubakri, *Migration and Cooperation for Development: the case of Egypt and Tunisia*, paper prepared for the Council of Europe's Joint Group of Specialists on Migration, Demography and Employment, (POSMG3.94E), Council of Europe, Strasbourg, 3 March 1993.

56 Ibid., p. 20.

57 I.J. Seccombe and R.J. Lawless, 'Some New Trends in Mediterranean Labour Migration: The Middle East Connection', *International Migration*, vol. 23, no. 1, March 1985.

58 Note the expulsions of Tunisian workers from Libya in 1969 (29,356), 1970 (33,939), 1972 (43,251), and 1976 (13,670). See Seccombe and Lawless, 'Some New Trends'.

59 Hassan Boubakri, *Migration and Cooperation for Development*, p. 17.

60 Note that Yugoslavia was also politically well placed to export workers to Libya. In the same month that the Turkish–Libyan agreement was signed, Libya and Yugoslavia signed a technical cooperation agreement which made provisions for the supply of Yugoslav technical and supervisory manpower. In 1982, there were some 12,700 Yugoslavs working in Libya. See Seccombe and Lawless, 'Some New Trends'.

61 M. Allefresde, 'Migration of Workers from the Mediterranean Countries to the Gulf States', OECD, Paris, 1984 (restricted). Quoted in Seccombe and Lawless, op. cit.

62 M. Allefresde, 'The Oil-Producing Countries of the Middle East and North Africa', in *The Future of Migration*, OECD, Paris, 1987, p. 293.

63 Ibid., p. 294; and OECD, *Continuing Reporting System on Migration (SOPEMI)*, Paris, 1987 and 1989.

64 The 'brain drain' or 'reverse transfer of technology' issue received a great amount of

attention during the 1960s and 1970s, and is again appearing as a major concern throughout the less developed world. The extent of the problem is indicated by the fact that sub-Saharan Africa lost an estimated 30% of its highly skilled manpower stock to the MDCs of the North (especially the European Community) between 1960 and 1984 (A. Adepoju, 'South–North Migration: the African Experience', *International Migration*, vol. 29, no. 2, p. 211). See also (for example) John Salt and Allan Findlay, 'International Migration of Highly-Skilled Manpower: Theoretical and Development Issues', and D. Chongo Mundende, 'The Brain Drain and Developing Countries', in Appleyard, ed., *The Impact of International Migration*, pp.159–81; and papers presented at the Tenth IOM Seminar on Migration, 'Migration and Development', Geneva, September 1992.

65   Council of Europe, 'Report on the New Countries of Immigration', Document 6211, Parliamentary Assembly, Strasbourg, 1990. See also John Salt, *Current and Future International Migration Trends Affecting Europe*, background document for the 4th Conference of European Ministers Responsible for Migration, Luxembourg, September 1991 (MMG-4 (91) 1 E), Council of Europe, Strasbourg, 1991, p.15.

66   Although, as noted in Chapter 6, recent ILO estimates are more modest.

67   For a discussion of current demographic pressures in North Africa, see, for example, Council of Europe, Committee on Migration, Refugees and Demography, 'Demographic Imbalances Between the Countries of the Mediterranean Basin' (rapporteurs: M. Mota Torres and Vazquez, assisted by Léon Tabah), restricted (AS/PR (42) 40), Council of Europe, Strasbourg, 22 May 1991 (AAR40.42). See also Raouf Daboussi, 'Economic Evolution, Demographic Trends, Employment and Migration Movements', synthesis report for the Mediterranean Information Exchange System on International Migration and Employment (MIES), International Labour Office, Geneva, February 1991.

68   Bimal Ghosh, 'Migration-Development Linkages: Some Specific Issues and Practical Policy Measures', paper presented at the Tenth IOM Seminar on Migration, Geneva, September 1992, p. 2.

69   Reginald T. Appleyard, *International Migration: Challenge for the Nineties*, paper published for the fortieth anniversary of the IOM, International Organization for Migration, Geneva, 1991, p. 83.

Chapter 6: Immigrant Minorities in Europe Today

1   Hartmut Esser and Hermann Korte, 'Federal Republic of Germany', in Tomas Hammar, ed., *European Immigration Policy: A Comparative Study*, Cambridge University Press, 1985, p. 180.

2   D. Tranhardt, 'Les relations ethniques et l'immigration en Allemagne après la réunification', in M. Martiniello and M. Poncelet, eds, *Migrations et minorités ethniques dans l'espace Européen*, De Boeck-Wesmael, Brussels, 1993, p. 49.

3   Czarina Wilpert, 'From One Generation to Another: Occupational Position and Social Reproduction – Immigrant and Ethnic Minorities in Europe', in C. Wilpert, ed., *Entering the Working World. Following the Descendants of Europe's Immigrant Labour Force*, Gower, Aldershot, 1988, p. 3.

4   Note for example that current Eurostat figures are based on census and other statistical sources which range from the mid-1980s to the early 1990s.

5   André Lebon, *Regard sur l'immigration et la présence étrangère en France, 1989/ 90*, Ministère des Affaires Sociales et de la Solidarité, Direction de la Population et

des Migrations, Paris, 1990, pp. 25–6.

6   Note also the relatively high incidence of dual nationality in Britain and France which blurs the distinction further. See Hammar, *Democracy and the Nation State. Aliens, Denizens and Citizens in a World of International Migration*, Avebury, Aldershot, 1990, pp. 111–13. There is little in the way of statistics on dual citizenship, but Hammar suggests a figure of at least one million dual citizens in France and notes the presence of over 600,000 residents in Britain born in the Irish Republic all of whom are potential dual-citizenship holders. Both countries have a comparatively relaxed attitude towards dual citizenship.

7   *Migration News Sheet* (monthly information bulletin on immigrants, refugees and ethnic minorities, European Information Network, Brussels), No. 133/94-04, April 1994, p. 8.

8   Annual reports. Generally provides data on select OECD countries and therefore does not provide comprehensive data for all European countries. See, for example, OECD, *SOPEMI 1993 (Annual Report). Trends in International Migration*, OECD, Paris, 1994.

9   See, for example, Eurostat, *Demographic Statistics 1993*, Luxembourg, 1994. Statistics confined to the EC member states. Less detailed data than that provided by SOPEMI.

10 OECD, *SOPEMI 1992. Trends in International Migration*, OECD, Paris, 1992. Tables 13, 14, 15 and 17.

11 See *Policies on Immigration and the Social Integration of Migrants in the European Community*, Experts' report drawn up on behalf of the Commission of the European Communities, Brussels, September 1990 (SEC(90)1813 final), p. 7.

12 Predominantly African (especially North African) and Latin American (particularly in Spain). Figure quoted by John Salt, *Current and Future International Migration Trends Affecting Europe*, paper presented at the Fourth Conference of European Ministers Responsible for Migration (Council of Europe), Luxembourg, 17–18 September 1991 (Council of Europe Document MMG-4 (91) 1 E), p. 15. *Source*: Council of Europe, *Report on the New Countries of Immigration*, Document 6211, Parliamentary Assembly, 1990.

13 W.R. Bohning, 'Integration and Immigration Pressures in Western Europe', *International Labour Review*, 1990. These figures are quoted in John Salt, *Migration and Population Change in Europe*, UNIDIR Research Paper No. 19, United Nations Research Institute for Disarmament, New York, 1993, p. 16.

14 OECD, *SOPEMI 1993 (Annual Report)*. Statistical tables. Note that the data for France are based on the 1990 census; for the UK, on the Labour Force Survey; and for Germany, on the population register.

15 Percentages for the Community as a whole. See Commission of the European Communities, *Policies on Immigration and the Social Integration of Migrants in the European Community*, SEC(90)1813 final, Brussels, 28 September 1990, statistical annex, pp. 42–8.

16 OECD, *SOPEMI 1991*, Paris, 1992, Table 10, p. 136. No breakdown provided by republic or religion, etc.

17 Estimate for 1985, which includes children born in France to Algerian parents (roughly 300,000), who are French according to French law but considered Algerian by Algeria. Ibid. See also Lebon, *Regard sur l'immigration*, p. 25.

18 OECD, *SOPEMI 1993*. Statistical tables.

19 Although this distinction is not entirely clear-cut. Note that France actively encour-

aged European immigration through agreements with sending countries and that North African immigration has also been facilitated by relative geographical proximity. On the other hand, Italian and Yugoslav migration to Germany began before the bilateral recruitment agreements were entered into, reflecting *inter alia* the significance of geographical proximity for migration patterns into Germany. Geographical position is particularly salient for Germany today in relation to migration from Eastern and Central Europe.

20 Referred to generally as New Commonwealth and Pakistan (NCWP) origin in most statistics, since Pakistan only rejoined the Commonwealth in 1989.

21 Note that this was the first census which included a question about ethnic origin.

22 More accurately American New Commonwealth, including the West Indies, Guyana, Belize and other NCW territories in the Americas.

23 John Haskey, *The Ethnic Minority Populations of Great Britain: Estimates by Ethnic Group and Country of Birth*, Demographic Analysis and Vital Statistics Division, Office of Population Censuses and Surveys, London, 1990. Note that East African Asians are registered as being of African ethnic origin.

24 The 1986 amnesty (Law 943) led to the registration of roughly 7,000 Senegalese, 3,000 Ghanaians, 1,000 Somalis, 1,000 Nigerians and nearly 500 citizens of the Ivory Coast. It can be assumed that the majority of African immigrants did not come forward to regularize their status (perhaps as many as 90%). See Roger Blackstone, *The Salt of Another's Bread: Immigration Control and the Social Impact of Immigration in Italy*, Report of a Western European Union Study Visit, Home Office, London, 1989.

25 Centro Studi Investimenti Sociali (CENSIS), *Atti Della Conferenza Nazionale dell'Immigrazione*, Editalia-Edizioni d'Italia, Rome, 1991.

26 See OECD, *SOPEMI 1990*, Paris, 1991, Table C1.2. Overall movements are almost certainly under-estimated.

27 On the basis of surveys carried out by CENSIS, the Bocconi University and ISTAT (Central Statistical Institute). See CENSIS, *Atti Della Conferenza*. See also OECD, *SOPEMI 1990*, p. 53.

28 See Heather Booth, *Guestworkers or Immigrants? A Demographic Analysis of the Status of Migrants in West Germany*, Monographs in Ethnic Relations, no. 1, Centre for Research in Ethnic Relations, Warwick, 1985. See also OECD, *SOPEMI 1986*, Paris, 1987.

29 OECD, *SOPEMI 1985*, Paris, 1986, p. 63.

30 Percentages and figures from the 1971 Census, the 1977 OPCS Monitor 77/1 and the 1986–8 Labour Force Survey.

31 Eurostat estimate for 1989 is 1.62 children per woman for the European Community as a whole. Italy has the lowest fertility rate in the Community (1.29). See Eurostat, *Demographic Statistics 1991*, Luxembourg, 1991.

32 'Evolution of Fertility of Foreigners and Nationals in OECD Countries', in *Migration. The Demographic Aspects*, OECD, Paris, 1991, pp. 29–41, at p. 39.

33 Stephen Castles, 'The Guests Who Stayed – The Debate on "Foreigners Policy" in the German Federal Republic', in *International Migration Review*, vol. 19, no. 3, Autumn 1985, pp. 517–34, at p. 519.

34 For example, a Turkish fertility rate of over 4 in Sweden cf. a Turkish fertility rate of under 3 in the FRG in 1985. See OECD, 'Evolution of Fertility', p. 37.

35 Ibid., p. 39. Low fertility rates also explain the declining size of West Indian minorities in Britain during the 1980s; cf. high fertility rates for minorities of

Pakistani and Bangladeshi origin. High fertility rates within the latter two groups are partly explained by low rates of female labour participation.

36   This is a trend visible in most immigrant groups, at least after two or three decades of settlement. Of course the rate at which fertility declines will vary from group to group. Certain groups, particularly those least integrated and coming from countries with high fertility rates, are likely to manifest slower convergence than others, rates possibly even levelling off at a higher level than that of the population as a whole. OECD, 'Evolution of Fertility', p. 40. See also J.J. Schoorl, 'Fertility Adaptation of Turkish and Moroccan Women in The Netherlands', *International Organization for Migration Quarterly Review*, vol. 28, 1990, pp. 477–95. The fact that immigrant fertility rates tend to decline is one of the reasons (leaving aside political or social factors) why immigration cannot be considered to be a potential solution to the problem of ageing in the populations of industrialized countries. The positive effect of immigration on birth rates would not be sustained if yearly inflows were not recurrent.

37   Eurostat, *Rapid Reports, Population and Social Conditions*, no. 4, 1990; and Eurostat, *Demographic Statistics 1992*, p. xxv.

38   Eurostat, *Rapid Reports, Population and Social Conditions*.

39   Figures taken from Anton Kuijsten, *International Migration in Europe: Patterns and Implications for Receiving Countries*, paper presented at the UNFPA/ECE Informal Expert Group Meeting on International Migration, Geneva, 1991, p. 14.

40   Eurostat, *Rapid Reports, Population and Social Conditions*.

41   See John Salt, *Current and Future International Migration Trends*, pp. 10–11.

42   OECD, *SOPEMI 1993*, Paris, 1994, p. 13.

43   Ibid.

44   This Act was strengthened by the second Race Relations Act passed in 1968 outlawing direct discrimination in employment, housing and the provision of commercial and other services. Implementation of both Acts was to be secured by the Race Relations Board established in 1966 under the 1965 Act. Both Acts proved weak, and the RRB had minimal impact. Recognition of race relations as a national issue of central importance was also reflected in the establishment of a Parliamentary Select Committee on Race Relations and Immigration in 1968. Note also the Community Relations Commission established the same year. See Zig Layton-Henry, *The Politics of Race in Britain*, Allen and Unwin, London, 1984, pp. 122–35.

45   See, for example, Paul White, 'The Migrant Experience in Paris', in Günther Glebe and John O'Loughlin, eds., *Foreign Minorities in Continental European Cities* (Erdkundliches Wissen, Heft 84), Steiner Verlag, Stuttgart, 1987, pp. 185–98, at p. 186.

46   Under the 1948 Nationality Act, all colonial and Commonwealth citizens were British subjects, and, as such, were free to hold a UK passport, to enter Britain to find work, to settle and to bring families without being subject to immigration controls. Once in the UK, all UK passport holders had the same rights and duties, including the right to vote in local and national elections. (Note that Irish nationals also enjoy full citizenship rights.)

47   Zig Layton-Henry, *The Politics of Immigration: Immigration, 'Race' and 'Race' Relations in Post-war Britain*, Making of Contemporary Britain Series (Institute of Contemporary History), Blackwall Publishers, Oxford and Cambridge MA, 1992, p. 9.

48   Ibid., p. 73.

49   Cf. the Netherlands, discussed below.

50   Quoted in Layton-Henry, *The Politics of Race in Britain*, p. 134.

51   Home Secretary, 1966, quoted in S. Patterson, *Immigration and Race Relations in Britain 1960–67*, Oxford University Press, 1969, p. 113.

52   Home Office, 'Policy Statement on the Criteria for Ethnic Minority Grants', Home Office, London, 1990.

53   The Commission for Racial Equality (CRE) is empowered to investigate complaints (individual or collective) of racial discrimination (direct or indirect) in all areas of housing, employment, education, provision of services, etc., and to take cases to court where appropriate (except in employment, where cases are dealt with by an industrial tribunal). The CRE received 1,381 applications for legal assistance in 1990 (CRE, *Annual Report 1990*, London, 1991, Appendix 6).

54   Commission for Racial Equality, *Review of the Race Relations Act 1976: Proposals for Change*, CRE, London, July 1985, paragraph 1.3. Survey carried out by the Policy Studies Institute in collaboration with the CRE.

55   Commission for Racial Equality, *Annual Report 1990*, p. 7.

56   R.D. Grillo, *Ideologies and Institutions in Urban France: The Representation of Immigrants*, Cambridge University Press, 1985, pp. 289 and 292.

57   For a discussion of the development of the concepts of '*insertion*', '*assimilation*' and '*intégration*' in France, see Patrick Weil and John Crowley, 'Integration in Theory and Practice: A Comparison of France and Britain', in *West European Politics*, vol. 17, no. 2 (April 1994) – Special issue on *The Politics of Immigration in Western Europe*, edited by Martin Baldwin-Edwards and Martin Schain (Frank Cass Publishers, London).

58   Ibid., p. 114.

59   Philip Ogden, 'The Legacy of Migration: Some Evidence from France', in Russell King, ed., *Mass Migration in Europe: The Legacy and the Future*, Belhaven Press, London, 1993, p. 114.

60   Grillo, *Ideologies and Institutions in Urban France*, p. 53.

61   Perceptions of Algerians are coloured by the French colonial experience, particularly the war of independence, and by the current political upheaval in Algeria.

62   Philip Ogden, 'The Legacy of Migration', p. 115.

63   See Gilles Verbunt, 'France', in Hammar, ed., *European Immigration Policy*.

64   See Patrick Weil and John Crowley, 'Integration in Theory and Practice', p. 113.

65   See OECD, *SOPEMI 1990*, Paris, 1991, p. 48.

66   See A. Lebon, *Regard sur l'immigration*, p. 66.

67   *Le premier rapport du Haut Conseil à l'Intégration*, 18 February 1991. Quoted in Philippe Farine, 'Les conditions juridiques et culturelles de l'intégration: le troisième rapport du Haut Conseil à l'Intégration', in *Migrations Société*, vol. 4, no. 20, 1992, p. 7. Translated by the author.

68   The new Aliens Law in France was adopted in November 1993. Its adoption was delayed by the Constitutional Court's ruling in August 1993 that, without an amendment to the Constitution, provisions relating to the right of asylum included in the Bill were unconstitutional. The Constitution was amended in November 1993 to qualify the constitutional right of asylum. This allowed voting on the Aliens Bill to continue. The new Law is extremely restrictive, including, for example, limitations on the right of family reunification, a number of restrictions to foreigners' access to residence permits, measures to increase the use of detention for undocumented immigrants and asylum-seekers, and a strengthening of expulsion rules. See *Migra-*

tion News Sheet, various issues, including No. 124/93-07, July 1993 and No. 129/93-10, December 1993.

69 See footnote on p. 115.

70 See Philippe Farine, 'Immigration, intégration et alternance', in *Migrations Société*, vol. 5, no. 27 (1993); and Antonio Perotti, 'Revue de Presse', in *Migrations Société*, vol. 5, no. 28–29 (1993).

71 Indeed, Britain stands out in Europe in respect of its comprehensive framework of anti-discrimination legislation and enforcement mechanisms. See UN Centre for Human Rights, *Second Decade to Combat Racism and Racial Discrimination. Global Compilation of National Legislation Against Racial Discrimination*, New York, 1991.

72 See, for example, Esser and Korte, 'Federal Republic of Germany'; and Castles, 'The Guests Who Stayed', pp. 517–34.

73 Stephen Castles, Heather Booth and Tina Wallace, *Here for Good. Western Europe's New Ethnic Minorities*, Pluto, London, 1984.

74 Castles, 'The Guests Who Stayed', p. 522.

75 Ibid.

76 Ibid.

77 Ibid.

78 See Esser and Korte, 'Federal Republic of Germany', p. 183.

79 See Ali Gitmez and Czarina Wilpert, 'A Micro-Society or an Ethnic Community? Social Organization and Ethnicity amongst Turkish Migrants in Berlin', in John Rex, Daniele Joly and Czarina Wilpert, eds., *Immigrant Associations in Europe*, Gower Publishing for the European Science Foundation, Aldershot and Vermont, 1987, p. 107.

80 Federal Minister of the Interior, *Survey of the Policy and Law Regarding Aliens in the Federal Republic of Germany*, V II 1-937020/15, Bonn, 1991, pp. 6–7.

81 Ibid.

82 Ibid.

83 Netherlands Scientific Council for Government Policy, 'Immigrant Policy: Summary of the 36th Report', Reports to the Government no. 36, NSCGP, The Hague, 1990.

84 Rinus Penninx, J. Schoorl and C. Van Praag, *The Impact of International Migration on Receiving Countries: the Case of the Netherlands*, Swets and Zeitlinger-NIDI CBGS Publications, Amsterdam, 1993, p. 160.

85 Ibid.

86 See Netherlands Scientific Council for Government Policy, 'Immigrant Policy', p. 57.

87 Ibid., p. 61.

88 Blackstone, *The Salt of Another's Bread*, p. 58. See also V. Melotti, 'Gli Immigrati Stranieri in Italia: Considerazione dopo la Sanatoria', in *Up and Down*, ISPES, February 1988.

89 Blackstone, *The Salt of Another's Bread*.

90 OECD, *SOPEMI 1990*, Paris, 1991, p. 53.

91 For example, a fear that registration would result in the loss of a job, since the majority of clandestine immigrants rely on work in the informal economy. (Many employers using irregular labour would be reluctant to employ legally registered immigrants.) Also significant is the fact that many immigrants in Italy do not intend to stay. According to a survey carried out by CENSIS in 1989/90, only about 30% of immigrants interviewed expressed a desire to remain in Italy. CENSIS, *Atti Della Conferenza*, p. 329. See also Salt, *Current and Future International Migration*

Trends, p. 16; and OECD, *Comparative Analysis of the Regularisation Experience in France, Italy, Spain, and the United States*, OECD, Paris, 1990.

92 ILO Migrant Workers (Supplementary Provisions) Convention of June 1975.

93 See Blackstone, *The Salt of Another's Bread*, Appendix A.

94 CENSIS, *Immigrati e Società Italiana*, Editalia-Edizioni d'Italia, Rome, 1991, p. 333.

95 CENSIS, *Atti Della Conferenza*.

96 CENSIS, *Immigrazione e Diritti di Cittadinanza*, Editalia-Edizioni d'Italia, Rome, 1991, pp. 462–3.

97 Commission of the European Communities, 'Policies on Immigration and the Social Integration of Migrants in the European Community', Experts' report drawn up on behalf of the Commission of the European Communities, Brussels, 1990, p. 14.

98 See, for example, Annie Phizacklea and Robert Miles, *Labour and Racism*, Routledge and Kegan Paul, London, 1980, Chapter 3; Malcolm Cross, *Migrant Workers in European Cities: Concentration, Conflict and Social Policy*, Working Papers on Ethnic Relations, no. 19, SSRC Research Unit on Ethnic Relations, Birmingham, 1983; D. Massey, *Spatial Divisions of Labour: Social Structures and the Geography of Production*, Macmillan, London, 1984.

99 See for example, John Rex and Sally Tomlinson, *Colonial Immigrants in a British City*, Routledge and Kegan Paul, London, 1979, Chapter 5.

100 Malcolm Cross, 'Ethnic Minority Youth in a Collapsing Labour Market: the UK Experience', in Wilpert, ed., *Entering the Working World*, p. 66.

101 See, for example, Grillo, *Ideologies and Institutions in Urban France*, pp. 117–18.

102 See, for example, Catherine Wihtol de Wenden, *Les immigrés et la politique: cent cinquante ans d'évolution*, Presses de la Fondation Nationale de Sciences Politiques, Paris, 1987.

103 White, 'The Migrant Experience in Paris', p. 195.

104 Attempted for a short period by Birmingham council. See Rex and Tomlinson, *Colonial Immigrants in a British City*, Chapter 5. Note also Ealing Council's attempts to disperse immigrant children by busing them to schools outside the area. See Zig Layton-Henry in Hammar, ed., *European Immigration Policy*. These measures also came in for considerable criticism, not least from immigrants themselves.

105 Note also the recent widespread use of the term *'seuil de tolérance'*, or 'threshold of tolerance', in France. See, for example, *Europe: Variations on a Theme of Racism, Race and Class*, vol. 32, no. 3, 1991, p. 50.

106 Helga Leitner, 'Regulating Migrants' Lives', in Glebe and O'Loughlin, eds, *Foreign Minorities in Continental European Cities*, pp. 71–89.

107 Netherlands Scientific Council for Government Policy, 'Immigrant Policy', p. 75. Note that a bill approving an expansion of this kind of 'positive action', including the obligation of employers to report on the numbers of minority members they employ, was approved in January 1994. See *Migration News Sheet* (monthly information bulletin on immigrants, refugees and ethnic minorities; European Information Network, Brussels), No. 131/94-02, February 1994.

108 Note that at the time of writing, a change in Belgium's anti-discrimination laws to cover discrimination against foreigners and ethnic minorities in employment and housing was under consideration.

109 Council of Europe (1991), 'Community and Ethnic Relations in Europe', Final Report of the Community Relations Project of the Council of Europe, (MG-CR (91) 1

final E), Council of Europe, Strasbourg, 1990, p. 66.

110 See, for example, the Resolution on Racism and Xenophobia adopted by the European Parliament in December 1993.

111 Czarina Wilpert, 'Work and the Second Generation: the Descendants of Migrant Workers in the Federal Republic of Germany', in Wilpert, ed., *Entering the Working World*, pp. 126–7. Note that young foreigners rely to a disproportionate extent on irregular and/or casual work.

112 Note for example that children of Indian ethnic origin tend to perform above the level of their white peers, whereas children of West Indian descent are more likely to underachieve. See Zig Layton-Henry in T. Hammar (ed.), 1984. Children of Turkish descent tend to underachieve to a greater extent than those of Yugoslav, Greek, Italian or Spanish descent. See Wilpert, 'Work and the Second Generation', pp. 118–19.

113 Women have also been targeted for language training. Note also 'mother-tongue' language teaching, which has often been supported by the state, either (in the past) to promote the preparedness of immigrants and their children to return to their country of origin (especially in the FRG), or to promote cultural identity within immigrant groups (usually this is left to immigrants themselves, but in the Netherlands, and to a lesser extent in France, the state has taken on direct responsibility for immigrant children's cultural education).

114 Note that Dutch language lessons will be mandatory for foreigners in the Netherlands after 1996 (at present they are voluntary). This reflects the shift away from 'minorities policy' towards 'anti-deprivation' policies in the Netherlands.

115 Wilpert, 'Work and the Second Generation', p. 127.

116 There is no consistent pattern as to whether the outcome is a de facto displacement of entire communities or whether the result is a break-up of existing concentrations. Immigrant concentration should not be seen as a static or finished process; communities are in a constant state of flux, and one area of concentration may all but disappear only to be replaced by another elsewhere. See, for example, White, 'The Migrant Experience in Paris'.

117 G.S. Cross, *Immigrant Workers in Industrial France: the Making of a New Laboring Class*, Temple University Press, Philadelphia, 1983, p. 16. Quoted in Philip Ogden, 'The Legacy of Migration', p. 111.

118 Wilpert, 'Work and the Second Generation'.

119 Tomas Hammar, *Democracy and the Nation State. Aliens, Denizens and Citizens in a World of International Migration*, Research in Ethnic Relations Series, Gower Publishing, Avebury, 1990, p. 3.

120 Ibid. pp. 12–13.

121 Including limited rights in Hamburg and Schleswig-Holstein in Germany; Spain (on the basis of reciprocal agreements); Ireland; the Netherlands; Portugal (nationals of Portuguese-speaking countries only); all five Scandinavian states; and Switzerland (certain cantons only).

122 Soledad Garcia, *Europe's Fragmented Identities and the Frontiers of Citizenship*, RIIA Discussion Paper no. 45, RIIA, London, 1992.

123 Wilpert, 'Work and the Second Generation'.

124 Uri Ra'anan, 'Nation and State: Order out of Chaos', in Uri Ra'anan, Maria Mesner, Keith Armes and Kate Martin, eds, *State and Nation in Multi-Ethnic Societies: The Breakup of Multinational States* (Institute for the Study of Conflict, Ideology and

Policy, Boston), Manchester University Press, Manchester, 1991, pp. 3–32. Based on Hans Kohn's 'western' model of national identity, summarized by Anthony Smith as being based on 'historic territory, legal-political community, legal-political equality of members, and common civic culture and ideology'. See Hans Kohn, *The Idea of Nationalism*, second edition, Collier Macmillan, New York, 1967; and Anthony Smith, *National Identity*, Penguin, London, 1991, pp. 11–12.

125 Uri Ra'anan, 'Nation and State', p. 13. Based on Hans Kohn's 'eastern' model of national identity, described by Anthony Smith as based on 'geneaology and presumed descent ties, popular mobilization, vernacular languages, customs and traditions'. See Anthony Smith, *National Identity*, p. 13.

126 Note, for example, the terminology used in the recent *Survey of the Policy and Law Regarding Aliens in the Federal Republic of Germany*, Federal Ministry of the Interior, much of which is devoted to a discussion of policy affecting the integration of so-called second and third generations. E.g., 'Approximately 60 per cent of aliens staying in the Federal Republic of Germany have been living here for ten years or more. More than two-thirds of foreign children and juveniles were born in the Federal Republic of Germany. The Federal Government assumes that most of them will stay for a considerable period of time or that some of them will even stay forever. This applies above all to those foreigners who were born and have grown up here.' (p. 5)

127 Council of Europe, 'Community and Ethnic Relations in Europe', p. 11.

128 Philip Ogden, 'The Legacy of Migration', p. 113.

129 Robin Oakley, *Racial Violence and Harassment in Europe*, report for the Council of Europe, Council of Europe document MG-CR (91) 3 rev. 2., Strasbourg, 1991, pp. 9–10.

130 Note that at the time of writing, laws against racist and xenophobic behaviour were *under consideration* in France (bill elaborated by the Justice Ministry in April 1994); Germany (a bill to combat the extreme right was adopted by the Bundestag in May 1994 but rejected by the Bundesrat in June 1994); Switzerland (the Penal Code was nearly amended to introduce provisions against racially motivated behaviour in June 1993, but because of pressure from the extreme right the amendment was made subject to a referendum); and Sweden (an amendment to the Penal Code to increase the punishment for racially motivated crimes was expected to come into force in July 1994). In the UK, the government has resisted pressure to make racially motivated violence a distinct crime. However, the importance of the impact of racially moti-vated violence and harassment on community relations has been more openly recognized than in other countries. A Government Action Group on Racial Violence was disbanded in 1992, but plans to reconvene the Group were being considered in early 1994 following an upsurge in violent attacks against ethnic minorities. See *Migration News Sheet*, various issues.

131 Ibid., p. 41.

132 Liz Fekete, 'Report of the European Committee on Racism and Xenophobia: a Critique', in *Race and Class (Special Issue: 'Europe: Variations on a Theme of Racism')*, vol. 32, no. 3. (1991), p. 148.

133 Robin Oakley, *Racial Violence and Harassment in Europe*, p. 13.

134 Council of Europe, 'Community and Ethnic Relations in Europe', p. 24.

135 Ibid., p. 25.

Chapter 7: Europe's Receiving States in the 1990s

1   A.R. Zolberg, 'Are the Industrial Countries Under Siege?', in G. Luciani, ed., *Migration Policies in Europe and the United States*, Kluwer, Dordrecht, 1993, p. 54.

2   Defined by the European Commission as 'the development of common rules and practices'. See Commission of the European Communities, *Communication from the Commission to the Council and the European Parliament on Immigration and Asylum Policies*, COM(94) 23 final, Commission of the European Communities, Brussels, 23 February 1994, p. 9.

3   Giuseppe Callovi, 'Regulation of Immigration in 1993: Pieces of the European Community Jig-Saw Puzzle', in *International Migration Review* 26(2), p. 356.

4   See Richard Plender, *International Migration Law*, Revised Second Edition, Nijhoff, Dordrecht, 1988, p. 251. The Convention was ratified by Portugal, Spain, Turkey, Sweden and the Netherlands. An additional problem, of course, was that this Convention sought an extension and/or a confirmation of states' obligations towards migrants at a time when the primary interest of those states was in restriction and control. At the time of writing, the only additional states to have ratified the Convention were France and Norway; the Convention had been signed by Belgium, Germany, Greece, Italy and Luxembourg. See Council of Europe, 'Activities of the Council of Europe in the Migration Field', CDMG(93) 10 E, Council of Europe, Strasbourg, 1993, p. 15. It is worth noting that all the West European delegations abstained from the adoption of a United Nations Economic and Social Council Resolution in February 1994 on measures to improve the situation and ensure the human rights and dignity of all migrant workers. This Resolution calls, *inter alia*, for all member states to ratify or accede to the International Convention on the Protection of the Rights of all Migrant Workers and Members of their Families adopted by the UN General Assembly on 18 December 1990 (this Convention requires 20 ratifications for its entry into force). See *Migration News Sheet*, No. 132/94-03, March 1994. See also EC Commission, *Communication on Immigration and Asylum Policies* (1994), Annex III.

5   E. Guild, *Protecting Migrants' Rights: Application of the EC Agreements with Third Countries*, CCME Briefing Paper No. 10, Churches Committee for Migrants in Europe (CCME), Brussels, 1992.

6   Article 8a.

7   This agreement was signed in 1985. It was motivated by a desire to make swifter progress towards the establishment of a unified market than was being made among the EC-Twelve.

8   Commission of the European Communities, *Communication from the Commission to the Council and the European Parliament on Immigration*, SEC(91) 1855 final, Commission of the European Communities, Brussels, 23 October 1991, p. 8.

9   Ministers Responsible for Immigration, 'Signing of the Convention determining the State responsible for examining applications for asylum lodged in one of the Member States of the European Communities', 6941/90 (Presse 87), Dublin, 15 June 1990. The Convention was signed by 11 member states; Denmark signed within a year.

10 This Convention had not been signed at the time of writing owing to a dispute between the United Kingdom and Spain over the status of the border between Gibraltar and Spain (the UK government considers the frontier to be internal; Spain considers it an external border). In November 1993, the European Commission submitted a new draft of the Convention to the Council of Ministers, which reflects institutional changes deriving from the entry into force of the Treaty on European

Union and the establishment of the European Economic Area. Whereas all previous drafts were confidential, the new draft, like all Commission proposals, has been published. See Commission of the European Communities, *Communication from the Commission to the Council and the European Parliament: (i) Proposal for a decision, based on Article K.3 of the Treaty on European Union establishing the Convention on the crossing of the external frontiers of the Member States; (ii) Proposal for a regulation, based on Article 100c of the Treaty establishing the European Community, determining the third countries whose nationals must be in possession of a visa when crossing the external borders of the Member States*, COM(93) 684 final, Commission of the European Communities, Brussels, 10 December 1993. It has also been published in the Official Journal (O.J. C11, 15 January 1994).

11 The Dublin Convention lays down provisions designed to prevent (1) multiple or successive applications being submitted by an asylum-seeker in more than one state; and (2) the problem of refugees in orbit caused by no state accepting responsibility for particular asylum-seekers. The draft External Borders Convention is primarily concerned with control arrangements at the external frontiers of the member states, visa policies for third-country nationals (including mutual recognition of visas and provisions for the development of a uniform visa) and rules governing secondary movement of third-country nationals within Union territory.

12 Note that the intergovernmental negotiations in this area are more open to public and parliamentary scrutiny under the new institutional structures brought about by the entry into force of the Treaty on European Union (TEU). Although these are considerably more secretive than decision-making procedures within the Community institutions, under the TEU the European Parliament must be regularly informed of and consulted on discussions concerning immigration and asylum issues listed under Title VI of the TEU (provisions on cooperation in the fields of Justice and Home Affairs). However, on 15 July 1993, the European Parliament adopted a Resolution regretting, under Title VI, the 'lack of effective parliamentary and judicial supervision and democratic procedures for decision-making in a field where the rights of the citizen are directly concerned'. The Resolution also requests that an agreement be signed with the Council with the aim of being allowed to send a delegation of Europarliamentarians as observers to certain intergovernmental meetings of ministers, and calls for the Rules of Procedure to be amended so as to provide for this procedure. See *Migration News Sheet*, No. 125/93-08, August 1993.

13 Note that prior to the entry into force of the TEU, intergovernmental cooperation in this area was theoretically reversible at any moment given that there was no Treaty commitment to cooperate. See EC Commission, *Communication on Immigration and Asylum Policy* (1994), p. 6.

14 Ad Hoc Group on Immigration, *Report from the Ministers Responsible for Immigration to the European Council Meeting in Maastricht on Immigration and Asylum Policy*, SN 4038/91 (WGI 930), Brussels, December 1991, p. 13.

15 EC Commission, *Communication on Immigration and Asylum Policies* (1994), pp. 1–2.

16 Ad Hoc Group, *Report from the Ministers Responsible for Immigration*.

17 Callovi, 'Regulation of Immigration in 1993', p. 370.

18 Commission of the European Communities: (i) *Communication from the Commission to the Council and the European Parliament on the right of asylum*, SEC(91) 1857 final, Commission of the European Communities, Brussels, 11 October 1991; (ii)

Communication on Immigration (1991). Note that the Commission issued a third Communication on these issues in February 1994. Whereas the issues of asylum and immigration were treated separately in the 1991 Communications, the 1994 Communication addresses the two subjects in a single document 'without losing sight of the characteristics of each which continue to make them distinct in nature'. See EC Commission, *Communication on Immigration and Asylum Policies* (1994), p. 1.

19 Luise Druke, *Asylum Policies in a European Community without Internal Borders*, CCME Briefing Paper No. 9, CCME, Brussels, 1992.

20 EC Commission, *Communication on Immigration* (1991), pp. 25 and 27.

21 Callovi, 'Regulation of Immigration in 1993', p. 371.

22 The determination of countries whose nationals need visas and the adoption of measures related to a uniform visa format.

23 Note that paragraph 7 of Article 100c provides for intergovernmental conventions, including the draft Convention on the Crossing of External Borders, to remain in force until their content is replaced by Community instruments.

24 Strictly a shared right of initiative with the member states, since the Commission does not have a monopoly over the right of initiative as it does in cases of full Community competence (such as in the area of visas under Article 100c).

25 A revised draft of the External Borders Convention which takes into account the entry into force of the TEU and the establishment of the European Economic Area.

26 Commission of the European Communities, *Communication from the Commission to the Council and the European Parliament: (i) Proposal for a decision, based on Article K.3 of the Treaty on European Union establishing the Convention on the crossing of the external frontiers of the Member States* ..., p. 6.

27 Commission of the European Communities, *Report to the Council on the possibility of applying Article K.9 of the Treaty on European Union to asylum policy*, SEC(93) 1687 final, Commission of the European Communities, Brussels, 4 November 1993, pp. 5 and 6.

28 EC Commission, *Communication on Immigration and Asylum Policies* (1994), p. 6.

29 Ibid.

30 Note that the Ad Hoc Group on Immigration has been replaced by a Steering Group (Steering Group I – asylum and immigration) under the Coordinating Committee (the so-called 'K.4 Committee') within the Committee of Permanent Representatives in the Council of Ministers. The K.4 Committee is responsible for coordinating the activities of the three Steering Groups working in the areas of Justice and Home Affairs (Steering Group I; Steering Group II – police and customs cooperation and cooperation in the fight against drugs; Steering Group III – judicial cooperation).

31 See *Migration News Sheet*, No. 131/94-02, February 1994, and No. 136/94-07. Not only will it be necessary to draft a convention to regulate the creation of the EIS, but at the time of writing the Council had still to decide on the competence of the European Court of Justice and the role of the European Parliament in this context (under Article K.3 of the TEU).

32 At the time of writing, it was not at all clear when the Schengen Implementing Convention would come into force. See *Migration News Sheet*, various issues.

33 See, for example, *Migration News Sheet*, No. 132/94-03.

34 Callovi, 'Regulation of Immigration in 1993', p. 366.

35 See *Migration News Sheet*, No. 133/94-04, April 1994, and No.135/94-06, June 1994. Note that the European Parliament recently decided to introduce a complaint before the European Court of Justice against the Commission for the latter's failure

to ensure the full implementation of free movement by the deadline of 31 December 1992.

36 The Resolution on Manifestly Unfounded Applications for Asylum and the Resolution on a Harmonised Approach to Questions Concerning Host Third Countries.

37 EC Commission, *Report on the possibility of applying Article K.9 to asylum policy*, p. 5.

38 Ibid., pp. 5–6.

39 EC Commission, *Communication on Immigration and Asylum Policies* (1994), p. 9.

40 Ad Hoc Group, *Report from the Ministers Responsible for Immigration*, p. 32.

41 Note that the latest draft of the External Borders Convention includes an undertaking on the part of member states to incorporate into their national legislation measures 'to oblige the carrier to take all the necessary measures to ensure that persons coming from third countries are in possession of valid travel documents and of the necessary visas, and to impose appropriate penalties on carriers failing to fulfil this obligation'. See Commission of the European Communities, *Communication from the Commission to the Council and European Parliament: (i) Proposal for a decision, based on Article K.3 of the Treaty on European Union establishing the Convention on the crossing of the external frontiers of the Member States...*, Title V, Article 14.

42 European Council document 10684/93 JAI 12, p. 3.

43 Note that Portugal is still a country of net emigration, but is also a 'receiver' of immigrants, particularly from South America and Africa.

44 Gildas Simon, 'Trends and Prospects on the Threshold of the Internal Market', in Commission of the European Communities, Directorate-General for Employment, Industrial Relations and Social Affairs, *Social Europe*, Brussels, 1990, pp. 20–33, at p. 31. Note that the increase in undocumented immigration into Germany over recent years is likely to have been associated with an expansion of the informal economy there, e.g. irregular employment in the construction industry. See *Migration News Sheet*, No. 131/94-02, February 1994, and No. 135/94-06, June 1994.

45 The UK's position as a densely populated island makes it relatively easy to control entries on the basis of strict controls at ports of entry. The UK's common law traditions, by defining what is prohibited rather than what is required, work against the idea of constant internal checks and controls on the movements and activities of residents (nationals and foreigners). Note, however, that more hidden forms of internal control play a role in the UK, e.g. information gathered from networks of 'devolved controllers', such as teachers, housing officials and health workers. The Asylum and Immigration Reform Act, passed in 1992, allows housing officials to check the immigration status of potential council tenants. See Anne Owers, 'The Age of Internal Controls?', in Sarah Spencer, ed., *Strangers and Citizens: A Positive Approach to Migrants and Refugees*, Institute for Public Policy Research/Rivers Oram Press, London, 1994, pp. 264–81.

46 Note that the Netherlands and Ireland are the only other Union member states not to use identity cards. However, a requirement to be able to provide proof of identity was introduced in the Netherlands on 6 December 1993. The Netherlands has resisted the introduction of identity cards because of the association with the Nazi occupation. Owers, 'The Age of Internal Controls?'

47 Note that the Parliamentary Home Affairs Select Committee and policing authorities appear to support the introduction of voluntary ID cards, whereas the Home Office and immigration service seem to be against their introduction. Support for ID cards may stem more from wider interests connected with crime detection and prevention

of terrorism than from a primary interest in immigration control. In addition to the political obstacles, however, the practical difficulties that would be encountered in any effort to introduce a system of ID cards aimed at controlling or monitoring immigration would be enormous. Note also that ID cards have been of dubious efficacy in preventing undocumented immigration into countries such as Italy and France. Owers, 'The Age of Internal Controls?'

48 A view shared by the governments of Ireland and Denmark.

49 See, for example, Commission of the European Communities, *Commission Communication to the Council and to Parliament: Abolition of Border Controls*, SEC(92) 877 final, Commission of the European Communities, Brussels, 8 May 1992. This is also the position of the Schengen states and the European Parliament.

50 18 November 1993. See *Migration News Sheet*, No. 129/93-12, December 1993.

51 Note that this surveillance is likely to have a discriminatory impact on legally resident immigrants, 'visible' migrants or visitors travelling on valid visas and members of established immigrant-origin ethnic minorities.

52 *Migration News Sheet*, various issues.

53 Ad Hoc Group, *Report from the Ministers Responsible for Immigration*, p. 28.

54 Most recently: Italy in 1989–90; Spain in 1991; and Portugal in 1992–3.

55 EC Commission, *Communication on Immigration* (1991), p. 14.

56 Who qualify for German citizenship.

57 Title VI of the draft submitted to the European Council by the European Commission in November 1993. See Commission of the European Communities, *Communication from the Commission to the Council and European Parliament: (i) Proposal for a decision, based on Article K.3 of the Treaty on European Union establishing the Convention on the crossing of the external frontiers of the Member States...*, Title VI, Articles 17–25.

58 *Treaty on European Union*, Article 100c.1.

59 Note that this list mirrors that drawn up by the Schengen Group.

60 Commission of the European Communities, *Communication from the Commission to the Council and the European Parliament ... (ii) Proposal for a regulation, based on Article 100c of the Treaty establishing the European Community, determining the third countries whose nationals must be in possession of a visa when crossing the external borders of the Member States.*

61 Ibid.

62 *Migration News Sheet*, No. 134/94-05.

63 *Treaty on European Union*, Article 100c.

64 Included as a provision of the draft External Borders Convention.

65 At 30 April 1993, only Denmark, Italy, Spain, Portugal and France did not require visas for Bosnian nationals. France required a letter of sponsorship.

66 *Migration News Sheet*, various issues.

67 European Council, doc. 10684/93 JAI 12.

68 For a discussion of these Resolutions, etc., see Amnesty International, *Europe: Harmonization of Asylum Policy: accelerated procedures for 'manifestly unfounded' asylum claims and the 'safe country' concept*, paper issue by the Amnesty International EC Project, Brussels, 1992. See also Sarah Collinson, *Beyond Borders: West European Migration Policy towards the 21st Century*, Royal Institute of International Affairs/Wyndham Place Trust, London 1993, pp. 79–85.

69 EC Commission, *Communication on Immigration and Asylum Policies* (1994), p. 24.

70 Ibid.

71 Note that the UNHCR also advised that Austria is not a safe country for asylum-seekers. See *Migration News Sheet*, No. 133/94-04, April 1994, and No. 134/94-05, May 1994.

72 See United Nations High Commissioner for Refugees, *Legal Factsheets on Asylum Procedures in Western Europe*, UNHCR, Regional Bureau for Europe, Geneva, 1993; and J. Gillespie, *Report on Immigration and Asylum Procedure and Appeal Rights in the 12 Member States of the European Community*, Immigration Law Practitioners Association, London, 1993.

73 I.e, the definition of the 1951 UN Convention on the Status of Refugees which covers persons with a well-founded fear of persecution in their country of origin by reason of their race, religion, nationality, political opinion or membership of a social group.

74 See, for example, Council of Europe Recommendation 773 (1976) and Recommendation R (84) 1 (1984).

75 Centre for Migration Research (University of Amsterdam), *Reception Policies for Persons in Need of International Protection in Western European States*, Research Project Commissioned by the United Nations High Commissioner for Refugees, UNHCR, Geneva, October 1993, p. 35.

76 European Council document 10684/93 JAI 12, p. 3.

77 Ibid., p. 2.

78 Ad Hoc Group, *Report from the Ministers Responsible for Immigration*, p. 34.

79 EC Commission, *Communication on the Right of Asylum* (1991); and *Communication on Immigration* (1991).

80 At the time of writing, the Dublin Convention had been ratified by Denmark, Greece, Italy, the UK, Portugal, Luxembourg and France.

81 As does the Ad Hoc Group's Resolution concerning host third countries, adopted at a ministerial meeting of the Ad Hoc Group on 30 November–1 December 1992.

82 *Migration News Sheet*, No. 129/93-12, December 1993. In respect of refugees from the former Yugoslavia, the UK has been arguing that it is sharing the 'burden' because it has contributed troops to the UN effort within the former Yugoslavia, and that countries which do not have troops there should be willing to take in more refugees.

83 European Council document 10684/93 JAI 12, p. 3.

84 Paragraph 7 of Resolution A3-0280/92 adopted by the European Parliament on 18 November 1992. Note that the Parliamentary Assembly of the Council of Europe also approved a set of measures on asylum in Europe in April 1994 which included the establishment of a fund to help over-burdened countries. See *Migration News Sheet*, No. 134/94-05, May 1994.

85 EC Commission, *Communication on Immigration and Asylum Policy* (1994), pp. 26–7.

86 Note that at a meeting of EU Ministers responsible for immigration in Thessalonika in May 1994 there was discussion of burden-sharing and the possible creation of a Union-wide fund to support Central and East European countries to slow down the departure of their nationals (ideas pushed by Germany and Greece), but opinions remained divided on both issues. *Migration News Sheet*, No. 135/94-06, June 1994.

87 Article A.2 (a) and (b). Article 8a of the SEA (Article 7a of the TEU) has been interpreted by the member state governments as applying to citizens of the European Community, as opposed to persons in general, and thus the determination of free movement rights that could potentially be enjoyed by third-country nationals in the European Union is left open to intergovernmental negotiation. However, this view

has not been shared by the European Commission. See Commission of the European Communities, *Abolition of Border Controls*, p. 2, where it is argued that 'any interpretation of Article 8a that confined its effects to Community nationals only would deprive that Article of any practical effectiveness'.

88 Ad Hoc Group, *Report from the Ministers Responsible for Immigration*, p. 6. Note that according to recent case-law of the European Court of Justice (n.b. the case of *Rush Portuguesa* of 27 March 1990), legally resident third-country nationals may work in another member state if they are sent by a firm to carry out services on behalf of the firm and if they have a visa for the specified amount of time. But this is on the basis of the rights of the firm, not of the workers. In such cases, the workers concerned do not have access to the labour market of the state in which they are not normally resident.

89 EC Commission, *Communication on Immigration* (1991), p. 25.

90 EC Commission, *Communication fon Immigration and Asylum Policy* (1994), p. 34.

91 Ibid.

92 Ibid., pp. 32–40.

93 See, for example, T. Hammar, *Democracy and the Nation-state: aliens, denizens and citizens in a world of international migration*, Gower Publishing, Aldershot, Avebury, 1990.

94 See, for example, Z. Layton-Henry, *The Political Rights of Migrant Workers in Western Europe*, Sage Modern Politics Series 25, Sage Publications, London, 1990. Note that clear agreement has yet to be reached on the question of voting rights for Union citizens.

95 Ad Hoc Group, *Report from the Ministers Responsible for Immigration*, p. 25.

96 EC Commission, *Communication on Immigration and Asylum Policy* (1994), p. 22.

97 *Migration News Sheet*, various issues. Note, however, that Spain's quota system has not proved particularly successful, due in part to the bureaucratic nature of the system, the relatively high costs to be borne by potential employers, and the fact that foreigners already working in Spain could not benefit from the system.

98 In 1991, roughly 200,000 workers benefited from this scheme. See John Salt, *Migration and Population Change in Europe* (UNIDIR Research Paper No. 19), United Nations Institute for Disarmament Research, New York, 1993, pp. 41–2. In May 1994, the Dutch employers organization FME (metal and electronic industries) complained that under this system German firms could recruit workers from Eastern Europe at lower wage levels, and that this amounted to unfair competition. See *Migration News Sheet*, No. 135/94-06, June 1994.

99 *Migration News Sheet*, No. 136/94-07, July 1994.

100 It should be noted, however, that the Schengen project itself has not been free of problems. Frustration over the delays in the implementation of the Schengen Agreement led Belgium, the Netherlands and Germany to discuss in April 1994 the possibility of applying the Schengen Agreement earlier (*Migration News Sheet*, No. 134/94-05, May 1994); and when it does finally come into force, it is likely initially to apply only to the five founding member states (Benelux, France and Germany). This indicates a 'two-speed' Schengen grouping, as well as a 'two-speed' Europe.

101 J. Widgren, 'The Need for a New Multilateral Order to Prevent Mass Movements from Becoming a Security Threat in Europe', paper prepared for the conference on 'The Security Dimensions of International Migration in Europe', organized by the Center for Strategic and International Studies (Washington DC) in Sicily, April 1993.

102 Note the Fourth Conference of European Ministers Responsible for Migration Policies, held in Luxembourg in September 1991, and the Fifth Conference, held in Athens in November 1993. These conferences, organized by the Council of Europe's European Committee on Migration (CDMG) looked into a wide range of migration issues. Particular note should also be made of the CDMG's Community Relations Project set up in 1987 and completed in 1991; and the Declaration and Plan of Action on combating racism, xenophobia, anti-Semitism and intolerance adopted by the Heads of State and Governments of the Council of Europe in Vienna in October 1993.

103 A process which emerged from the Council of Europe's Ministerial Conference on the Movement of Persons coming from Central and Eastern Europe, held in Vienna in January 1991. This grouping currently has 37 members. Five follow-up meetings were held between January 1991 and December 1993. The discussions within this grouping reflect the relatively wide range of interests among the states represented, with a focus on migration control, freedom of movement, exchange of information, visa practices and burden-sharing. Little progress has been made since mid-1993, reflecting disagreements among participating states, particularly over the issue of burden-sharing.

104 This grouping stems from the Intergovernmental Conference on European Coopera-tion to Prevent Uncontrolled Migration convened in Berlin in October 1991, attended by the European Community and EFTA states plus the Soviet Union and Central and East European states. The result of this conference was the establishment of a Working Party chaired by Austria in cooperation with Hungary and the chairman of the Schengen Group, with the task of developing proposals to implement measures to prevent or check undocumented immigration. The Working Party drew up a list of recommendations which were adopted at the second intergovernmental conference, held in Budapest in February 1993. Like the recommendations developed in negotia-tions among the EC-Twelve, those of the Budapest meeting amount essentially to political agreements, although with less force than those reached among the EU member states.

105 Agreements imposing a mutual obligation for one state to readmit from the other state undocumented or 'irregular' immigrants and/or rejected asylum-seekers who originate from or have transited through its territory.

106 Note that, at the time of writing, the Schengen states were negotiating a multilateral readmission agreement with Switzerland.

107 See Justice and Home Affairs Council, doc. 10655/93 JAI 11 (Annex).

Chapter 8: Conclusion

1 See Wolfgang Ochel and Kurt Vogler-Ludwig (IFO Institute for Economic Research), 'International Migration: a New Challenge for the Industrialised Countries', paper presented at the Conference of the Tokyo Club Foundation for Global Studies, Tokyo, June 1992.

2 OECD (Continuous Reporting System on Migration), *SOPEMI 1993 (Annual Report). Trends in International Migration*, OECD, Paris, 1994, p. 13.

Select Bibliography

Ad Hoc Group on Immigration, *Report from the Ministers Responsible for Immigration to the European Council Meeting in Maastricht on Immigration and Asylum Policy*, SN 4038/91 (WGI 930), Brussels, 3 December 1991.

Adler, Stephen, *International Migration and Dependence*, Saxon House, Farnborough Hants, 1977.

Adler, Stephen, *Swallow's Children – Emigration and Development in Algeria*, Geneva, ILO, 1980.

Amnesty International, *Europe: Harmonization of Asylum Policy: accelerated procedures for 'manifestly unfounded' asylum claims and the 'safe country' concept*, paper issue by the Amnesty International EC Project, Brussels, 1992.

Appleyard, R., ed., *The Impacts of International Migration on Developing Countries*, OECD, Paris, 1989.

Appleyard, R., ed., *International Migration Today. Vol. 1: Trends and Prospects*, UNESCO, Paris, 1988.

Appleyard, ed., *The Impact of International Migration.*

Baubock, R., 'Immigration and the Boundaries of Citizenship', Monographs in Ethnic Relations 4, Warwick, Centre for Research in Ethnic Relations, 1992.

Bevan, Vaughan, *The Development of British Immigration Law*, Croom Helm, London, 1986.

Blackstone, *Salt of Another's Bread: Immigration Control and the Social Impact of Immigration in Italy*, Report of a Western European Union Study Visit, Home Office, London, 1989.

Böhning, W.R., *Studies in International Migration*, International Labour Office, London, 1984.

Castles, S., 'The Guests Who Stayed – The Debate on "Foreigners Policy" in the German Federal Republic', in *International Migration Review*, vol. 19, no. 3, 1985.

Castles, S., Booth, H. and Wallace, T., *Here For Good: Western Europe's New Ethnic Minorities*, London, Pluto Press, 1984.

Castles, S. and Kosack, G., *Immigrant Workers and Class Structure in Western Europe*, Oxford, Oxford University Press, 1973.

Callovi, Giuseppe, 'Regulation of Immigration in 1993: Pieces of the European Community Jig-Saw Puzzle', in *International Migration Review* 26(2).

Charles W. Stahl, ed., *International Migration Today. Vol. 2: Emerging Issues*, UNESCO, Paris, 1988.

CENSIS (Centro Studi Investimenti Sociali) *Atti Della Conferenza Nationale dell' Immigrazione*, Editalia-Edizioni d'Italia, Rome, 1991.

CENSIS, *Immigrati e Società Italiana*, Editalia-Edizioni d'Italia, Rome, 1991.

CENSIS, *Immigrazione e Diritti di Cittadinanza*, Editalia-Edizioni d'Italia, Rome, 1991.

Centre for Migration Research (University of Amsterdam), *Reception Policies for Persons in Need of International Protection in Western European States*, Research Project Commissioned by the United Nations High Commissioner for Refugees, UNHCR, Geneva, October 1993.

Coles, G., 'Changing Perspectives of Refugee Law and Policy', in V. Gowlland and K. Samson, eds., *Problems and Prospects of Refugee Law*, The Graduate Institute of International Studies, Geneva, 1992.

Collinson, Sarah, *Beyond Borders: West European Migration Policy Towards the 21st Century*, Royal Institute of International Affairs/Wyndham Place Trust, London, 1993.

Commission for Racial Equality, *Review of the Race Relations Act 1976: Proposals for Change*, London, CRE, 1985.

Commission for Racial Equality, *Annual Report 1990*, London, CRE, 1991.

Commission of the European Communities, *Communication from the Commission to the Council and the European Parliament: (i) Proposal for a decision, based on Article K.3 of the Treaty on European Union establishing the Convention on the crossing of the external frontiers of the Member States; (ii) Proposal for a regulation, based on Article 100c of the Treaty establishing the European Community, determining the third countries whose nationals must be in possession of a visa when crossing the external borders of the Member States*, COM(93) 684 final, Commission of the European Communities, Brussels, 10 December 1993.

Commission of the European Communities, *Communication from the Commission to the Council and the European Parliament on Immigration*, SEC(91) 1855 final, EC Commission, Brussels, 23 October 1991.

Commission of the European Communities, *Communication from the Commission to the Council and the European Parliament on Immigration and Asylum Policies*, COM(94) 23 final, EC Commission, Brussels, 23 February 1994.

Commission of the European Communities, *Policies on Immigration and the Social Integration of Migrants in the European Community*, Experts' report drawn up on behalf of the Commission of the European Communities, Brussels, September 1990 (SEC(90)1813 final).

Council of Europe, *Activities of the Council of Europe in the Migration Field* (CDMG (93) 10 E), Council of Europe, Strasbourg, 1993.

Council of Europe, *Final Communiqué of the Conference of Ministers on the Movement of Persons From Central and Eastern European Countries*, Council of Europe, Vienna, 25 January 1991.

Council of Europe, *Community and Ethnic Relations in Europe: Final report of the Community Relations Project of the Council of Europe*, (MG-CR (91) 1 final E), Council of Europe, Strasbourg, 1991.

Cross, M., *Migrant Workers in European Cities: Concentration, Conflict and Social*

Policy, Working Papers on Ethnic Relations, no. 19, Birmingham, SSRC Research Unit on Ethnic Relations, 1983.

Curtin, Philip D., *The Atlantic Slave Trade: A Census*, University of Wisconsin Press, Madison, 1969.

Davis, Kingsley, 'The Migrations of Human Populations', *Scientific American*, no. 231, September 1974.

Dowty, Alan, *Closed Borders*, Yale University Press, New Haven and London, 1987.

Druke, Luise, *Asylum Policies in a European Community without Internal Borders*, CCME Briefing Paper no. 9, Churches Committee for Migrants in Europe (CCME), Brussels, 1992.

Esser, H. and Korte, H., 'Federal Republic of Germany', in Tomas Hammar, ed., *European Immigration Policy: A Comparative Study*, Cambridge, Cambridge University Press, 1985.

European Council, 'Declaration on Principles Governing External Aspects of Migration Policy' in the Conclusions of the Presidency (SN 456/1/92 REV 1), Edinburgh, December 1992.

European Parliament, *Report of the Committee of Enquiry into Racism and Xenophobia*, (Rapporteur: Mr Glyn Ford), Brussels, European Parliament Sessions Document A3-195/90, Brussels, 1989.

Federal Minister of the Interior, *Survey of the Policy and Law Regarding Aliens in the Federal Republic of Germany* (V II 1-937 020/15 [Translation]), Bonn, 1991.

Garcia, Soledad, *Europe's Fragmented Identies and the Frontiers of Citizenship*, RIIA Discussion Paper no. 45, RIIA, London, 1992.

Gieseck, A., Heilemann, U. and Dietrich von Loeffelholz, H., Economic and Social Implications of Migration into the Federal Republic of Germany, RWI-Papiere No. 35, Essen, Rheinisch-Westfülisches Institut für Wirtschaftsforschung, 1993.

Gillespie, J., *Report on Immigration and Asylum Procedure and Appeal Rights in the 12 Member States of the European Community*, Immigration Law Practitioners Association, London, 1993.

Grillo, R.D, *Ideologies and Institutions in Urban France: The Representation of Immigrants*, Cambridge University Press, 1985.

Hall, Stuart, 'Migration from the English-speaking Caribbean to the United Kingdom, 1950–80', in Charles W. Stahl, ed., *International Migration Today. Vol. 2: Emerging Issues*, UNESCO, Paris, 1988.

Hammar, Tomas, ed., *European Immigration Policy*, Cambridge University Press, 1985.

Hammar, Tomas, *Democracy and the Nation State. Aliens, Denizens and Citizens in a World of International Migration*, Avebury, Aldershot, 1990.

Johnston, H. J. M., *British Emigration Policy 1815–1830: Shovelling out Paupers*, Clarendon Press, Oxford, 1972.

Justice and Home Affairs Council, doc. 10655/93 JAI 11.

Kritz, M.M., Keely, C.B., and Tomasi, S.M., eds., *Global Trends in Migration: Theory and Research on International Population Movements*, Center for Migration Studies, New York, 1983.

Kubat, Daniel, ed., *The Politics of Migration Policies. Settlement and Integration: the First World into the 1990s* (Second Edition), New York, Center for Migration Studies, 1993.

Kulischer, Eugene, *Jewish Migrations: Past Experiences and Post-War Prospects*, American Jewish Committee, New York, 1943.

Kulischer, Eugene, *Europe on the Move. War and Population Changes 1917–1947*, Columbia University Press, New York, 1943.

Layton-Henry, Z., *The Political Rights of Migrant Workers in Western Europe*, Sage Modern Politics Series 25, London, Sage Publications, 1990.

Layton-Henry, Z., *The Politics of Immigration. Immigration, 'Race' and 'Race' Relations in Post-war Britain*, Making of Contemporary Britain Series (Institute of Contemporary History), Oxford and Cambridge MA, Blackwell Publishers, 1993.

Lebon, André, *Regard sur L'immigration et la présence étrangère en France, 1989/90*, Ministère des Affaires Sociales et de la Solidarité, Direction de la Population et des Migrations, Paris, 1990.

Leitner, H., 'Regulating Migrants' Lives', in Günther Glebe and John O'Loughlin, eds., *Foreign Minorities in Continental European Cities* (Erdkundliches Wissen, Heft 84), Stuttgart, Steiner Verlag, 1987.

LeMay, Michael C. ed., *The Gatekeepers. Comparative Immigration Policy*, Praeger, New York, 1989.

Loescher, Gil and Monahan, Laila, (eds.), *Refugees and International Relations*, Oxford University Press, 1989.

Loescher, Gil, *Refugee Movements and International Security*, Adelphi Paper 268, Brassey's for the International Institute for Strategic Studies, London, 1992.

Marrus, Michael, *The Unwanted; European Refugees in the Twentieth Century*, Oxford University Press, New York and Oxford, 1985.

Martin, Philip L., *The Unfinished Story: Turkish Labour Migration to Western Europe*, Geneva, ILO, 1991.

Migration News Sheet, various issues, Brussels, European Information Network.

Netherlands Scientific Council for Government Policy, 'Immigrant Policy: Summary of the 36th Report', Reports to the Government 36, The Hague, 1990.

Oakley, R., *Racial Violence and Harassment in Europe*, report for the Council of Europe, Strasbourg, Council of Europe document MG-CR (91) 3 rev. 2, 1991.

Ochel, Wolfgang, and Vogler-Ludwig, Kurt, (IFO Institute for Economic Research), 'International Migration: a New Challenge for the Industrialised Countries', paper presented at the Conference of the Tokyo Club Foundation for Global Studies, Tokyo, June 1992.

OECD Continuous Reporting on System on Migration (*SOPEMI*), OECD, Paris, various dates.

OECD, *Migration. The Demographic Aspects*, OECD, Paris, 1991.

Ogden, P., 'The Legacy of Migration: Some Evidence from France', in Russell King, ed., *Mass Migration in Europe. The Legacy and the Future*, London, Belhaven Press, 1993.

Owers, Anne, 'The Age of Internal Controls?', in Sarah Spencer, ed., *Strangers and Citizens. A Positive Approach to Migrants and Refugees*, Institute for Public Policy Research / Rivers Oram Press, London, 1994.

Paine, Suzanne, *Exporting Workers: the Turkish Case*, Cambridge University Press, 1974.

Penninx, R., Schoorl, J. and Van Praag, C., *The Impact of International Migration on Receiving Countries: the Case of the Netherlands*, Amsterdam, Swets and Zeitlinger – NIDI CBGS Publications, 1993.

Phizacklea, A. and Miles, R., 'Class, race, ethnicity and political action', *Political Studies*, vol. 25, no. 4, 1977.

Phizacklea, A., and Miles, R., *Labour and Racism*, Routledge and Kegan Paul, London, 1980.

Piore, M., *Birds of Passage: Migrant Labour and Industrial Societies*, Cambridge University Press, 1979.

Plender, Richard, *International Migration Law*, Revised Second Edition, Nijhoff, Dordrecht, 1988.

Presidenza del Consiglio dei Ministri, *Norme Urgenti in Materia di Asilo Politico, Ingresso e Soggiorno dei Cittadini Extracomunitari e di Regolarizzazione de Cittadini Extracomunitari ed Apolidi Già Presenti Nel Territorio Dello Stato*, Law of 28 February 1990, no. 39, converting Decree no. 416 of December 1989, Collana de Testi e Documenti, Dipartimento per L'Informazione e L'Editoria (Istituto Poligrafico e Zecca Dello Stato), Rome, 1990; (including English translation).

Race and Class (Special Issue: 'Europe: Variations on a Theme of Racism'), vol. 32, no. 3, 1991.

Ravenstein, E. G., 'The Laws of Migration', *Journal of the Royal Statistical Society*, no. 52, London, 1889.

Rex, J., 'The Concept of a Multi-Cultural Society', Occasional Papers in Ethnic Relations 3, Warwick, Centre for Research in Ethnic Relations, 1985.

Rex, J., Joly, D., and Wilpert, C., eds., *Immigrant Associations in Europe*, Gower, Aldershot, 1987.

Rex, J. and Tomlinson, S., *Colonial Immigrants in a British City*, Routledge and Kegan Paul, London, 1979.

Rystad, Göran, ed., *The Uprooted: Forced Migration as an International Problem in the Postwar Era*, Lund University Press, Lund, 1990.

Salt, John, *Current and Future International Migration Trends Affecting Europe*, background document for the 4th Conference of European Ministers Responsible for Migration, Luxembourg, September 1991 (MMG-4 (91) 1 E), Council of Europe, Strasbourg, 1991.

Salt, John, *Migration and Population Change in Europe* (UNIDIR Research Paper No.19), United Nations Institute for Disarmament Research, New York, 1993.

Schmitter Heisler, Barbara, 'Sending Countries and the Politics of Emigration and Destination', in *International Migration Review* (Special Issue: 'Civil Rights and the Socio-political Participation of Migrants'), vol. 19, 1985.

Seccombe, I.J., and Lawless, R.J, 'Some New Trends in Mediterranean Labour Migration: The Middle East Connection', *International Migration*, vol. 23, no. 1, March 1985.

Serageldin, Socknat, Birks, Li, and Sinclair, *Manpower and International Labour Migration in the Middle East and North Africa*, Oxford University Press for the World Bank, Oxford, 1983.

Simon, G., 'Industrialisation, Emigration et Réinsertion de la Main-d'Oeuvre Qualifiée au Maghreb – le cas de la Tunisie et de l'Algérie', *Hommes et Migrations*, no. 902, 1976.

Smith, A., *National Identity*, London, Penguin Books 1991.

Stanton Russell, S., and Teitelbaum, M.S., *International Migration and International Trade*, World Bank Discussion Paper, no. 160; World Bank, Washington DC, 1992.

Tapinos, Georges, *L'immigration étrangère en France, 1946–1973*, Institut National d'Etudes Démographiques no. 71, Presses Universitaires de France, Paris, 1975.

Thistlethwaite, Frank, 'Migration from Europe Overseas in the Nineteenth and Twentieth Centuries', *Rapports*, vol. 5, 1960.

Thomas, Brinley, *Migration and Economic Growth. A Study of Great Britain and the
Atlantic Economy*, Cambridge University Press, 1954.

UNHCR, *Legal Factsheets on Asylum Procedures in Western Europe*, UNHCR,
Regional Bureau for Europe, Geneva, 1993.

US Committee for Refugees, *World Refugee Survey 1993*, American Council for
Nationalities Service, Washington DC, 1993.

Van Praag, C.S., 'Minderheden voor en na de nota' (Minorities before and after the
Policy Document), *Migrantenstudies* 2/4, 1986.

Verbunt, Gilles, 'France', in Tomas Hammar, ed., *European Immigration Policy: A
Comparative Study*, Cambridge, Cambridge University Press, 1985.

Weiner, Myron, *International Migration and Security*, Westview, Boulder CO and
Oxford, 1993.

Weiner, Myron, 'On International Migration and International Relations', in *Population
and Development Review*, vol. 2, no. 3, 1985.

White, Paul, 'The Migrant Experience in Paris', in Günther Glebe and John
O'Loughlin, eds., *Foreign Minorities in Continental European Cities*
(Erdkundliches Wissen, Heft 84), Steiner Verlag, Stuttgart, 1987.

Wihtol de Wenden, Catherine, *Les immigrés et la politique*, Presses de la Fondation
Nationale des Sciences Politiques, Paris, 1988.

Wilpert, C., ed., *Entering the Working World. Following the Descendants of Europe's
Immigrant Labour Force*, Gower, Aldershot, 1988.

Wilpert, C. and Gitmez, A., 'A Micro-Society or an Ethnic Community? Social Organi-
zation and Ethnicity amongst Turkish Migrants in Berlin', in John Rex, Daniele
Joly and Czarina Wilpert, eds., *Immigrant Associations in Europe*, Aldershot and
Vermont, Gower Publishing for the European Science Foundation, 1987.

Zolberg, A. R., Suhrke, A., and Aguayo, S., *Escape from Violence: Conflict and the
Refugee Crisis in the Developing World*, Oxford University Press, New York and
Oxford, 1989.

Zolberg, A. R., 'Are the Industrial Countries Under Siege?', in G. Luciani, ed.,
Migration Policies in Europe and the United States, Kluwer, Dordrecht, 1993.

Zolberg, Aristide R., 'Contemporary Transnational Migrations in Historical Perspec-
tive: Patterns and Dilemmas', in Mary M. Kritz, ed., *US Immigration and Refugee
Policy. Global and Domestic Issues, USA and Canada*, Lexington Books,
Lexington MA, 1983.

Index